The Economics of Property-Casualty Insurance

A National Bureau
of Economic Research
Project Report

The Economics of Property-Casualty Insurance

Edited by   David F. Bradford

The University of Chicago Press

Chicago and London

DAVID F. BRADFORD is professor of economics and public affairs at Princeton University, a research associate of the National Bureau of Economic Research, and adjunct professor of law at New York University.

The University of Chicago Press, Chicago 60637
The University of Chicago Press, Ltd., London
© 1998 by the National Bureau of Economic Research
All rights reserved. Published 1998
Printed in the United States of America
07 06 05 04 03 02 01 00 99 98   1 2 3 4 5
ISBN: 0-226-07026-3 (cloth)

Library of Congress Cataloging-in-Publication Data

The economics of property-casualty insurance / edited by David F. Bradford.
     p. cm. — (A National Bureau of Economic Research project report)
   Includes bibliographical references and index.
   ISBN 0-226-07026-3 (cloth : alk. paper)
   1. Insurance, Property—United States.   2. Insurance, Casualty—United States.   I. Bradford, David F., 1939–   .   II. Series.
HG8531.E86   1998
368.1'01'0973—DC21   97-37801
                                                      CIP

Relation of the Directors to the
Work and Publications of the
National Bureau of Economic Research

1. The object of the National Bureau of Economic Research is to ascertain and to present to the public important economic facts and their interpretation in a scientific and impartial manner. The Board of Directors is charged with the responsibility of ensuring that the work of the National Bureau is carried on in strict conformity with this object.

2. The President of the National Bureau shall submit to the Board of Directors, or to its Executive Committee, for their formal adoption all specific proposals for research to be instituted.

3. No research report shall be published by the National Bureau until the President has sent each member of the Board a notice that a manuscript is recommended for publication and that in the President's opinion it is suitable for publication in accordance with the principles of the National Bureau. Such notification will include an abstract or summary of the manuscript's content and a response form for use by those Directors who desire a copy of the manuscript for review. Each manuscript shall contain a summary drawing attention to the nature and treatment of the problem studied, the character of the data and their utilization in the report, and the main conclusions reached.

4. For each manuscript so submitted, a special committee of the Directors (including Directors Emeriti) shall be appointed by majority agreement of the President and Vice Presidents (or by the Executive Committee in case of inability to decide on the part of the President and Vice Presidents), consisting of three Directors selected as nearly as may be one from each general division of the Board. The names of the special manuscript committee shall be stated to each Director when notice of the proposed publication is submitted to him. It shall be the duty of each member of the special manuscript committee to read the manuscript. If each member of the manuscript committee signifies his approval within thirty days of the transmittal of the manuscript, the report may be published. If at the end of that period any member of the manuscript committee withholds his approval, the President shall then notify each member of the Board, requesting approval or disapproval of publication, and thirty days additional shall be granted for this purpose. The manuscript shall then not be published unless at least a majority of the entire Board who shall have voted on the proposal within the time fixed for the receipt of votes shall have approved.

5. No manuscript may be published, though approved by each member of the special manuscript committee, until forty-five days have elapsed from the transmittal of the report in manuscript form. The interval is allowed for the receipt of any memorandum of dissent or reservation, together with a brief statement of his reasons, that any member may wish to express; and such memorandum of dissent or reservation shall be published with the manuscript if he so desires. Publication does not, however, imply that each member of the Board has read the manuscript, or that either members of the Board in general or the special committee have passed on its validity in every detail.

6. Publications of the National Bureau issued for informational purposes concerning the work of the Bureau and its staff, or issued to inform the public of activities of Bureau staff, and volumes issued as a result of various conferences involving the National Bureau shall contain a specific disclaimer noting that such publication has not passed through the normal review procedures required in this resolution. The Executive Committee of the Board is charged with review of all such publications from time to time to ensure that they do not take on the character of formal research reports of the National Bureau, requiring formal Board approval.

7. Unless otherwise determined by the Board or exempted by the terms of paragraph 6, a copy of this resolution shall be printed in each National Bureau publication.

(Resolution adopted October 25, 1926, as revised through September 30, 1974)

Contents

Acknowledgments

A great many people were involved in the development of the research reported in this volume. I would particularly like to acknowledge the roles of Gordon Stewart, president of the Insurance Information Institute (III), and Martin Feldstein, president of the National Bureau of Economic Research (NBER). The ongoing project on the economics of the property-casualty insurance industry is their joint conception and the product of their joint leadership. At a more mundane but also critical level, the financial support of the III provided the wherewithal to carry the project through the first phase constituted by the papers collected in this volume.

The researchers were aided in their tasks by the generous participation of a number of individuals with expertise in the industry. Especially important were economists Sean F. Mooney, senior vice president of the III, and Orin Kramer of Boston Provident Partners. Among others who contributed their inside knowledge were Frederick Yohn of Aetna Life and Casualty, Stephen Collesano and Khan Zahid of American International Group, Michael P. Daly of CIGNA Corporation, Charles A. Parker and Martin Haber of Continental Corporation, Mark L. Ricciardelli of Employers Reinsurance Corporation, James Moor of the Hartford Insurance Company, Frederic W. Hickman and Bradford L. Ferguson of Hopkins and Sutter, Michael Fusco of the Insurance Services Office, Inc., Robert Klein of the National Association of Insurance Commissioners, and Michael E. Hogue of the PW Group.

The papers benefited as well from the academic expertise of Stewart Myers of MIT and a referee for the University of Chicago Press, both of whom read the entire manuscript and provided helpful feedback. Academic and industry critiques were provided as well for four of the papers in connection with their presentation at a Franco-American seminar on uncertainty, risk, and insurance in Pauillac near Bordeaux during the summer of 1994. Jointly organized by the NBER and the Insurance Chairs ENSAE-Delta and Paris X–Nanterre–

Cepremap in Paris, the conference was sponsored by the Fédération Française des Sociétés d'Assurances and AXA France.

A project of this sort requires a great deal of organizational support as well, and I would especially like to thank NBER conference director Kirsten Davis and her assistants Rob Shannon and Lauren Lariviere for making the various meetings and final conference, in several locations, run so smoothly. The bureau's Deborah Kiernan and Christina McFadden coordinated the papers and shepherded the manuscripts into the University of Chicago Press system, where Anita Samen and Christine Schwab efficiently and courteously supervised the details of publication.

To all of these, my heartfelt thanks.

David F. Bradford

Introduction

David F. Bradford

Although there has long been a community of scholars focusing on the study of insurance, it is fair to say that (pensions and life insurance aside) there has been relatively little attention paid to the subject in the economics profession more broadly. In this, insurance differs from banking, for example. In the hope of expanding the network of economists who work on insurance and the stock of empirical knowledge useful to those who develop policies related to the industry (both within companies and at the federal and state governmental levels), Gordon Stewart, president of the Insurance Information Institute (III), proposed to Martin Feldstein, president of the National Bureau of Economic Research (NBER), that the bureau undertake, with III support, a series of studies of the industry. Early in 1993, I was invited to direct for the bureau the first phase of a new program of empirical research addressed to the role of commercial insurance (nonlife and nonhealth) in the U.S. economy.

In a series of meetings and conferences over the next three years, several scholars who had not worked in the area before engaged in discussions with representatives of the industry and scholars with prior research experience in insurance about the industrial organization, regulation, and taxation of the industry, about its relationship to capital markets, about the accounting conventions so critical to understanding industry statistics, and about the sources of data for empirical work. The meetings were also sounding boards for successive versions of the papers collected in this volume, which represent the first fruit of the NBER's ongoing efforts.

In commissioning this initial round of papers we set as our objective studies

David F. Bradford is professor of economics and public affairs at Princeton University, a research associate of the National Bureau of Economic Research, and adjunct professor of law at New York University.

relating to a series of broad topics, including competition and profitability in the property-casualty insurance industry, accounting and taxation issues, determinants of insurance availability, the role of guarantee funds, the relation between government and insurance, the reinsurance market, and the connection between the insurance industry and the process of national capital accumulation.

As work went along, these broad objectives were refined into specific empirical studies and became more particular. One topic, reinsurance, was postponed to the second phase of the project. Of the other topics, profitability is addressed in the paper by Gron and Lucas, which explores the "insurance cycle." Taxation and insurance accounting are at the heart of Bradford and Logue's paper on the impact of tax reform on insurance pricing. Availability is the underlying theme of Jaffee and Russell's and Suponcic and Tennyson's quite different papers on rate regulation. These papers, and especially the Jaffee-Russell paper, also contribute to understanding the connection between government and the industry. Bohn and Hall tell us about guarantee funds, and the team of Born, Gentry, Viscusi, and Zeckhauser contributes insights into the way the insurance industry, with its peculiar mixture of mutual and stock company forms, fits into the national financial puzzle.

To preview the papers in somewhat more detail:

In their paper, "External Financing and Insurance Cycles," Anne Gron and Deborah Lucas take a close look at the behavior of stock companies, asking whether the cost of raising external finance can plausibly explain the phenomenon of periods of high prices and rationing of insurance policies followed by periods of expanding coverage and lower prices. A natural question is why, given the implication that there is a predictable increase in profitability of writing policies in the time of high prices, suppliers of capital do not rush to fill the profit opportunity vacuum. Having established the chronology of the insurance cycle in the past, Gron and Lucas assemble a variety of data bearing on the extent to which stock companies took steps to attract fresh capital coming out of the troughs of the cycle. Looking specifically at the incidence of dividend cuts, repurchases or retirement, and fresh issues of equity and debt, they find evidence that companies respond in the predicted direction but conclude that the magnitudes of the responses are surprisingly small. In addition to the theoretical reasoning and empirical conclusions, readers will find highly informative the wealth of information on trends and patterns in the financial structure of the property-casualty insurance industry presented in the paper.

During the 1980s, federal income tax treatment of property-casualty insurers and their policyholders underwent several important changes, the most significant of which came in 1986. David Bradford and Kyle Logue's paper, "The Effects of Tax Law Changes on Property-Casualty Insurance Prices," develops theoretical predictions of how these changes should have affected the equilibrium prices of property-casualty insurance policies and explores the extent to which the theoretical predictions are realized in data on industry experience.

The paper is devoted mainly to a careful specification of the income tax rules, and to deriving the connection between predictions about simple forms of insurance policy and industry data on "premiums earned." The predicted impact of the changes in the tax rules enacted in 1986 translates into a tax on premiums that varies strongly with the length of the tail of policies. For medical malpractice, the longest tail line of insurance, the impact might have been as much as a 13 percent tax. Using data on industry aggregates for 1976–93 and assuming no biases in insurers' loss-reserving practices, the authors conclude, however, that tax law changes do not explain much of the large swings in the loss ratios observed in the industry.

Two of the papers focus on the impact and origins of rate regulation in a major component of the industry, the market for auto insurance. The studies by the teams of Jaffee and Russell and Suponcic and Tennyson can both also be recommended for the broad overviews they offer of the structure and economics of the insurance industry. In their paper, "The Causes and Consequences of Rate Regulation in the Auto Insurance Industry," Dwight Jaffee and Thomas Russell provide a compact review of what economic theory says about what a competitive auto insurance market ought to look like, an insightful discussion of the ways in which theory fails to predict reality, and a contribution to the economic theory of regulation. Their paper takes as its point of departure an explanation of the strong expansionary trend in the extent and detail of state regulatory control over the auto insurance industry, focusing on the case of Proposition 103 in California. Proposition 103 was a ballot initiative, passed in 1988, that put in place several restrictions on auto insurers, including a rollback of auto insurance rates, limits on the factors that companies could use in placing policyholders in risk classes, and a requirement that companies accept applications for insurance from "good drivers." Noting that prices of most goods and services are not regulated in California, the authors consider explanations based on distributional equity, welfare enhancement (regulatory intervention based on market failure), and fairness for the imposition of regulation on automobile insurance. The first two might be described as conventional economic motives for regulation. Jaffee and Russell, however, identify several reasons for thinking that fairness, the idea that price dispersion should bear some relationship to differences in cost, may play an important role in explaining both the structure of the automobile insurance industry and the politics of Proposition 103.

In "Rate Regulation and the Industrial Organization of Automobile Insurance," Susan Suponcic and Sharon Tennyson consider the theory and evidence relating to the impact of regulation on the number and types of companies operating in a state. To develop their hypotheses, the authors take the reader through data on the composition of the industry in terms of sizes of companies, types of distribution ("direct writers" versus companies that market through independent agents), extent of geographic coverage, and degree of specialization in automobile insurance. The authors relate these characteristics of companies to the predicted strategic approaches they would take to differences in, and changes in, the stringency of rate regulation by states. Using annual data on state aggregates for the period 1987–92 and various measures of regulatory stringency, the authors find support for the conclusion that increased regulation lowers the number of companies, especially low-cost national companies, operating in a state.

James Bohn and Brian Hall take up the problem of who insures the insurers in "The Costs of Insurance Company Failures." Under the decentralized system of regulating insurance companies practiced in the United States, each state operates some form of guarantee or solvency fund, whereby surviving companies are assessed to cover the claims of state residents holding policies of a failed property-casualty company. Likening the system to a tax and social insurance program, Bohn and Hall point out that it raises the usual efficiency and moral hazard issues of such programs. Since the size of the problem has grown sharply, their exploration of the costs, time path, and determinants of resolving insolvency is timely. By painstakingly correlating data from a variety of sources, the authors are able to develop a detailed picture of a large fraction of resolutions of insolvent companies between 1986 and 1993. Their surprising finding is that the costs incurred to resolve insurance company insolvencies are remarkably high—roughly 100 percent of the book value of the assets in the year before the company was declared insolvent. They note that this is nearly three times as high as the costs of resolving bank failures. The implied question for further work, relevant for the design of policy in this area: Why is this so?

In "Organizational Form and Insurance Company Performance: Stocks versus Mutuals," Patricia Born, William Gentry, W. Kip Viscusi, and Richard Zeckhauser take a fresh look at the way the organizational form of an insurance company affects its responses to different situations, including changes in profitability of lines and in regulatory climate. Based on a compact overview of the implications of the theory that a particular form will prevail in an industry if it offers the most effective solution to the industry's particular agency problem, they argue that firms organized as for-profit stock companies will respond more quickly and, in a sense, more opportunistically to changes in their environments. Using data on individual companies in the National Association of Insurance Commissioners records of property-casualty companies' annual financial statements, the authors conclude that in many respects, there is little difference between the performance of stock and mutual companies. They conclude, however, that their central hypothesis of the quicker reactions of stock companies to changes in their circumstances is consistently supported in the data.

1 External Financing and Insurance Cycles

Anne Gron and Deborah Lucas

1.1 Introduction

The property-casualty insurance industry is characterized by an "insurance cycle"—periods of high prices and rationing followed by periods of expanding coverage and lower prices. One might expect that the high-price, restricted-supply phase would be short lived due to competition between insurers for profitable new business. In fact, this phase is persistent enough that it can be observed in annual data. A number of possible explanations for this phenomenon have been suggested. In this paper we test the hypothesis that these episodes are due to temporary capital shortages that reduce the industry's ability to back risk (Winter 1988; Gron 1990). Such shocks to industry net work may arise either from reductions in asset value (e.g., a drop in the stock market) or from unanticipated increases in claims payments.

Past empirical studies of the cycle provide evidence that is consistent with the capital shortage hypothesis: industry capacity measures have a significant, negative relationship with price-claims margins, and large increases in price-claims margins are followed by increases in industry capacity as measured by net worth (Winter 1991a; Gron 1994a, 1994b). Yet this evidence does not explain why capital shortages would not be quickly corrected by an infusion of new capital, particularly when profit margins are high. Unlike many industries, there appears to be no reason for a significant lag between the arrival of new capital and increased capacity. That is, the required "time to build" is short

Anne Gron is assistant professor of management and strategy at the Kellogg Graduate School of Management, Northwestern University. Deborah Lucas is Household International Professor of Finance at the Kellogg Graduate School of Management, Northwestern University, and a research associate of the National Bureau of Economic Research.

The authors thank Susan Chaplinsky, Robert Korajczyk, Mitchell Petersen, and participants at the 1994 Franco-American Economics Conference for helpful comments, and Kate Evert and Dino Faleschetti for careful research assistance. Bob Spatz provided valuable technical assistance.

because financial capital serves primarily as a buffer against high claims costs or poor asset performance.[1] This intuition is captured in models of insurance pricing without capital market frictions where price is equal to the present value of expected claims (see, e.g., Fairley 1979; Hill 1979; Myers and Cohn 1987). In order to explain periods of unusually high profitability, any model of capital constraints for this industry must rely on some mechanism that delays capital inflows when industry net worth is low.[2]

A primary reliance on internally generated funds to finance business expansion is not special to the property-casualty industry. Most firms prefer to use internally generated funds since they avoid the costs associated with external financing. Models attempting to explain this phenomenon typically postulate that capital market imperfections such as asymmetric information increase the cost of external funds. Thus, even if insurers can earn what appear to be abnormal returns on new policies, the cost of raising external funds may exceed the potential benefits from the high returns earned on new policies. The question, then, is whether plausible issue costs can explain the persistence of high-price periods.

To date there has been little empirical research that systematically examines insurer financing decisions in relation to periods with and without likely capital shortages. This paper provides such an overview of insurer financing behavior and its relation to the cycle. In particular, we look for evidence that might support the notion that the cost of external capital for the property-casualty industry is sufficiently high to explain the persistence of high-price, constrained-output periods. Much of our focus is on stock insurers since these insurers should have greater access to external capital and because of data availability.

Section 1.2 begins with a description of the cyclic nature of the insurance industry over the period 1967–90, using aggregate industry and financial statistics for a sample of stock insurers. Since reducing cash payments to stockholders is an alternative to issuing debt or equity, we look for evidence of changes in payout policy over the cycle. In section 1.3 we describe the sample of public debt and equity issues used in the analysis of external financing and summarize the evidence on how much insurers raise in the capital markets, what types of instruments are used, whether reliance on external sources has changed over time, and how financing varies with the relative abundance of capital in the industry and overall market conditions.

Evidence on the cost of external financing is examined in section 1.4. A key indicator of this cost is the stock price reaction to a security issue announcement since it reflects the revision in the market's expectations about the value of an issuing firm. To evaluate the hypothesis that external finance is unusually

1. It has been suggested, however, that in the aftermath of a major disaster, the disruption in established policyholder relationships may result in a longer time to build.
2. See also the models of insurance pricing with possible capital shortages by Cummins and Danzon (1991), Cagle and Harrington (1995), and Doherty and Garven (1995).

costly for the property-casualty industry, we measure the stock price reaction to insurer announcements of equity issues and debt issues and compare these price changes to those for other industries. We focus primarily on equity issues since these are a relatively costly form of external finance. Asquith and Mullins (1986) find that industrial firms announcing an equity issue experience a stock price decline of 2–3 percent on average, which for a typical issuer represents a drop in market value equal to about 20 percent of the total cash raised.[3] If stock price reactions to stock issues by property-casualty insurers are unusually negative, this would provide evidence that insurers face a relatively high cost of external funds.[4] Section 1.5 concludes with a discussion of explanations for the insurance cycle that are alternatives to the capital shortage hypothesis.

1.2   Industry Measures

In this section we summarize the performance of stock property-casualty insurers over the period 1967–90. Using data from a variety of sources, the time path of profitability, capital structure, and payout policy is related to the insurance cycle.

1.2.1   Measures of Profitability, Capacity, and Prices

Insurance market conditions are usually described in terms of accounting profitability. Industry profitability, measured as net income divided by revenues, is graphed in figure 1.1 for the 1967–93 period.[5] A change from declining to increasing profitability marks the beginning of a high-price, restricted-output period.[6] During these years, there are three episodes of high price and restricted output: 1969–70, 1975–76, and 1985–86. Premium price changes, net worth series, and stock indexes follow a similar pattern. Gron (1994b) finds that large increases in price-claims indexes coincide with changes from de-

---

3. One explanation for the price drop is that the riskiness of equity exacerbates problems of asymmetric information since purchasers anticipate issues by predominantly overvalued firms (Myers and Majluf 1984).

4. This research also contributes to the literature on the link between firm financing and real market outcomes, much of which explores the effect of decreased liquidity on real firm decisions. Recent theoretical and empirical work (e.g., Fazzari, Hubbard, and Petersen 1988; Chevalier and Scharfstein 1994) suggests that competition among firms is weaker, and price–noncapital cost margins are higher, when firms and the industry are more liquidity constrained. A similar pattern is observed in the property-casualty industry: when industry capacity is low the price of insurance relative to noncapital costs is higher, perhaps reflecting a temporary increase in the opportunity cost of capital.

5. Unless otherwise noted, the data described here are from *Best's Aggregates and Averages* (A. M. Best Company, various years).

6. Price and quantity data would be preferable for describing market conditions, but they are not available. Other profitability series show the same time-series pattern (Stewart 1984). Due to accounting practices, income from insurance premiums tends to reflect pricing conditions for the previous as well as the current accounting period. Therefore, the greatest increase in profitability will not necessarily coincide with the largest increase in prices. Anecdotal evidence confirms that pricing changes occur around the time accounting profitability changes. Gron (1994a) and Cummins and Outreville (1986) provide useful discussions of insurance accounting.

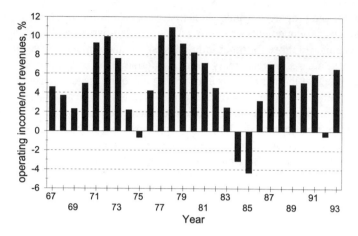

Fig. 1.1   Industry operating income

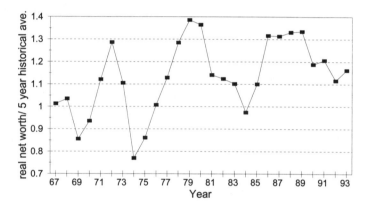

Fig. 1.2   Industry capacity

creasing to increasing accounting profitability. Large increases in the price-claims margin occur in 1969–70, 1975–76, and 1985.

Capacity is related to the volume of policies that can be supported by the industry's capital base. Although a precise regulatory measure of capacity does not exist, the time-series pattern of various proxies for industry capacity are consistent with the capital shortage hypothesis (see fig. 1.2). For instance, here industry capacity is measured as the ratio of industry net worth to its five-year historical average. The series has relative minima at 1969, 1974, and 1984, suggesting that capacity is low immediately before price-claims margins rise. The figure also reveals that large declines in capacity immediately precede low-capacity years.[7]

---

7. Net worth divided by a historical average is also used in Winter (1991) and in Gron (1994b). A different measure of capacity, industry net worth divided by GNP, displays a similar pattern and

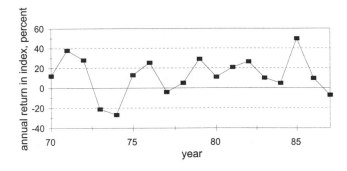

Fig. 1.3   Property-casualty stock returns, 1970–87

Finally, figure 1.3 displays annual returns for A. M. Best's property-casualty company stock index for the years 1970–87.[8] Data for more recent years are unavailable. The stock return series shows a pattern similar to the other industry aggregates: returns of property-casualty firms reach relative minima in 1974 and 1984, with substantial increases in annual returns in the years immediately following these relative minima.

For comparison to the above aggregates, we also collected data on a sample of large property-casualty and multiline insurers listed in quarterly and/or annual Compustat for the 1970–92 period. Data for 38 different insurers are available from this source, but not all insurers were listed for the entire period. Data for 1970–72 are particularly sparse, and for the remainder of the 1970s there are an average of 21 observations per year. Observations per year increase to about 30 in the early 1980s and to 35 by the end of the period.[9]

Figure 1.4 shows the annual means of income normalized by sales or assets for this Compustat sample. The pattern found in the aggregate industry ratios is also seen here. Clearly, 1985 was a year of particularly low income. Income was relatively low as well in 1970 and 1974. The mean annual ratio of liabilities to assets is generally increasing over the period. While the ratio declines somewhat in the latter part of the 1970s, there is really only one distinct feature, which is the significant increase in liabilities relative to assets in 1985.

1.2.2   Payout Policy

Internally generated funds represent by far the largest source of capital for U.S. corporations.[10] The primary advantage of internal financing is that it

---

is used in Gron (1994a, 1994b). For a more detailed exploration of the capacity-price time-series relationship, see Gron (1994b).

8. Stock index data are from van Aartrijk (1985) and A. M. Best Company (1988).

9. Two firms had negative equity for one year: Mission Insurance in 1985 and Ambase in 1990. Mission was declared insolvent and liquidated in 1985. Ambase was reorganized in 1990. These observations were dropped from the sample.

10. The OECD reports that internal funds comprise almost 80 percent of financing for U.S. firms in the period 1984–88.

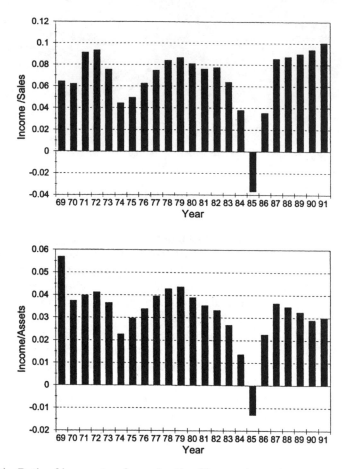

Fig. 1.4   Ratio of income to sales and ratio of income to assets

avoids the direct and indirect costs associated with issuing new securities. Clearly, one way for firms to increase available internal funds is to cut back on payouts to shareholders, that is, by reducing dividends or repurchases. While stock repurchases are considered discretionary, managers appear reluctant to reduce dividends except when under strong financial pressure to do so, in part because of the negative stock price reaction to dividend cuts. As a result, we expect to see an overall reduction in dividend growth rates and repurchase activity during periods of industry-wide capital shortages, with a potentially larger response of repurchases than of dividends.

One measure of dividend policy is the payout ratio, which measures the dollar dividend per share divided by earnings per share. Figure 1.5 plots the payout ratio for the period 1972–90 using data from quarterly Compustat on property-casualty insurers, as described above. Notice that the payout ratio

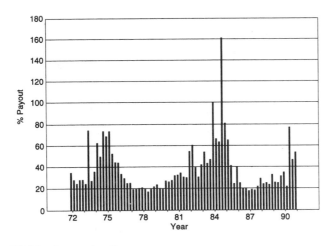

Fig. 1.5   Dividend payout ratio

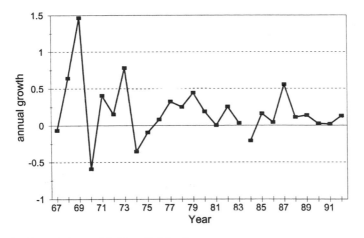

Fig. 1.6   Growth in stockholder dividends

hovers between 25 and 60 percent for most of this period, with a noticeable increase in the payout ratio in the two years preceding the earnings crash of 1984–85. As in other industries, it appears that insurers follow a fairly smooth payout policy. The exception to this was the period 1984–85, at which time dividends clearly fell by much less than earnings. If 1975–76 and 1985–86 are taken to be periods of capital shortage, the graph is consistent with the idea that payout ratios were somewhat reduced in the years immediately following these episodes, perhaps in an effort to rebuild capital. Similar conclusions can be drawn from the time-series behavior of the dividend yield (dividend divided by price).

To look more closely at these changes, figure 1.6 shows the proportional

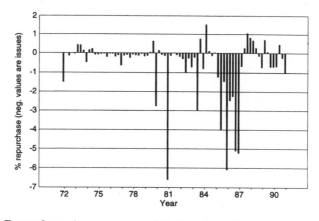

Fig. 1.7   Repurchases (as percentage of stock outstanding)

changes in aggregate stockholder dividends over the 1967–92 period.[11] Consistent with the idea that dividends are only reduced under duress, negative growth is rarely observed. In fact, years with dividend cuts coincide with turning points in the cycle—1970, 1974–75, and 1984—suggesting some attempt was made to conserve scarce capital.

As discussed above, an alternative to dividends is to use share repurchases to distribute cash. Although still less important than dividends, the volume of repurchases by U.S. firms has grown steadily over the past several decades. Figure 1.7 plots equity repurchases and issues over the 1972–90 period, also using data from quarterly Compustat for firms classified as property-casualty insurers. The data again support the idea that insurers were trying to rebuild capital following the 1984–85 shock. In particular, no repurchases for the 32 firms in the sample were reported from 1985–87, but repurchase activity resumed in 1988 and thereafter. Interpreting repurchase activity for the earlier period is more problematic because repurchases are less prevalent and because data are available for only 12 firms. The increase in repurchase activity in 1983–84 is consistent with the rise in dividend payout ratios in the same years, but it is somewhat surprising in light of the drop in net worth that appears at about the same time.

1.3   Firm Financing Behavior

The statistics presented in the previous section suggest that profitability in the property-casualty industry has varied markedly over time, with episodes of high prices and restricted output in 1969–70, 1975–76, and most notably in

11. The data are from *Best's Aggregates and Averages*. The pre-1983 series consists of aggregate stock company measures. The post-1983 series consists of consolidated data for all insurers. The large increase in 1969 is most likely a one-time adjustment due to the passage of the Holding Company Act.

1985–86. Although payouts to shareholders grew at a slower rate in the high-price, restricted-output phases, the large fluctuations in capital do not appear to be substantially offset by efforts to conserve internally generated funds via changes in payout policy.

An alternative to financing with retained earnings is to raise capital externally. Here we focus on public debt and equity issues as sources of external funds and examine how the volume of new issues in the property-casualty industry has varied over time and with market conditions. We concentrate on debt and equity because of data availability and because these sources are likely to account for a large fraction of external financing. It should be noted, however, that other sources of external finance, including bank loans, private placements of debt and equity, and other types of securities such as convertible bonds or warrants, are also potential sources of capital.

1.3.1   Data

We obtained all SEC-registered debt and equity announcement and issue dates for the property-casualty industry from the Securities Data Company (SDC). Since 1970, this sample includes 171 equity issues by 100 different property-casualty companies, reinsurers, and holding companies, totaling over $11.5 billion. We also obtained information on companies in these categories for 142 debt issues that yielded over $13.6 billion. The data obtained include the total value of the issue, the number of shares issued in the case of equity, and the type of debt or equity issued (e.g., preferred, common, subordinated). For companies with a listed issue date but no announcement date, the announcement date was obtained when possible from the *Wall Street Journal Index*. The sample does not include companies that announce an issue but then do not follow through with it.

1.3.2   Volume of Equity Issues over Time

The time-series pattern of external financing in the property-casualty industry can be related to potentially explanatory variables such as changes in firm and industry net worth, stock market returns, and economy-wide financing behavior. Table 1.1 shows the number of firms issuing equity each year and the total dollar value of issues, while figure 1.8 shows the annual dollar volume of equity issues as a fraction of industry net worth. For all series the data display two peaks: a larger peak at 1985–86 and a smaller peak at 1971–72. These correspond to two of the three periods of high price and restricted output. In the third period in which industry data suggest a capital shortage, 1975–76, there is not such a clear peak. While total equity offered relative to industry net worth increases slightly in 1976, the number of firms issuing equity is not significantly different from other years. As with the earlier series, the activity during the 1980s is significantly greater than that of the preceding period.

The question arises of whether insurers issue more during certain periods because of conditions particular to the property-casualty industry, or whether

Table 1.1   **Equity and Debt Issues**

Year	No. of Equity Issues	Value of Equity Issues (million $)	No. of Debt Issues	Value of Debt Issues (million $)
1970	1	3.5	3	172.2
1971	14	191.9	2	26.1
1972	18	313.1	5	130
1973	1	0.6	3	213.3
1974	0	0	2	200.4
1975	0	0	1	0.4
1976	2	78.8	3	105
1977	4	15.6	4	103.6
1978	5	23.1	4	157.3
1979	0	0	2	22.7
1980	4	72	3	66.9
1981	2	35.2	3	116
1982	2	71.5	5	241.5
1983	7	404.5	4	322.8
1984	4	222.7	2	99.8
1985	29	2,787.9	9	947.5
1986	29	3,067.5	15	1,816.6
1987	6	386	12	1,369.7
1988	4	69.5	13	1,443
1989	1	15.5	7	1,445.3
1990	4	272	1	99.9
1991	6	669.3	15	1,813
1992	14	1,968.5	11	1,338.2
1993	14	860.9	13	1,408.6

they were simply following broad-based financing trends in the market. For industrial firms, the volume of equity issues varies substantially over time, with the bulk of issues clustered in "hot" market periods. One prominent characteristic of hot market periods is that aggregate stock market returns are above average.

To examine whether property-casualty issues are clustered with those of industrial issuers, we use the classification of historical hot and cold market periods identified by Bayless and Chaplinsky (1994). For their sample of industrial firms they find that 60 percent of the issues occur in hot periods (28 percent of the months considered) while only 13 percent of the issues occur in cold periods (29 percent of these months). Why this pronounced clustering of equity issues occurs remains somewhat mysterious; some have attributed it to temporal variations in adverse selection while others point to fads in financing mechanisms and waves of market optimism. Whatever the explanation, the average stock price drop for industrial firms is lower during hot periods by about 2 percent, a substantial cost differential that appears to benefit hot market issuers (Bayless and Chaplinsky 1994). For the 137 issues in our sample that occurred over this time period, 66 occurred in hot periods while only 10 occurred in

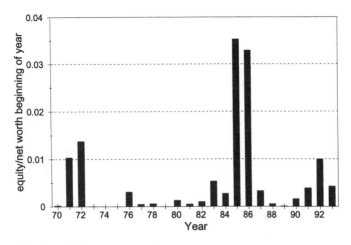

Fig. 1.8   Equity relative to net worth

cold periods.[12] This suggests issue behavior temporally similar to other equity issuers and may explain the relatively low volume of issues in 1975–76 despite the apparent capital shortage in the property-casualty industry.

1.3.3   Volume of Debt Issues over Time

The time-series properties of our sample of debt issues is summarized in figures 1.9, 1.10, and 1.11. As with equity issues, the most activity occurs in 1986, and there is more activity generally toward the end of the period. In contrast to equity issues, however, the peaks of financing activity are less pronounced. Issue volume patterns also vary across debt maturities. Short-term debt issues are rare in the 1970s but are used quite frequently in the last five or six years of the period. Even in the later period, however, short-term debt accounts for a small fraction of total proceeds.[13] The issue pattern of medium-term debt over time is similar to that for equity, with proceeds as a fraction of industry net worth peaking in 1971, 1976, and 1986. Notice that the issue volume in 1976 is large relative to equity, perhaps because firms were substituting debt issues for equity issues in this cold market period. Long-term debt issues, like short-term issues, do not exhibit any particular correlation with industry-wide changes in net worth or market conditions.

Data on long-term debt are also available from quarterly Compustat for many of the firms in the smaller sample examined in section 1.2. For comparison, figure 1.12 shows the average percentage changes in long-term debt over the 1974–90 period for the Compustat firms (which number 12 in 1974 and

12. The relatively large number of issues in 1992 and 1993 also appears to be consistent with high overall issue volume in this period.
13. This measure of short-term debt does not include bank loans, which could be an important source of additional short-term capital.

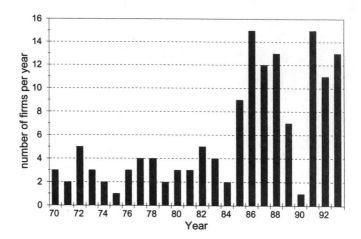

Fig. 1.9   Debt issues

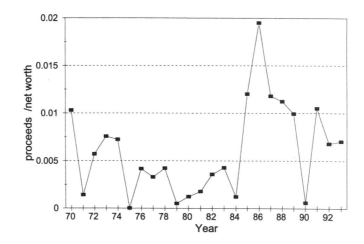

Fig. 1.10   Debt issues relative to net worth

increase to 28 firms in 1989). As for the larger SDC sample, on average changes to debt were positive but show no particular pattern in relation to the insurance cycle. Notice that the large percentage increases in the earlier part of the period reflect the low base of debt at that time. Figure 1.13 shows the ratio of long-term debt to total assets over the same period, where total assets is measured as the sum of market equity and book liabilities. In this graph the increase in the ratio of debt to value in 1984–85 primarily reflects the drop in stock price rather than an increase in debt.

As in the case of equity issues, it is difficult to disentangle increases in external financing due to events particular to the property-casualty industry from increases due to broader market trends. The growth of debt financing in the

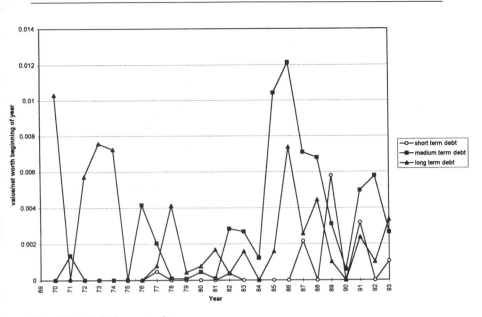

Fig. 1.11 Debt by maturity

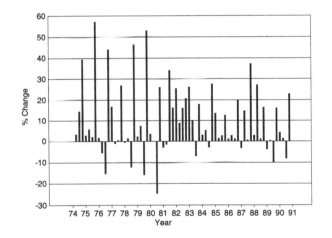

Fig. 1.12 Changes in debt

middle to late 1980s is consistent with large economy-wide increases in lever-age, due in part to the more favorable tax treatment of debt following the Tax Reform Act of 1986.

1.3.4 Evaluating the Importance of External Finance

As we have seen, the observed pattern of debt and equity issues is consistent with the idea that insurers use external finance to offset reductions in capital,

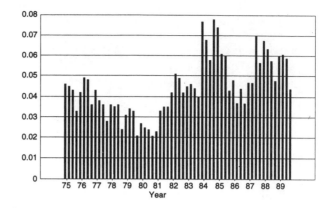

Fig. 1.13   Long-term debt (as fraction of firm value)

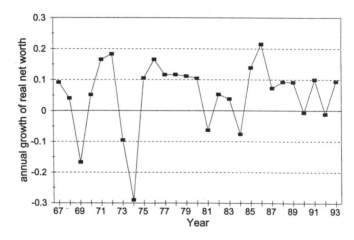

Fig. 1.14   Growth in industry net worth

but it could also be attributed to broader market trends. To evaluate the quantitative importance of external finance in offsetting the cycle, we compare the total amount of externally generated financing to changes in total net worth. The annual growth in real net worth for the industry is shown in figure 1.14. Negative-growth years are 1969, 1973, 1974, 1981, 1984, 1990, 1992, where the last two are quite close to zero. High-growth years generally follow those with negative growth and include 1971, 1972, 1975, 1976, 1985, and 1986. The use of external financing is actually greater in these high-growth years, which might be explained by the lead time needed to arrange an issue. The delay could also arise if insurers wait for the market to recognize the potential for profitable expansion before issuing. Interestingly, the amount of total capital raised in equity and debt markets is not large relative to the total increase in net worth in these years. The ratio of total debt and equity funds generated to the increase in stock insurers' net worth is 13 percent in 1970, 4 percent in 1976, and 33.6 percent in 1985. Of course, the amounts raised represent a much larger fraction of the net worth of the issuing firms.

To evaluate whether the relationship between issues and capacity is statistically significant, we performed the regression analysis presented in table 1.2. For both equity and debt issues, we examined three measures: the number of issues, the real value of funds issued, and the value of funds issued relative to industry net worth at the beginning of the year. Our explanatory variables are capacity at the beginning of the year, measured as industry net worth as of the beginning of the year divided by the five-year historical average, and the ratio of industry liabilities to assets, as of the beginning of the year.[14] The results in table 1.2 show there is a negative relationship between industry capacity and the various measures of equity financing. This relationship is generally significant at or above the 15 percent confidence level. In addition, there is a positive relationship between measures of equity financing and the ratio of liabilities to assets at the beginning of the period, although this relationship is less precisely measured. On the other hand, there is no statistically significant relationship between capacity and measures of debt financing. Debt financing, like equity financing, is positively related to industry leverage as measured by liabilities relative to assets.

An often-cited "capacity" statistic in the industry is the ratio of premium revenue to net worth. This ratio reflects the industry's leverage in terms of premium revenue. Under the assumption that premium revenue primarily reflects the expectation of uncertain claims costs, this ratio reflects expected costs relative to the funds available if realized costs exceed their expectations. If there is some maximum ratio of premium revenue to net worth and if insurers are at or near that limit after declines in net worth, then the percentage increase in net worth following a security issue translates into the same percentage increase in premium revenue supported. As seen from the discussion above, the increase in premium revenue that can be supported by the externally generated funds is relatively small for all years but 1985–87.

1.4 The Announcement Effect of Equity and Debt Issues

As discussed earlier, there are significant direct and indirect costs to security issues that can discourage firms from financing otherwise attractive investment opportunities. Direct costs include underwriters' fees, SEC filing requirements, distribution costs, bank charges, and so on. The largest indirect cost, usually associated with the issue of risky securities such as equity, is the negative market price reaction to the announcement of an issue. The argument that high-price, restricted-output periods in the property-casualty industry are due to capital shortages implicitly rests on the idea that raising capital is prohibi-

14. Industry data are from *Best's Aggregates and Averages,* as described in section 1.2.

Table 1.2   External Financing and Industry Capacity

Explanatory Variable	Dependent Variables					
	No. of Equity Issues	Real Value of Equity Issues	Value of Equity Issues / Net Worth	No. of Debt Issues	Real Value of Debt Issues	Value of Debt Issues / Net Worth
Capacity	−13.54	−1,471.68	−.017	−3.50	−455.30	−.006
	(−1.54)	(−1.69)	(−1.72)	(−.81)	(−.82)	(−1.12)
Liability / assets	49.58	7,612.00	.06	58.61	6,530.88	.03
	(1.33)	(2.06)	(1.45)	(3.20)	(2.79)	(1.43)
R^2	.13	.21	.16	.33	.27	.11

Notes: Numbers in parentheses are *t*-statistics. All regressions have 24 observations.

tively expensive as a result of these direct and indirect costs. To see whether there is evidence of unusually high financing costs, in this section we measure the stock price reaction to insurance company issues of debt and equity and compare the reaction to that for other financial and industrial firms.

1.4.1 Equity Issues

We focus primarily on equity issues because they provide capital in a form that is clearly acceptable to regulators and because they are a relatively expensive form of financing. Not only are there significant direct costs involved in equity issues, estimated to range from 1 to 5 percent of the value issued, but issuers typically experience a significant drop in their stock price as well.

One commonly accepted explanation for the announcement-day price drop is that asymmetric information between managers and potential shareholders creates an adverse selection problem (Myers and Majluf 1984). Firms that realize their stock is overvalued have an incentive to issue additional stock since their current shareholders will benefit at the expense of the new buyers. Similarly, managers who believe their stock is undervalued will avoid issuing equity. Potential buyers, realizing these incentives, react to the announcement of an equity issue as a signal that the stock is overvalued, and hence the market price falls. Consequently, many firms whose stock is not undervalued would forgo or postpone valuable investment opportunities or rely more on internal financing rather than issue equity at a depressed price.[15]

Empirical studies of stock price behavior around equity issues (e.g., Masulis and Korwar 1986; Mikkelson and Partch 1986; Korajczyk, Lucas, and McDonald 1990) reveal a number of regularities that are consistent with this basic adverse selection story. For industrial firms, stock prices fall an average of 2–3 percent at the announcement of an issue. Following this, there is a further drop of about 0.5 percent for firms that follow through with an issue. Studies have also found that issuing firms have abnormally high returns in the months preceding the announcement of an issue, an observation that also can be explained by the impact of adverse selection in a multiperiod setting (Lucas and McDonald 1990). More recent evidence suggests that issuing firms experience negative abnormal returns in the three to five years after they issue, suggesting that the price drop at announcement underestimates the bad news associated with the average issue (Loughran and Ritter 1996).

The price behavior for financial firms and utilities is somewhat different. For instance, the announcement-day stock price drop for public utilities is considerably lower than for industrial firms. The differential may be due to the facts that utilities issue more frequently so the announcement is more likely to be anticipated and that they have more easily observable investment projects.

---

15. This argument presumes that undervalued firms have no way to credibly and inexpensively convey this information to the market. One might also argue that the price drop does not represent a cost to firms that are overvalued. Even for this group, however, firms acting in the interests of shareholders who would prefer to see their stock at a higher price will be reluctant to issue.

The fact that their rate of return is regulated may also have an impact. In a study of the banking industry, Cornett and Tehranian (1994) conjecture that the stock price reaction to equity issues by commercial banks will be more pronounced for "voluntary" than for "involuntary" issues, and they find some evidence supporting this claim. An involuntary issue is defined as occurring when the issuing bank is in violation of regulatory capital adequacy requirements.[16]

On a priori grounds it is not clear how the indirect costs of equity issues should be expected to change over the insurance cycle. In analogy to the case of commercial banks studied by Cornett and Tehranian (1994), one might expect the stock price reaction to equity issues to be less negative during the high-price, constrained-supply phase because investors can observe the need for capital and the potential for profitable investment. This suggests that insurers would face relatively low costs of issuing equity in these periods, making it more puzzling that supply shortages persist. On the other hand, insurance is an information-intensive business, and it is plausible that managers have a much better idea of the value of their assets and liabilities than does the market. Even during a high-price, constrained-output phase, an equity issue could reveal that a firm was hit with a particularly large number of costly claims or low asset returns, forcing it to go to the equity market.

Results

To assess the market price reaction to an insurer equity issue, we calculate abnormal returns over the 20-day window surrounding the announcement of an equity issue. The abnormal return is calculated as the daily return of the issuing company minus the daily return of a value-weighted market index.[17] These returns are taken from the Center for Research on Security Prices (CRSP) data tapes, which provide information on NYSE/AMEX and NASDAQ stocks. Of the 171 equity issue events obtained from SDC and after excluding brokerages, we were able to match 113 to CRSP data using CUSIP identification numbers. Cumulative abnormal returns were calculated by compounding the average daily abnormal returns over the 20-day window.

On day 0 (the announcement day) the average price drop across the 113 events for which data were available was 1.1 percent, with a standard deviation of 2.69 percent. Although the drop is not statistically significant, it is much larger than the typical daily abnormal return in other days in the event window, which never exceeds 0.45 percent. In contrast to previous studies on industrial firms, no apparent price drop is observed on day −1, suggesting little information leakage prior to the announcement. The standard deviation of abnormal returns is fairly constant over the event window. Figure 1.15 summarizes the

---

16. A parallel experiment for property-casualty insurers is complicated by the absence of a well-specified regulatory capital requirement.

17. The results are unchanged if an equally weighted index is used to calculate abnormal returns. It is also possible to calculate β-adjusted abnormal returns, but this requires more financial data and generally makes little difference in this type of event study.

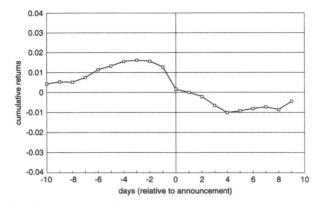

Fig. 1.15   Equity issues (cumulative abnormal returns)

behavior of abnormal returns for issuing firms. As a robustness check, we also calculated the price reaction excluding firms that were classified as primarily brokerages or health and accident and including all firms for which data were available. The price drop and variance for the different samples were almost identical.

Because of the small sample size, it is hard to draw strong conclusions about how this price reaction compares to that for other industries. It appears, however, that the price drop is relatively small compared to the experience of industrial firms, which typically drop 2–3 percent in value. It is more similar to the price drop in response to bank equity issues of 1.56 percent for voluntary issues and 0.64 percent for involuntary issues found by Cornett and Tehranian (1994). This relatively small price drop exacerbates the puzzle of why insurers do not rely more on external financing during the high-price, constrained-supply phase of the insurance cycle.

The Effect of Market Climate

Recall that many property-casualty industry issues occur during economy-wide hot market periods, and that for industrial firms the price drop is lower at these times. To see whether insurers issuing in hot markets also gain a price advantage, we divide the sample between "hot" and "not hot" issuers, again using the date classifications suggested by Bayless and Chaplinsky (1994):[18]

Hot	Not Hot
11/80–03/84	03/69–10/80
07/85–09/87	04/84–06/85
04/88–10/88	10/87–03/88
	11/88–10/89

18. Because of the small number of issue events in each year, it is not possible to identify systematic changes in the price drop over time more finely.

In our sample 52 announcements occur in identified hot periods and 26 announcements occur in not hot periods. Consistent with the findings for industrial firms, the average price drop for the hot market issuers was only 0.7 percent while for not hot market issuers the drop was 1.6 percent. For the unclassified post–October 1989 period, the average price drop for the 36 events in our sample is 1 percent. In none of the subperiods is the price drop statistically significantly different from zero, although (with the exception of the hot market group) they are at least twice as large as the average price change on any other day in the 20-day window.[19]

Cross-Sectional Influences

The price drop at issue announcement is potentially affected by cross-sectional factors such as the size of the issue. In a regression of the price drop on issue size, however, no significant relationship was detected.

1.4.2   Debt Issues

In comparison to most other companies insurers have little ordinary debt in their capital structure. One explanation for this is that policyholders already have debtlike claims on a firm's cash flows, making additional fixed obligations less attractive. Still, issuing debt that is junior to the claims of policyholders is a viable way to increase capital, particularly as a short-term measure. For most firms issuing debt is a less costly alternative to issuing equity because of both lower direct costs and lower indirect costs. Indirect costs are lower because it is fairly easy for management and the market to agree on the value of a low-risk security such as debt. This implies that one would not expect to see a large price drop on the announcement of a debt issue, a conjecture that has been confirmed by earlier empirical work on industrial firm issues.

To see how the market responds to property-casualty industry debt issues we follow the methodology of the previous section, computing average abnormal returns in the 20-day window centered on debt issue announcement days (see fig. 1.16). For the 82 debt issues for which announcement days could be matched to stock return data, the price drop on the announcement day averaged 0.5 percent. As expected, the drop was statistically insignificant and similar in magnitude to abnormal returns on other days in the window. It appears that the market receives property-casualty debt issues similarly to those of other firms.

1.5   Concluding Remarks

In this paper we have explored the conjecture that the periodic episodes of high prices and constrained supply in the property-casualty industry are the

19. It would be interesting to compare these statistics to the price response to issues in high-price, constrained-supply periods that do not correspond the hot market periods. Unfortunately only a few of the issues fall into this category, so no meaningful comparison can be made.

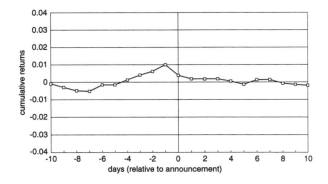

Fig. 1.16   Debt issues (cumulative abnormal returns)

result of temporary capital shortages. To do this we looked for increases in activities aimed at increasing capital at these times: dividend cuts, repurchase cuts, equity issues, and debt issues. We also looked for evidence that the costs of raising external capital are unusually high relative to other industries by examining the market price response to security issues.

There is some evidence of payout policy changes in the expected direction, and also of an increased volume of debt and equity issues following low-capacity periods. The total amount of capital obtained by security issues or reduced payouts, however, appears to be small relative to the observed drops in net worth, suggesting that insurers rely primarily on future retained earnings to rebuild their capital positions. When property-casualty insurers do go to the capital markets we find no evidence that they receive an unusually poor reception. In fact, the market price reaction to equity issues appears to be considerably less negative than for industrial issuers, but similar to that for banks and utilities.

These findings make the seeming reluctance of property-casualty insurers to rely more heavily on external capital markets somewhat surprising and suggest several possibilities to be explored in future research. One interpretation of our evidence is that the cycle should not be attributed to periodic shortages of capital, but instead to another factor(s) that remains to be identified. For instance, one explanation of the cycle that does not rely on capital market imperfections is that premiums rise in response to new information about expected cost increases. Changes in loss distributions produce large reductions in industry net worth, and insurers update their estimates of expected claims and increase prices accordingly. Since current cost data do not fully reflect this new information, the relation between industry capacity and operating margins temporarily shifts. Under this alternative hypothesis, we would not expect insurers' cost of external financing to be unusually high, nor would insurance prices necessarily increase with low capital.

On the other hand, although the incorporation of new public information into prices may be a factor in the cycle, new information alone is unlikely to explain a number of phenomena that appear to be related to the cost of capital or other asymmetric information problems. For one, periods of high prices also appear to be periods of rationing. The fact that insurers temporally concentrate their equity issues during periods in which other firms are issuing equity and in periods following an increase in industry profitability also suggests that asymmetric information is a factor.

A second possibility is that the costs of raising external capital are much higher than the observed price reactions to equity issues suggest, particularly for the firms that choose not to issue securities. A shortcoming of our method is that we can only observe costs for the firms that find it profitable to go ahead with an issue, and even in this case we rely on an indirect measure of the costs (i.e., the market price response). Several aspects of the data do point toward high costs: the propensity of firms to issue in hot markets, the somewhat higher cost of issuing in cold markets, and the small volume of equity and debt issues overall.

Finally, an interesting trend in the data is the significant increase in the use of debt and equity issues by insurers over time. If capital availability did play a major role in past fluctuations, we would expect to see less pronounced cycles in the future as the size and informational efficiency of capital markets continue to increase.

References

A. M. Best Company. Various years. *Best's aggregates and averages: Property-casualty.* Oldwick, N.J.: A. M. Best Company.
———. 1988. 1987 Insurance stock trends. *Best's Review: Property-Casualty Insurance Edition* 88 (11): 34–38, 42.
Asquith, Paul, and David W. Mullins, Jr. 1986. Equity issues and offering dilution. *Journal of Financial Economics* 15 (January/February): 61–89.
Bayless, Mark, and S. Chaplinsky. 1994. Favorable pricing and hot and cold equity issue markets. Working paper. Evanston, Ill.: Northwestern University.
Cagle, Julie A. B., and Scott E. Harrington. 1995. Insurance supply with endogenous insolvency risk. *Journal of Risk and Uncertainty* 11:219–32.
Chevalier, J., and D. Scharfstein. 1994. Capital market imperfections and countercyclical markups: Theory and evidence. NBER Working Paper no. 4614. Cambridge, Mass.: National Bureau of Economic Research, January.
Cornett, M. M., and H. Tehranian. 1994. An examination of voluntary versus involuntary security issuances by commercial banks. *Journal of Financial Economics* 35:99–122.
Cummins, J. David, and Patricia Danzon. 1991. Price shocks and capital flows in liability insurance. In *Cycles and crises in property/casualty insurance: Causes and implications for public policy,* ed. J. D. Cummins, S. E. Harrington, and R. W. Klein. Kansas City, Mo.: National Association of Insurance Commissioners.
Cummins, J. David, and J. François Outreville. 1986. An international analysis of un-

derwriting cycles in property-liability insurance. *Journal of Risk and Insurance* 54:246–62.

Doherty, Neil, and James Garven. 1995. Insurance cycles: Interest rates and the capacity constraint model. *Journal of Business* 68:383–404.

Fairley, William B. 1979. Investment income and profit margins in property-liability insurance. *Bell Journal of Economics* 10 (spring): 192–210.

Fazzari, F. M., R. G. Hubbard, and B. C. Petersen. 1988. Financing constraints and corporate investment. *Brookings Papers on Economic Activity,* no. 1, 141–95.

Gron, Anne. 1990. Property-casualty insurance cycles, capacity constraints, and empirical results. Ph.D. diss., Massachusetts Institute of Technology, Cambridge.

———. 1994a. Capacity constraints and cycles in property-casualty insurance markets. *Rand Journal of Economics* 25:110–27.

———. 1994b. Evidence of capacity constraints in property-casualty insurance. *Journal of Law and Economics* 37:349–77.

Hill, R. D. 1979. Profit regulation in property-liability insurance. *Bell Journal of Economics* 10 (spring): 172–91.

Korajczyk, R., D. Lucas, and R. McDonald. 1990. Understanding stock price behavior around the time of equity issues. In *Asymmetric information, corporate finance, and investment,* ed. R. Glenn Hubbard. Chicago: University of Chicago Press.

Loughran, Tim, and Jay Ritter. 1996. Long-term market overreaction: The effect of low-priced stocks. *Journal of Finance* 51: 1959–70.

Lucas, Deborah, and Robert L. McDonald. 1990. Equity issues and stock price dynamics. *Journal of Finance* 45 (4): 1019–43.

Masulis, Ronald W., and Ashok N. Korwar. 1986. Seasoned equity offerings: An empirical investigation. *Journal of Financial Economics* 15 (January/February): 91–118.

Mikkelson, Wayne H., and M. Megan Partch. 1986. Valuation effects of security offerings and the issuance process. *Journal of Financial Economics* 15 (January/February): 31–60.

Myers, S. C., and R. A. Cohn. 1987. A discounted cash flow approach to property-liability rate regulation. In *Fair rate of return in property-liability insurance,* ed. J. D. Cummins and S. E. Harrington. Boston: Kluwer Nijhoff.

Myers, Stewart C., and Nicholas S. Majluf. 1984. Corporate financing and investment decisions when firms have information that investors do not have. *Journal of Financial Economics* 13:187–221.

Stewart, Barbara D. 1984. Profit cycles in property-liability insurance. In *Issues in insurance,* vol. 2, ed. John D. Long and Everett D. Randall. Malvern, Pa.: American Institute for Property and Liability Underwriters.

van Aartrijk, Peter. 1985. 1984 Insurance stock trends. *Best's Review: Property-Casualty Insurance Edition* 85 (10): 13–15, 103–4.

Winter, Ralph A. 1988. The liability crisis and the dynamics of competitive insurance markets. *Yale Journal on Regulation* 5:455–500.

———. 1991. The dynamics of competitive insurance markets. Toronto: University of Toronto. Mimeograph.

2 The Effects of Tax Law Changes on Property-Casualty Insurance Prices

David F. Bradford and Kyle D. Logue

An insurance company is a financial intermediary whose main line of business is the sale of a particular type of contingent contract, called an insurance policy. Under this contract, the insurer promises to pay some amount to the policyholder, or to some other beneficiary, following the occurrence of an insured event. In the context of property-casualty insurance, the relevant insured events include, for example, the accidental destruction of the insured's property or the award of a liability judgment against the insured. In return for this promise the insured pays the insurer a premium. The premium and the earnings on the premium are then used by the insurer to cover its administrative costs, to pay the eventual loss claims that arise under the policy, and to provide a profit to the owners of the insurance company.

During the 1980s, the federal income tax treatment of property-casualty insurers and their policyholders underwent several important changes, the most significant of which came in 1986. A priori reasoning suggests that the income tax treatment of insurance companies should affect equilibrium prices of insur-

David F. Bradford is professor of economics and public affairs at Princeton University, a research associate of the National Bureau of Economic Research, and adjunct professor of law at New York University. Kyle D. Logue is assistant professor of law at the University of Michigan.

This paper is a part of the project on the Economics of the Property and Casualty Insurance Industry of the National Bureau of Economic Research, supported by the Insurance Information Institute. During its preparation, Bradford enjoyed the hospitality of the Economic Policy Research Unit at the Copenhagen Business School. He would also like to express appreciation for the support of the John M. Olin Foundation and Princeton University's Woodrow Wilson School and Center for Economic Policy Studies. Logue thanks his colleagues at the University of Michigan Law School, Ted Sims in particular, for many helpful discussions regarding the issues discussed in the paper. He also received generous research support from the Cook Research Fund at the University of Michigan Law School. Both authors thank Sean Mooney of the Insurance Information Institute for helpful comments and suggestions. Stuart Thiel of the University of Michigan and Ryan Edwards of Princeton University provided extraordinary research assistance. The usual caveats apply.

ance. In this article we develop theoretical predictions for how these changes should have affected the equilibrium prices of property-casualty insurance policies, and we explore the extent to which the theoretical predictions are reflected in the available data on industry underwriting experience.

One initial challenge presented by our study is conceptual: In the case of property-casualty insurance, it is not clear what one means by "price" or "quantity." The annual premium received by an insurance company in exchange for the sale of a single one-year occurrence-based policy (i.e., a policy that covers losses arising out of insured events that occur during the one-year period in which the policy is in force) can be understood as the product of a unit price for that type of coverage and the quantity of insurance embodied in the policy. But neither the price nor the quantity is directly observed. We take as a measure of the quantity of insurance contained in such a policy the total value of all the loss indemnity payments and loss expenses (such as attorneys' fees) that the insurer expects to pay in connection with that policy. The price of the policy, then, is the ratio of the premium to this measure of quantity. Our analysis thus addresses the role of taxes in the determination of this ratio.

For purposes of relating the predictions of theory to industry experience, we suffer from a lack of information about what insurance companies actually *expect* to pay. What we have instead are the companies' reported premiums earned and their *reported* estimates of what they expect to pay in the future as a result of covered events that have occurred as of the date of the report. These estimates are provided annually both to state regulators and to the public on forms called "annual statements." Annual statement (or "statutory") accounting data are also used by insurers in calculating their federal income tax liability, which, of course, is reported to the Internal Revenue Service (IRS). (Our discussion of insurance accounting, of which there will necessarily be a fair amount, draws primarily from Mooney and Cohen 1991 and Troxel and Bouchie 1990.)

We divide the paper into four sections. In section 2.1 we set forth a precise, albeit stylized, description of a property-casualty insurance policy and a detailed taxonomy of insurance prices and quantities. Understanding this taxonomy will require a measure of patience and perseverance of the reader, but in our view, it is worth the effort; in any event, the taxonomy will be used throughout the remainder of the paper as well as in the appendixes. In section 2.2 we use the taxonomy to describe two methods of accounting for the financial results of a property-casualty insurer: statutory, or annual statement, accounting and nominal economic income accounting. In section 2.3 we summarize the federal income tax treatment of property-casualty insurance companies, with an emphasis on certain important changes that were made as part of the Tax Reform Act of 1986 (TRA86). (The most important changes made by TRA86 for our purposes were the introduction of the loss-reserve discounting requirement and the inclusion in taxable income of 20 percent of unearned premiums.) In section 2.3 we also discuss briefly the tax treatment of liabilities that are not funded through property-casualty insurance, and we describe a significant change in those rules that was enacted in 1984. In section 2.4 we develop the theory of how income taxes affect the break-even prices of insurance (with special attention to the changes made by TRA86). In section 2.5 we present calculations of break-even prices based on the theory from section 2.4, and we compare those calculations with the historical record of the industry. The data consist of the losses incurred and loss adjustment expenses incurred (i.e., estimated loss payouts on existing policies) and the premiums earned by U.S. property-casualty insurers during the period 1976–93. The source of the data is the aggregated annual statement information published in *Best's Aggregates and Averages: Property-Casualty.* Various details of our procedures are described in appendixes.

Our predictions regarding the effect of the TRA86 changes can be summarized as follows: (1) For all tax years after 1986 we would expect to see some increase in the break-even price of insurance, and we would expect the size of the increases to be positively correlated with the level of market interest rates and with the length of the "tail" of the given line of insurance. The predicted impact of the changes in the tax rules enacted in 1986 translates into a tax on premiums (net of the cost of acquisition) of up to 13 percent (on medical malpractice, the longest tail line of insurance). (2) For the 1986 tax year, owing to a special transition rule in TRA86 called the "fresh start," we would expect a one-time reduction in premiums, as the fresh start essentially provided property-casualty insurers in 1986 with an extra incentive to issue policies during that year. Although we calculate economically meaningful impacts on the break-even terms of insurance policies, data on industry performance that we present show a sufficiently high degree of year-to-year variation (presumably reflecting the true riskiness of insurance, even in the aggregate) to swamp the impact of the changes in tax rules.

2.1 Describing an Insurance Policy

We begin our detailed description of a theoretical insurance policy by introducing the concept of a *spot policy:* an insurance contract that covers the policyholder for the stream of future loss payments that will arise out of a single specified loss event that has already occurred. A *standard policy* is our term for a group of spot policies sold by an insurance company to a single insured as a package for a given *policy period,* typically one year. Thus, under a standard policy, in exchange for a premium payment from the insured, the insurer agrees to issue individual spot policies for any insured loss event that occurs during the policy period.[1] We treat the premium for a standard policy as being

---

1. The standard policy is the formalization of a typical insurance policy, such as a one-year occurrence-based commercial general liability policy. Such a policy, when issued, in effect obligates the insurer to issue what we call spot policies during the year to "fund" losses as they occur. Insurers rarely issue individual spot policies outside of the context of a standard policy, although

paid to the insurer on the date that the policy is written. This premium can be understood as a forward purchase of a package of spot policies. With a real insurance contract, the stream of loss payments associated with a covered event will not be known with certainty. Since the tax law changes we consider have related solely to the treatment of the timing of cash flows and not to the treatment of risk, we focus on the special case in which the loss profile is known with certainty to the insurance company.[2]

We describe the losses covered by a spot policy or standard policy in terms of the policy's *cumulative loss payments, L(·)*, where $L(t)$ specifies the cumulative cash outflow of loss payments made by time t, measured from the date of writing the policy. (Except where we specify otherwise, the term *loss payment* should be understood as gross of the insurance company's allocated loss adjustment expenses.) We use the term *loss profile* to refer to the function that describes the increases in L over time, that is, the function that describes the actual cash outflows. We denote by $l(t)$ the path of such payments as a function of time elapsed since the moment of writing. This may be a continuous function that expresses the rate of payment per unit time (so that the payment during the short time, dt, after t is given by the product $l(t)dt$) or, more typically for our application, may consist of a sequence of payments at specified time points. (The loss profile bears the same relationship to the cumulative loss payments as does a density or probability function to a cumulative distribution function.)

2.1.1 Insurance Quantity Defined: Spot Policies

$L(\infty)$ is the sum of all the loss payments on the policy, which, if the meaning is clear from the context, we denote as simply L. Then the *normalized loss profile, $l(t)/L$*, sums to one. If two different policies, characterized by loss profiles $l^1(t)$ and $l^2(t)$, have the same normalized loss profiles, we say they are in the same *line* of insurance policies. This terminology is intended to capture the idea that a line of insurance (such as medical malpractice) consists of policies with similar anticipated time profiles of payouts (with the same length of tail, e.g.). We refer to the loss profile in a line that sums to one as the *unit profile* for that line; a policy that has the unit profile is a *unit policy* in a line. The loss profile of any policy in a line is then a multiple, L, of the unit profile, and so it

---

something approximating such policies does exist. E.g., retroactive insurance policies, which are issued after a loss event has occurred as a means of funding the liability through a property-casualty insurer, are relatively rare but not unprecedented. Such a policy approximates the economics of a spot policy, although a retroactive policy can still entail a fair amount of uncertainty regarding the total amount and the timing of loss payments. For the sake of simplicity, our analysis assumes away such uncertainty.

2. For discussions of the pricing of the risk associated with loss and unearned premium reserves, see Butsic (1991), D'Arcy (1988), and Kraus and Ross (1982). For arguments that the tax law changes we are considering should have had their principal, if not their only, impact on the purely intertemporal aspects of transactions, see, e.g., Gordon (1985) and Bradford (1995).

Table 2.1   **Loss Profile for Automobile Liability**

Time Relative to Accident Year (AY)	Payment during Year
AY + 0	.34
AY + 1	.31
AY + 2	.15
AY + 3	.09
AY + 4	.05
AY + 5	.03
AY + >5	.02
Total	.99

Source: Authors' calculations based on A. M. Best Company (various years).

is meaningful to speak of L as the quantity of insurance embodied in a policy in a line.

Any given spot policy can be understood as a quantity of unit policies in the relevant line. A unit policy in a line, such as automobile liability, pays a total of $1 over time, with the time pattern characteristic of the line. For example, the industry average unit loss profile for an auto liability spot policy in the period we are studying is shown in table 2.1.

2.1.2   Insurance Prices Defined: Spot Policies

Let P stand for the premium received by the company (net of selling costs) at the moment of writing a spot policy with a particular loss profile $l(\cdot)$. The single premium buys a whole profile of loss payments. (When we want to emphasize that the premium pays for losses that have already been incurred as of the date of writing, we refer to it as a spot premium, in contrast with the premium paid on a standard insurance policy.) Just as it is meaningful to speak of the quantity of insurance in a spot policy within a given line, so we can speak of the price of insurance implicit in the policy. It is simply the ratio of the premium to the total anticipated losses:

$$p = \frac{P}{L}.$$

In our terminology, the premium on a given policy is not the price. It is like the amount paid for a quantity of potatoes, the product of a per unit price and a number of units purchased. The price of a policy in a line of insurance is the premium on a unit policy.

A *unit single-payment policy* in a line pays off exactly one at the payoff time characteristic of the line, which, by analogy with bond terminology, we refer to as the policy's *maturity*. In fact, we shall make great use of the analogy, noted by others, between the sale of a policy by an insurance company and a loan from policyholder to company, the premium being lent against repayment in the form of policy payoffs (see, e.g., Cummins and Grace 1994). The unit single-payment policy that pays off at T corresponds to a discount $1 bond maturing at T. Each unit policy, in turn, can be understood as composed of a sum of quantities of single-payment unit policies.

2.1.3 Standard Policies: Prices and Quantities

Just as a spot policy can be understood as a package of single-payment policies, as discussed above, a standard policy can be understood as a package of spot policies. Thus, for example, under an auto liability policy written on 1 September 1987, a company might have expected to accumulate $40 in incurred losses for each passing day, or $40 × 365 = $1,460 in incurred losses during the policy year. We can think of the premium as a forward purchase of the package of spot policies. The parties to a standard policy are generally uncertain about the size of the spot policies that will come into being as a result of events during the policy year (e.g., a fire that damages a factory), and for each of those spot policies, they will generally be uncertain about the amount and time profile of the loss payments and expenses (it takes time to determine the amount of the covered damages, which may be paid out over a course of years). Of course, the company has a good idea of what those losses are going to be, and we might express this idea in probabilistic terms. As was the case for the description of a spot policy, however, it eases exposition and analysis to assume it known that each day (or moment) during the policy year will add one identical spot policy to the company's liabilities. And each of those spot policies involves a known and certain profile of loss payments.

Thus a standard policy can be built up from unit spot policies, which can in turn be built up from unit single-payment spot policies. By direct analogy with a spot policy, we define as a *unit standard policy* in a line a policy on which the losses over the policy year aggregate to one.

2.2 Accounting for Insurance Policies

To understand the taxation of an insurance company and to interpret the available data, we need to express the ideas just discussed in terms of the financial, regulatory, and tax accounting of the company. Our eventual goal is to be able to account for a standard policy, but we will begin with the accounting for a spot policy and build from there.

2.2.1 Accounting for a Spot Policy

Thus we start with the simplified example of an insurance company that issues a spot policy characterized by loss profile $l(\cdot)$. At that moment, the insurer will add to its balance sheet a new asset, the premium receivable, P, and a new liability, the obligation to pay out $l(\cdot)$ over time. In terms of statutory accounting, the balance sheet entry corresponding to this new liability is the *unpaid losses* account, sometimes referred to as the insurer's *loss reserve*. If the sole purpose of the insurer's reported loss reserve were to reflect the market value of the new liability, the reserve would presumably be carried as the discounted value of the loss payouts, $\int_0^\infty l(t)e^{-rt}dt$, where r is the going interest rate (for simplicity, assumed constant in this formula). As we discuss below, that amount also represents the break-even spot premium for this policy in a system without taxes. Therefore, when an insurer writes a break-even spot policy under these assumptions, it would have no net effect on the insurer's balance sheet, as the values of the new liability and the new asset would be directly offsetting. More generally, the *discounted loss reserve* associated with a policy represents the discounted value of the payments remaining to be made as of any particular time in the life of the policy.

Note, however, that the rules of statutory accounting applied by state regulators require the use of *undiscounted loss reserves* for regulatory reporting purposes. Thus, when reporting the loss reserve for a given spot policy as of time t' (relative to the date of the loss) on its regulatory balance sheet, the insurer must use the simple sum of all anticipated future loss payments associated with that policy, $\int_{t'}^\infty l(t)\, dt$. The value of this undiscounted loss reserve will exceed the value of the discounted loss reserve, and the amount of the difference will depend on the applicable interest rate and the length of the tail of the spot policy in question. As we show in considerable detail below, at interest rates that are high but within historical precedent and for a long-tailed policy (such as medical malpractice), the difference can be substantial.[3]

An insurance company's loss reserve is a stock concept; it is a liability, the value of which can be measured at any given time. The income calculation of a company, corresponding to this balance sheet accounting, is obtained by taking year-to-year differences. Thus the premiums taken in during the year will be added in, and the increase in outstanding loss reserves will be deducted. This is the conceptual basis for the *loss reserve deduction* in the calculation of taxable income.

An insurance company's total annual income is the sum of its *underwriting income* and *investment income*. Investment income is simply the amount

---

3. If we let $R(t)$ stand for the amount remaining to be paid on a policy, then writing the policy increases the company's net worth according to statutory accounting rules by $P - R$ (0). Time-value of money considerations lead us to expect $R(0)$ to be greater than P, so the effect of writing a policy is expected to reduce net worth under statutory accounting. In order to meet statutory solvency requirements, the company must have some capital of its own to balance sufficiently the negative effect of writing a policy. Thus the conservative accounting conventions imposed by regulation, coupled with accounting net worth restrictions, have the effect of obliging companies to hold collateral against their more distant obligations to pay out under the policy. We offer two justifications for not attempting to model the impact of the corporation income tax system on the yield of this obligatory collateral. First, for an insurance company that is part of a larger group, the collateral requirement is unlikely to add to the equity desired by the group as a whole (so there is no extra tax cost). Second, under the "Miller equilibrium" hypothesis (Miller 1977), shareholders are indifferent between the after-tax returns on debt and on equity. For them, the collateral, taxed at the corporate level, yields a competitive rate of return.

earned by the insurer on invested premiums and reinvested earnings, net of investment expenses. Underwriting income is calculated by taking the difference between premiums earned and underwriting expenses incurred during the year. And typically one of the largest underwriting expense deductions, the loss reserve deduction, is the increase in outstanding loss reserves during the year.

2.2.2 Accounting for a Standard Insurance Policy

When we move from the accounting for a spot policy to the accounting for a standard policy, things get more complicated. The sale of a standard policy is, in essence, the advanced sale of a series of spot policies to be issued as time passes. Thus, at the precise moment the standard policy is issued to the insured, assuming the premium is paid at the moment of issuance, the insurance company for a brief time has an asset (in the form of the premium) with no off-setting loss reserve liabilities. Those liabilities are incurred only as time passes and as the implicit (or hypothetical) spot policies are issued over the course of the policy period (which, again, is typically one year). Therefore, at the moment the standard policy is issued, the offsetting liability is the obligation to provide the implicit spot policies over time. Statutory accounting deals with this obligation through a balance sheet entry called the *unearned premium reserve*.

By convention, the premium on a standard insurance policy is treated as earned, and the unearned premium reserve is correspondingly reduced, pro rata during the policy year. During that time, spot policy loss liabilities are incurred, giving rise to loss payments and loss reserves for unpaid losses. In arriving at its annual underwriting income, an insurer deducts from premiums accrued the year-over-year increase in the company's unearned premium reserve (in addition to the year-over-year increase in loss reserves).

2.2.3 From Spot Prices to Earned Premiums and Incurred Losses by Accident Year

Statutory accounts present reports on an insurance company's earned premiums and incurred losses, categorized by *accident year*. The term accident year refers to the calendar year during which losses were incurred under policies issued by the company. The premiums earned during an accident year consist of the allocated fractions of the premiums on standard policies that cover any part of the calendar year in question. Because of the convention of assuming that a premium is earned at an even rate over the policy year, if the spot premiums are changing the premiums earned during an accident year may not be exactly the same as the sum of implicit spot premiums charged for the coverage. (The way we deal with this in our calculated prices is detailed in appendix B.)

2.2.4 Accounting and Economic Income Concepts

As mentioned above, under the insurance accounting rules that govern the calculation of annual income for regulatory purposes, property-casualty insurers take loss reserve deductions on an undiscounted basis. Accordingly, statutory accounting has the effect of accelerating deductions when compared with *nominal economic income accounting.* As we define the term, the *nominal economic income* of a company is the sum of all cash payments to the company's owners and the increase in the market value of the company's assets net of liabilities during the year. For a company that makes no distributions to its owners, nominal economic income is simply the year-to-year change in its net worth when all assets and liabilities are accounted for at their current market value. Nominal economic income may be contrasted with *economic income,* as the term is often used in discussions of tax policy. As applied to a firm, economic income means the sum of distributions to owners and the annual change in the firm's net worth, *corrected for inflation*—that is, with all the elements measured in constant purchasing power units. For our purposes, nominal economic income is the relevant concept, since all ordinary borrowing and lending transactions are accounted for in the tax law according to nominal economic income rules.[4]

The effect of the inconsistency between nominal economic income accounting and statutory accounting can be seen in the following simple example. Imagine an insurance company that issues one identical insurance policy every year, that invests all cash inflows at the going constant rate of interest, and that, contrary to the regulatory requirements, has no capital of its own other than accumulation from premiums and earnings on premiums (i.e., the insurer maintains no surplus). If we then look at the balance sheet of this company at the end of any given year, we will see a stock of assets consisting of the accumulations from past and current premium receipts, plus interest earned on those invested premiums, net of loss (and loss expense) outlays. In a competitive market, the assets on hand will just equal the discounted value of the unpaid losses on the stock of policies. Thus, the market value of this package of assets and liabilities will be zero every year. What is more, the company's nominal economic income (the annual change in the market value of its assets and liabilities—the company is paying out nothing to its owners) will also be zero.

In contrast, the net worth of the company understood in statutory accounting terms will be negative. Indeed, under the assumptions of the example, it will be the same negative amount each year (since the company issues identical policies each year). Moreover, after the start-up years, the statutory annual income of the insurer will also be zero. (During the start-up years, the statutory income would be negative.) If the insurer were then to stop writing these hypothetical yearly policies, statutory accounting and nominal economic accounting would diverge. Under nominal economic income accounting, the value of the insurer's portfolio of assets and liabilities would remain at zero, and the insurer's nominal economic income would continue to be zero from year to year as the old policies were paid off. Under statutory accounting, however,

4. When other transactions are accounted for on other bases, tax arbitrage will give rise to biases in the portfolios of taxpayers in different situations and to differences in market yields on various financial products according to the tax circumstances of the holder (Bradford 1981).

the insurer's income would be positive, since it would have earnings on its assets and any loss payment would be associated with an offsetting reduction in the stock of unpaid losses, with a corresponding addition to statutory income at that point. Conversely, if the company started expanding its business, its nominal economic income would remain zero, but its statutory income would be negative.

The inconsistencies between nominal economic accounting and statutory accounting are especially significant because, before TRA86, the federal income tax treatment of property-casualty insurance companies essentially replicated statutory accounting. Section 2.3 summarizes the federal income tax treatment of property-casualty insurance companies, and it emphasizes how that treatment was changed by TRA86. Section 2.3 also discusses briefly a change that took place in 1984 in the tax treatment of liabilities not funded through property-casualty insurance policies.

2.3   Federal Income Tax Treatment of Property-Casualty Insurance

2.3.1   Tax Treatment of Property-Casualty Insurance Companies

The federal income tax treatment of property-casualty insurance companies is governed by a special set of rules that are collected in subchapter L of the Internal Revenue Code (IRC). Under subchapter L, insurers are generally required to calculate their taxable income using the same statutory accounting conventions required by state regulators, which we described in section 2.2. As mentioned in that section, statutory accounting requires an insurer to calculate its annual income by taking into account both its net underwriting profit (or loss) and its net investment income (or loss) for a given *reporting year,* that is, the year for which the annual statement report is filed—which coincides with the insurer's *tax year.* Consistent with statutory accounting, an insurer's year-end underwriting income is determined roughly as follows:

1. Start with *premiums written* during the reporting year (in our model, these are the premiums received on issuance of a standard policy) *less*

2. *Premium acquisition expenses* incurred during the reporting year (these are the up-front costs of selling the policy such as commissions) *less*

3. The increase in the insurer's *unearned premium account* during the reporting year *less*

4. The increase in the insurer's *unpaid losses* account during the reporting year (this is the *loss reserve deduction* mentioned section 2.2, i.e., the net increase during that reporting year in the insurer's estimate of its future claim payments) *less*

5. Any actual *paid losses* that occurred during the reporting year[5]

---

5. The sum of items 4 and 5 for a given reporting year is referred to in statutory accounting as the *losses incurred.*

The result of this calculation—the insurer's net underwriting income—is then added to net investment income (which is simply the difference between investment earnings and investment expenses) to get taxable income.

Until the enactment of TRA86, subchapter L permitted property-casualty companies to calculate their loss reserve deductions on an undiscounted basis, just as they have always been required to do for regulatory purposes. That is, for tax purposes an insurer simply deducted the difference between the beginning balance and ending balance in its unpaid losses account, without taking into account the fact that those liabilities represented payments to be made in the future. This rule had the effect of giving property-casualty insurers the benefit of the inconsistency between statutory accounting and nominal economic income accounting described above.

In the early and mid-1980s, in various reports to Congress it was argued that, as a result of this inconsistency between statutory accounting and nominal economic income accounting, (1) the property-casualty industry had for years been paying less in federal income taxes than it should have been and (2) a bias in favor of funding risks through property-casualty companies had been created.[6] At least in part on the basis of such arguments, Congress included in TRA86 a requirement that for all tax years after 1986, all loss reserve deductions must be calculated on a discounted basis. For any post-1986 tax year, the loss reserve deduction is determined by taking the difference between the discounted value of the beginning balance in the unpaid losses account and the discounted value of the ending balance in that account.

Thus the post-1986 treatment of loss reserves approximates the treatment required by nominal economic income accounting. Differences remain, however. For example, TRA86 and the Treasury regulations that have been promulgated under it contain fairly specific rules limiting how the discounting requirement may be implemented. The insurer must use discount factors that are published periodically by the Treasury Department. (Those discount factors may diverge from the actually prevailing rates.) And the insurer must, with some exceptions, use the "loss payment patterns" (or, to use our terminology, the loss profiles) that are also published every few years by the Treasury. Those loss profiles—there is a separate profile for each line of insurance—are calculated by the Treasury using data from previously filed annual statements for the entire industry. Under some circumstances an insurer can elect to use its own historical loss experience in calculating the profile for purposes of discounting; however, many insurers cannot qualify for that option.[7]

---

6. This argument was made, for example, in a very influential report to Congress issued by the General Accounting Office (GAO 1985). The loss-reserve discounting requirement ultimately enacted by Congress (discussed below in the text) essentially adopted the GAO proposal.

7. In applying the Treasury's discount factors to its statutory loss reserves, the insurer is allowed to take into account the extent to which the reserves were already discounted on the annual statement. As we have already noted, however, most state regulatory authorities do not permit discounting of reserves for annual statement purposes.

In addition, a special transition rule—called the *fresh start*—was inserted in TRA86. This rule essentially permitted insurers a second deduction (spread out over a number of years) equal to the difference between the discounted value and the undiscounted value of the total year-end 1986 loss reserves. In the absence of the fresh-start rule, the introduction of the reserve-discounting requirement would have produced a large lump-sum tax on property-casualty insurers for the 1986 tax year. When total year-end reserves were required to be discounted to present value, instead of a fresh start there would have been a large loss reserve inclusion in gross income equal to the amount of the discount.[8] However, Congress chose to permit insurers to exclude that amount from gross income.

In addition to the loss-reserve discounting requirement, TRA86 also made a number of other changes in the tax treatment of property-casualty insurers. Prominent among these for our purposes was the change in the treatment of the unearned premium reserve.[9] Before TRA86, subchapter L permitted insurers to deduct the full value of the annual increase in their unearned premium reserve, thereby excluding from income revenue that had not yet been accrued. In both committee reports accompanying TRA86, it was contended that this ability to exclude unearned premiums, coupled with the allowance of an up-front deduction for premium acquisition expenses, resulted in a mismatching of income and expenses (U.S. Congress 1984). Therefore, in an effort to produce a rough matching of income and expense, a provision was included in TRA86 in effect reducing the annual unearned premium reserve deduction by 20 percent.

We would, a priori, expect both of these changes in the tax treatment of property-casualty insurers—the loss-reserve discounting requirement and unearned premium inclusion—to have effects on break-even prices in the property-casualty market. In section 2.4 below, where we discuss the effect of taxes on break-even prices generally, we also set forth specifically our predictions regarding the effects of these changes. (In general, we would expect a decrease in prices in 1986—due to the fresh start—and an eventual increase in break-even prices in the years thereafter owing to the switch to discounted reserves.) Then in section 2.5 we explore the extent to which the actual industry-wide aggregate data—taken from *Best's Aggregates and Averages*—match our predictions.

8. This inclusion would have been required by IRC section 481(a). When there is a change in accounting methods that would otherwise permit double deductions, section 481(a) provides a method by which the effect of the second deduction can be eliminated or at least reduced. Therefore, absent the fresh-start rule in TRA86, section 481(a) would have required all property-casualty insurers either to include the amount of the discount in income in 1986 or, at least, to include the amount of the discount over a period of years. The fresh-start rule essentially trumped the effect of section 481(a).

9. One change that we will not deal with in this paper involved insurers' tax-exempt income. TRA86 required property-casualty insurers to include 15 percent of what was previously exempt interest income from state and local government bonds and from untaxed dividends. Other major tax changes in 1986 that affected property-casualty insurers were the reduction in corporate rates (from 46 percent in 1986 to 40 percent in 1987 and to 34 percent in 1988) and the introduction of the alternative minimum tax.

Before turning to section 2.4, however, we briefly summarize another interesting change in the tax laws that occurred in the 1980s—specifically in 1984—which we would expect to have some (albeit small) effect on equilibrium property-casualty prices, although we do not attempt to model this effect in section 2.4.

2.3.2   Tax Treatment of Liabilities *Not* Funded through Property-Casualty Insurance Companies

Thus far we have been discussing the economics and accounting of how a business or an individual might fund certain types of liabilities through a property-casualty insurance policy. And in the previous subsection we explained how the pre-TRA86 tax rules for property-casualty companies created a bias in the direction of funding risks in that manner (at least as compared to the incentives that would have existed under a nominal economic income tax). In this subsection we explain how a fundamental change in the tax treatment of liabilities accrued by noninsurance companies—that is, liabilities *not* funded through a property-casualty company—that was enacted in 1984 should have *increased,* if only temporarily, that bias in favor of property-casualty risk funding.

Before the enactment of the Tax Reform Act of 1984 (TRA84), businesses that used the accrual method of accounting for federal tax purposes could, in a very rough way, approximate the accelerated deductions available to property-casualty insurance companies. This acceleration of deductions resulted from the application of the traditional "all-events test," which determines generally the timing of deductions taken by accrual method taxpayers. Under the pre-TRA84 version of this test, an accrual method taxpayer could deduct a liability in the year in which (1) all events necessary to fix the liability had occurred and (2) the amount of the liability could be determined with reasonable accuracy. Thus, for example, whenever the taxpayer entered into a binding contract to make a fixed payment in the future, the taxpayer could—in the year of contracting—deduct the undiscounted face value of the future payment, even if the payment was not to be made for several years.

To illustrate the effect of this rule, consider the following example of a structured settlement arrangement that might have occurred before TRA84: An individual is injured on 1 January in year 1 by a product manufactured by Company X. Assume that the company and the individual agree to settle the claim for $823 to be paid by the company to the individual on 31 December of that year. Assume further, for the sake of the example, that the before-tax rate of interest on all investments is 10 percent, that all investments (of both the company and the injured individual) are subject to income tax, and that the marginal tax rate for all taxpayers is 50 percent. Thus the after-tax interest rate of return on all investments is 5 percent.

Under the all-events test (as it was applied before the enactment of TRA84), these facts would give rise to the following tax-planning opportunity: The parties could agree that, instead of the $823 cash payment in year 1, the company would pay the injured party $1,000 four years later, at the end of year 5. Provided that the company was solvent and likely to remain solvent, the injured party would be indifferent between these two payment options because they have the same present value, discounting at the after-tax interest rate. If the parties agree to this deferred payment arrangement, the company could then take the full $1,000 deduction on its year 1 tax return.

Assuming the company has income in year 1 against which to offset the deduction, the deduction would save the insurer $500 in taxes in that year. The company then combines this $500 with $323 of its own money and invests the sum at the after-tax rate of 5 percent per year. By the end of year 5, the money will have grown to $1,000 under the current assumptions, the amount necessary to satisfy the company's obligation to the injured party. Thus, the out-of-pocket after-tax cost to the taxpayer of this liability would be only $323.

Under the nominal economic income treatment of this structured settlement transaction, the company would be permitted a deduction of $683 on its year 1 tax return ($1,000 discounted for four years at the 10 percent before-tax interest rate) and an additional deduction each year (through year 5) equal to the annual increase in the present value of the liability resulting from the passage of time. The discounted present value of the tax saving amounts to $458 in year 1. Thus, by investing these tax savings and $365 of its own money in year 1 (at 5 percent after tax), the company could generate the necessary $1,000 by the end of year 5. Thus, one measure of the tax-deferral effect of this particular structured settlement agreement is the difference between the after-tax cost to the taxpayer under nominal economic income taxation ($365) and the after-tax cost to the taxpayer under the pre-TRA84 all-events test ($323)—the difference being $42 in this example.

The structured settlement represents an extreme example of the tax deferral available under the old all-events test. To achieve the degree of tax deferral described in the example above, however, it was necessary for the company not only to be aware of the liability but also to enter into the structured settlement contract with the injured party. Such contracts probably accounted for a relatively small portion of the total amount of risk funding in the pre-TRA84 years. Note, however, that a structured settlement was not the only means of accelerating deductions under the pre-TRA84 all-events test. In addition, there was a considerable amount of pre-TRA84 case law that had the effect of allowing accrual method taxpayers to deduct certain liabilities that called for the taxpayer to make payouts far into the future.

For example, one court held that the all-events test was satisfied—the liability was fixed—with respect to a company's self-insured workers' compensation liabilities in the year in which the injury occurred, provided that those liabilities were uncontested.[10] Moreover, courts have generally held that the

10. *Crescent Wharf & Warehouse Co.* v. *Commissioner,* 518 F.2d 772 (9th Cir. 1975). Generally, a taxpayer may not deduct amounts set aside as a self-insurance reserve for expected future costs. The deduction can be taken only when the all-events test is satisfied.

length of time between accrual and payment does not affect whether the deduction could be taken or for how much. As will be discussed below, this result approached (without quite equaling) the treatment available to insurers under pre-TRA86 subchapter L. (The main difference was that an insurer could have deducted the workers' compensation liability even if the claims had been contested.)

Thus, for workers' compensation liabilities, to a lesser extent for tort liabilities, and for other liabilities as well, taxpayers before TRA84 could exploit the old all-events test and defer taxes by taking deductions years in advance of payments (U.S. Congress 1984).

In 1984 Congress introduced the "economic performance" requirement, which largely eliminated the tax-deferral opportunities described above in connection with the old all-events test.[11] The economic performance requirement, found in IRC section 461(h), altered the timing of large classes of deductions under the old all-events test. Section 461(h) provides generally that an accrual method taxpayer can deduct an expense *no earlier than* the year in which economic performance occurs with respect to that expense.[12] With respect to the timing of deductions for tort liabilities, workers' compensation liabilities, and breach-of-contract liabilities specifically, however, the economic performance requirement essentially placed all taxpayers on the cash-receipts-and-disbursements method of accounting. Thus, for post-1984 tax years, liabilities arising out of tort claims, workers' compensation claims, or contract claims can be deducted only when payment is actually made by the taxpayer to the party to whom the liability is owed: a tort liability, for example, may be deducted no earlier than the year in which the taxpayer actually pays the tort award (or settlement amount) to the tort plaintiff.

Note that under the economic performance rule, the company in the structured settlement example above would been required to delay the $1,000 tax deduction until the year of actual payment—year 5. In that case (holding all other assumptions the same), the after-tax cost to the self-insurer of the structured settlement arrangement would have been $411. This is because the present value in year 1 of the delayed tax deduction would be $411, and as noted above, a total of $823 is needed in year 1 to fund the $1,000 payment in year 5.

Finally, consider how the manufacturer in the structured settlement example above could have funded its tort liability through a property-casualty insurance

---

11. Under IRC section 468B, companies that have tort liabilities can still generate tax benefits by making qualified payments to a "designated settlement fund." However, the companies must comply with a set of complicated and restrictive regulatory requirements, and the size of the tax savings of a designated settlement fund are considerably smaller than the tax savings that were possible under the old all-events test.

12. The general rules for determining when economic performance occurs are straightforward: If the taxpayer's expense arises out of the provision of services to (or by) the taxpayer, economic performance occurs as the services are rendered. If the expense arises out of the provision of property to (or the use of property by) the taxpayer, economic performance occurs as the property is provided to (or used by) the taxpayer.

company rather than through self-funding. Make the following assumptions: (1) Just before the occurrence of the injury (at the end of year 1), the manufacturer purchased an occurrence-based commercial general liability insurance policy from a property-casualty insurance company. (2) The injury (caused by the manufacturer's product) is covered under the policy. (3) The insurer estimates that the covered injury will give rise to a single $1,000 payment to be made four years later, at the end of year 5.[13] (4) The premium charged by the insurer is equal to $645, the break-even premium, given statutory accounting for insurance company income.[14] (5) The insurance premium is deductible as an ordinary and necessary business expense on the manufacturer's year 1 tax return. Under these assumptions, the $645 deduction would save the manufacturer $322 in taxes. Thus the after-tax cost to the manufacturer of funding the liability through the property-casualty policy is $323. Under these assumptions, then, the after-tax cost of funding the liability through the property-casualty insurer and the after-tax cost of self-funding it (in the event a structured settlement could be arranged) were the same.

Because of the changes made by TRA84 (which were made effective for deductions that would have been allowable after 18 July 1984 under the prior rules), we would expect the cost of self-funding certain types of liabilities (especially tort, workers' compensation, and breach-of-contract liabilities) to have increased in 1984 and subsequent years. Likewise, the relative cost of funding such liabilities through property-casualty insurance policies should have decreased around that time. Therefore, we would expect to see an increase in the quantity of liability insurance (especially in the general liability and workers' compensation lines) that was supplied and demanded in 1984, 1985, and 1986.

That quantity effect, however, might be de minimis because of the relatively small magnitude of the change. That is, it may be that the discussion above overstates the extent to which non–insurance company taxpayers were, pre-TRA84, able to accelerate the deduction of accrued liabilities. Also, the quantity effect may be offset to some extent by the price effects caused by the changes in TRA86, which will be discussed in section 2.4.

2.4   Effect of Taxes on Break-Even Prices

As mentioned in section 2.3, one would expect generally that tax rules will influence both the break-even spot prices of property-casualty insurance (where the treatment of loss reserves is critical) and the relationship between break-even spot prices and break-even standard premiums (where the main issue is the treatment of unearned premium reserves). We treat the two pieces

---

13. Perhaps it will take five years for the litigation to run its course; or, in some cases, it may take five years for the victim to discover the injury.

14. In section 2.4 we explain how the insurance premium depends on the tax treatment of the insurance company; the example applies the pre-TRA86 rules.

separately, starting with the effect of taxes on break-even spot prices. Note one critical assumption of this section and of the paper as a whole: we assume throughout that in setting their *reported* loss reserves and unearned premium reserves insurers show no systematic bias. That is, we assume they are not influenced in any direction by the possible effects of these reported numbers on their tax liabilities, their likelihood of regulatory review, or their financial status in the capital markets. In future work, we hope to isolate the discretionary element in loss-reserving decisions and to measure the direction and extent of various biasing factors, such as taxes and regulatory concerns. But for now, an absence of bias is assumed.[15]

2.4.1   Break-Even Spot Prices

Break-Even Spot Prices with No Taxes

By a simple arbitrage argument, the break-even premium on a spot policy with known loss profile is simply the discounted value of the losses. Let $r(t)$ be the yield curve in the bond market at the time of writing a single-payment policy, understood as the average annual yield on a zero-coupon bond that pays off t years in the future. Then, the break-even condition is

$$P(l(\cdot)) = \int_0^\infty l(t)e^{-r(t)t}\, dt.$$

This condition expresses the effect of a time-varying discount rate. Note that there is no question of predicting future interest involved. The valuation of the cash flow of losses is based on the interest rates at the time of writing the policy.

Provided the time shape is fixed, the price of a spot policy at any given time is determined in this simple model by the yield curve at that time. The framework permits analysis of the effects of changes in the yield curve on different standardized time shapes (e.g., medical malpractice, workers' compensation), as well as variation in the time shape of policies, for example, a lengthening of the payment tail on some line. If the discount rate in the market is the same, r, for all maturities, the break-even condition is

$$P(l(\cdot)) = \int_0^\infty l(t)e^{-rt}\, dt.$$

For the special case of a unit single-payment spot policy, that is, a policy that pays off at exactly one point in time, maturing at T (measured from the time of writing), the break-even premium (the unit price for that line) is

$$P(T) = e^{-rT}.$$

---

15. For a review of aggregate industry data suggesting that reported loss reserves may be biased by taxes, see Bradford and Logue (1997) and Logue (1996).

Break-Even Spot Prices with Taxes

In the calculation of the company's taxable income, gross underwriting income consists of premiums earned. A deduction is allowed on account of any increase in the liabilities for future loss payments; that is the loss reserve deduction. We may start by considering the case in which taxable income is the same as nominal economic income, as defined above. We then consider significant deviations in the rules from the nominal economic income standard.

Taxes with nominal economic income accounting. When we introduce an income tax, we must translate the analysis of cash flows in a single-payment spot policy to net-of-tax terms. If the income tax were actually based on nominal economic income, then the insurance company that issued a policy on break-even terms in the absence of taxes, and fully hedged its position by buying a portfolio of bonds with maturities matching its payment obligations, would not have any income at any point and would not pay any tax. So, under those circumstances, the tax would not affect the equilibrium price of insurance (except possibly indirectly, through an effect on the level of interest rates). Translated into terms of gross income and deductions, the premium, P, would be included as gross income and the addition to loss reserves of an exactly equal amount (because it is a break-even policy) would be taken as a deduction. Over time, there would be additional deductions for successive loss payments, but they would be matched by equal and opposite changes in the level of loss reserves. In addition, there would be deductions as the value of discounted loss reserves increased by virtue of the approach to future payout points. These deductions would give rise to negative underwriting income. They would be matched by the yield on the use of funds up until the time of payout, which would give rise to positive investment income, offsetting underwriting losses. So the company's net taxable income would be zero throughout the life of the contract. (In appendix A, we provide further discussion of the discount rate appropriate for use in setting loss reserves, drawing on the analogy between a single-payment spot policy and a discount bond.)

Taxes with statutory accounting for loss reserves. With statutory accounting for loss reserves, the story is different. The premium comes in as gross income when received, but the simultaneous deduction is of the *undiscounted* reserve. The increase in liability on a discounted basis that takes place as the time of future payment approaches has no tax consequences. As with nominal economic income accounting, loss payments give rise to a deduction when made, offset by a simultaneous reduction in the deduction for loss reserves as the stock of undiscounted liabilities for losses incurred is reduced by the amount paid out. So, with statutory accounting used for tax purposes, writing what would be a break-even insurance policy in the absence of taxes results in a stream of changes in tax liabilities with positive discounted value to the taxpayer.

In working out the details, we need to take account of the fact that the company will evaluate cash flows on the basis of their after-tax consequences, using the after-tax discount rate. In the case of a constant tax rate, τ, the after-tax discount rate applicable to a cash flow t years in the future is $(1 - \tau)r(t)$.

With statutory accounting, there is a deduction for the undiscounted loss reserve at the time of writing the policy, $R(0) = L$. The cash flow associated with the policy is thus $(1 - \tau)P + \tau L$ at time of issue, followed by the flow $-l(t)$ at subsequent time t consisting of the actual loss payout. Since the payout is deducted and the corresponding increase in loss reserves is included in taxable income, there are no tax consequences at payout time. Denoting the break-even premium under statutory accounting by P^s, it must satisfy the break-even condition

$$(1 - \tau)P^s + \tau L = \int_0^\infty l(t)e^{-(1-\tau)r(t)} \, dt.$$

Two important characteristics of the impact of taxes using statutory accounting can be inferred from this break-even condition. First, the tax rate matters. As we show next, the higher the tax rate, the lower the break-even premium, given the term structure of before-tax interest rates. Second, the time pattern of tax rates matters. For example, other things equal, the lower the tax rate anticipated in the future, relative to the time of writing the policy, the lower the break-even premium. Conversely, an anticipated increase in the rate of tax will result in an increase in the break-even premium.

We may contrast this break-even condition with the condition that would apply under nominal economic income accounting, which would involve an initial deduction of the discounted value of the anticipated loss, followed by a stream of deductions for any increase in that discounted value due to the approach of the payment date. (There is a further stream of deductions for the payments themselves that is offset by exactly equal reductions in the stock of reserves.) Letting R^d stand for the discounted value of loss reserves, the cash flow at the time of writing the policy would be $(1 - \tau)P + \tau R^d(0)$, or

$$(1 - \tau)P + \tau \int_0^\infty l(t)e^{-rt} \, dt.$$

Under our assumption that the losses on the policy are known at the outset, the discounted value of losses remaining to be paid at a time t' subsequent to the date of issue would be given by

$$R^d(t') = \int_{t'}^\infty l(t)e^{-r(t-t')} \, dt.$$

The *change* in discounted reserve is a deduction in calculating nominal economic income and so would induce a stream of tax savings under a system of nominal economic income taxation. The rate of cash flow at t' would then be

$$-l(t') + \tau r R^d(t'),$$

where we have used the fact that, net of payouts, the stock of discounted reserves will grow instantaneously at the rate of interest. Denoting the break-even premium under nominal economic income accounting by P^e, it must satisfy the break-even condition

$$(1 - \tau)P^e + \tau R^d(0) = \int_0^\infty [l(t') - \tau r R^d(t')]e^{-(1-\tau)rt'} \, dt'.$$

Relying on the discussion in appendix A, we know that this break-even condition implies $P^e = R^d(0)$.

The relationship between the two break-even premium levels can be expressed in simple form in the case of a single-payment policy. The after-tax cash flow from the break-even premium under statutory accounting must have a discounted (at the after-tax discount rate) value of zero:

$$P^s - \tau(P^s - 1) - e^{-(1-\tau)rT} = 0,$$

$$(1 - \tau)P^s = e^{-(1-\tau)rT} - \tau,$$

$$P^s = \frac{e^{-(1-\tau)rT} - \tau}{1 - \tau}.$$

A somewhat startling implication of the calculation is that the break-even loan proceeds to justify a repayment of one after a time period T could actually be *negative* for large enough values of T, r, or τ. The insurer could afford to pay the policyholder to accept coverage, taking its return in the form of tax savings.

This may be contrasted with the corresponding break-even premium, P^e, under nominal economic income accounting for tax purposes,

$$P^e = \tau e^{-rT}.$$

The ratio of the two

$$\frac{P^s}{P^e} = \frac{\left(\dfrac{e^{-(1-\tau)rT} - \tau}{1 - \tau}\right)}{e^{-rT}} \quad \text{and}$$

$$\frac{P^s}{P^e} = \frac{e^{\tau rT} - \tau e^{rT}}{1 - \tau}$$

depends on the tax rate, the discount rate, and the time to maturity (length of the tail for an insurance policy). If the tax rate is zero or the discount rate is zero or the time to maturity is zero, the two amounts are the same. Increasing the tax rate, the discount rate, or the time to maturity lowers the ratio, that is, lowers the break-even amount under statutory relative to that under nominal economic income accounting. For a high enough discount rate, tax rate, or time to maturity, the competitive premium level is negative, whereas the premium is always positive under nominal economic income accounting.

The relationship between the various parameters (tax rate, discount rate, time to maturity) and the ratio between break-even premium levels under statutory and nominal economic income accounting is highly nonlinear. Table 2.2 shows that, with a tax rate of 30 percent, the impact increases dramatically as the interest rate goes above 10 percent and the time to payoff goes beyond 10 years. Since the relevant discount rate is the nominal interest rate, it is clear that the recent history of interest rates in the United States includes periods in which the premiums on long-tailed lines of insurance might have been significantly affected by tax factors.

Aside on tax-exempt interest. In the analysis thus far we have assumed that the rate at which the company discounts after-tax cash flows is the after-tax interest rate. In practice, an important feature of the tax landscape is the option to hold state and local tax-exempt bonds. We propose not to explore in any depth the maximizing financial portfolio choices by insurance companies. However, to the extent that tax-exempt interest applies at the margin to financial choices by the company, it would be substituted for the after-tax interest rate in our analysis. Essentially, the effect is to substitute for the actual marginal tax rate the, lower, implicit marginal tax rate embodied in the difference between tax-exempt and taxable bond yields. So, for example, if the tax-exempt interest rate is 8 percent and the taxable interest rate is 10 percent, the tax rate implicit in the tax-exempt yield would be 20 percent. If the relevant margin for the insurance company is the tax-exempt bond, then the formulas above should employ the implicit marginal tax rate of 20 percent (as applied to the taxable interest rate) rather than the statutory tax rate.

An insurance company that is well managed from a tax point of view will, however, try to assure that the marginal source of funds for the insurance business is fully taxable income. Note that whereas the insurance company's tax rate does not enter the determination of the break-even premium level under nominal economic income accounting, it does enter under statutory accounting. In the latter case, the higher the tax rate, the lower the break-even premium, other things equal. It is characteristic of situations in which the yield from an investment according to taxable income measurement rules incorporates deferral relative to nominal economic income rules that the taxpayer with the higher marginal tax rate will be willing to pay the higher price for a given investment opportunity (Bradford 1981). In those situations, there will be a tendency for higher marginal rate taxpayers to drive exempt or low-rate taxpayers out of activities. In the case of insurance companies, with statutory accounting used for tax purposes, the same tendency is present. To the extent that an insurance business can be arranged so that the marginal underwriting loss comes out of fully taxable income, the company will be able to take full advantage of the deferral effect of the statutory accounting. (For a thorough treatment of these issues, in particular the financial portfolio choices of insurance companies, see Cummins and Grace 1994.)

Table 2.2   **Break-Even Premiums for Statutory versus Nominal Economic Income Accounting**

Maturity	τ = 0.1				τ = 0.3				τ = 0.5			
	r = 0.05	r = 0.1	r = 0.15	r = 0.2	r = 0.05	r = 0.1	r = 0.15	r = 0.2	r = 0.05	r = 0.1	r = 0.15	r = 0.2
1	1.00	1.00	1.00	1.00	1.00	1.00	1.00	0.99	1.00	1.00	0.99	0.99
3	1.00	0.99	0.99	0.98	1.00	0.98	0.96	0.93	0.99	0.97	0.94	0.88
10	0.98	0.93	0.79	0.54	0.95	0.76	0.32	−0.56	0.92	0.58	−0.25	−1.95
20	0.93	0.54	−0.73	−4.41	0.76	−0.56	−5.09	−18.66	0.58	−1.95	−11.12	−39.82

Source: Authors' calculations.

Note: Table reports ratio of break-even premium for single-payment policy under statutory accounting relative to that under nominal economic income accounting.

Taxes with statutorily prescribed discounted reserves. As described in section 2.3, since TRA86, insurance companies have been required to use discounted reserves in calculating taxable income. As far as spot policies are concerned, it would be reasonable to describe the post-TRA86 rules as taxing companies roughly on a nominal economic income basis. As described above, however, the rules limit the flexibility of insurance companies to vary the loss profile assumed in calculating income, and they incorporate an assumed interest rate that may be different from the one actually prevailing. To illustrate, suppose the prescribed profile were "too long," T' instead of T for our single-payment example, and the interest rate "too low," r' instead of r. Then, unlike the case of consistent nominal economic income accounting, the tax rate and interest rates would influence the break-even premium, P. As a consequence, it is necessary to model the determination of break-even premiums using an explicit specification of the Treasury discount factors.

2.4.2   From Break-Even Spot Prices to Earned Premiums

The theoretical analysis developed above relates to the economics of a spot policy. A standard policy incorporates a year's worth of spot policies, paid for at the beginning of the year. To get from spot policy prices to standard policy prices requires discounting the anticipated spot policy amounts. The income tax also affects the relationship between break-even spot prices and break-even standard policies, via the treatment of unearned premium reserves (which was changed in 1986).

Industry data on premiums take the form of amounts earned during the reporting year. The amount earned during a reporting year constitutes the pro rata portions of premiums on standard policies that commenced during the previous year or that extend into the next accounting year. These amounts may be differentially affected by changes in the rates of tax during these years.

Appendix B describes how we deal with these and many other details in the process of developing the figures presented in the next section, which describes the empirical results.

2.5   Empirical Results

2.5.1   Profiles, Tax Rates, Discount Rates, and IRS Reserve
Discount Factors

To implement the formulas derived above we require data on loss profiles, taxes, discount rates, and IRS discount factors (for unpaid loss reserves).

Profiles

A unit loss profile in a line of insurance is assumed to take the form of a sequence of discrete payments, l_j, occurring at times, t_j, measured from the

Table 2.3   **Unit Spot Policy Loss Profiles Based on Treasury Data (percent)**

Tax Year	Auto Liability	Other Liability	Workers' Compensation	Medical Malpractice	Farmowners, etc.
AY + 0	34.32	9.20	25.92	3.02	55.74
AY + 1	30.88	16.19	28.61	9.96	23.39
AY + 2	15.03	14.69	13.33	10.45	7.33
AY + 3	8.82	15.13	7.74	12.15	4.75
AY + 4	4.76	10.99	4.47	9.90	3.05
AY + 5	2.73	8.92	3.50	8.27	2.43
AY + 6	1.24	5.11	1.88	7.03	1.05
AY + 7	0.64	4.28	1.73	6.47	0.38
AY + 8	0.23	2.16	1.50	5.13	0.68
AY + 9	0.32	1.02	0.62	2.74	0.32
AY + 10	0.32	1.02	0.62	2.74	0.32
AY + 11	0.32	1.02	0.62	2.74	0.32
AY + 12	0.32	1.02	0.62	2.74	0.25
AY + 13	0.06	1.02	0.62	2.74	0.00
AY + 14	0.00	1.02	0.62	2.74	0.00
AY + 15	0.00	7.23	7.58	11.20	0.00
Total	100.00	100.00	100.00	100.00	100.00

Source: Derived from A. M. Best Company (1988).

time of writing. Since this is a unit profile, the payments sum to one. The specific profiles we use are based on those promulgated by the IRS in connection with the development of reserve discount factors. Those profiles are derived by the Treasury in a somewhat ad hoc manner from data on the percentage of incurred losses paid by the end of the reported accident year and successive years, using the historical record as an approximation to the forward-looking profiles one would actually like to know.

We distinguish five unit spot policy loss profiles, based on the aggregation of industry data by the lines of insurance as they were defined by the industry until 1989 (at which point data began to be reported in somewhat finer detail and the lines were disaggregated into more categories). The pre-1989 lines are "auto liability," "other liability," "workers' compensation," "medical malpractice," and "farmowners, homeowners, and commercial multiple peril, ocean marine, aircraft (all perils), and boiler and machinery."

Table 2.3 presents the Treasury profiles as specified in connection with deriving the reserve discount factors applicable after 1986. We have extended the profiles to 16 years, assuming all losses are paid by the end of the fifteenth year after the accident year.

As discussed in appendix B, we translate these profiles into assumed spot policies by treating the first payout as occurring as a discrete amount exactly three months after the time of writing, and the successive payouts as discrete amounts occurring on the anniversary dates. So a typical profile in this applica-

Table 2.4   **Average Time to Payout by Line**

Line	Average Time to Payout (years)
Auto liability	1.57
Other liability	4.38
Workers' compensation	3.12
Medical malpractice	6.34
Farmowners, etc.	1.17

Source: Authors' calculations based on data from A. M. Best Company (1988).

tion involves a payout at the .25, 1, 2, . . . , etc. year points. It is immediately apparent from the table that there is considerable variation in the length of the tails of the different lines. Based on our assumed timing, the average times to payout implicit in the data are shown in table 2.4. Referring to table 2.2, showing the effect of the difference between statutory and discounted reserve accounting for tax purposes, we can see that the only line for which we might look for a significant effect is medical malpractice.

Anticipated Tax Rates

Tax rates have changed from time to time. The break-even premium under statutory accounting depends on the company's anticipation of future tax rates. Sometimes tax legislation specifies the future course of tax rates. For purposes of this exercise, we assume that companies know the tax rate that will, in fact, apply to the year of writing the policy (the first of two accident years that will be touched by the policy) and for future years believe the tax rates specified in legislation as of the end of the accident year. (We also assume in this paper that companies do not manipulate their loss reserves.) Table 2.5 specifies the tax rates used in our calculations for each year. The rates shown on the diagonal are the rates that actually applied in the years in question. The last column, for 1993, is repeated for all future years required in the calculations.

Discounting

In determining the spot price at any time, discounting is at the then-current term structure of interest rates. The interest rate data that we use are in the form of yields on Treasury securities of different maturities. Although such a yield is derived as an internal rate of return on securities that make periodic coupon payments between issue date and maturity, we treat the rates as applying to zero-coupon bonds with various maturities. So, if the five-year yield is reported as 7 percent, we assume $1 payable in five years can be bought for $e^{-.07*5} = e^{-.35}$. The after-tax interest rate applicable to a 40 percent bracket taxpayer would be 4.2 percent. We use the notation $r(t)$ to designate the interest rate applicable to a zero-coupon bond of maturity t. Where the relevant maturity does not correspond exactly to a maturity available in the data (e.g., four

Table 2.5   Federal Income Tax Rates Used in Calculating Break-Even Premiums

Tax Rates Anticipated in	Tax Rates in																	
	1976	1977	1978	1979	1980	1981	1982	1983	1984	1985	1986	1987	1988	1989	1990	1991	1992	1993
1976	.48	.48	.48	.48	.48	.48	.48	.48	.48	.48	.48	.48	.48	.48	.48	.48	.48	.48
1977		.48	.48	.48	.48	.48	.48	.48	.48	.48	.48	.48	.48	.48	.48	.48	.48	.48
1978			.48	.46	.46	.46	.46	.46	.46	.46	.46	.46	.46	.46	.46	.46	.46	.46
1979				.46	.46	.46	.46	.46	.46	.46	.46	.46	.46	.46	.46	.46	.46	.46
1980					.46	.46	.46	.46	.46	.46	.46	.46	.46	.46	.46	.46	.46	.46
1981						.46	.46	.46	.46	.46	.46	.46	.46	.46	.46	.46	.46	.46
1982							.46	.46	.46	.46	.46	.46	.46	.46	.46	.46	.46	.46
1983								.46	.46	.46	.46	.46	.46	.46	.46	.46	.46	.46
1984									.46	.46	.46	.46	.46	.46	.46	.46	.46	.46
1985										.46	.46	.46	.46	.46	.46	.46	.46	.46
1986											.46	.4	.34	.34	.34	.34	.34	.34
1987												.4	.34	.34	.34	.34	.34	.34
1988													.34	.34	.34	.34	.34	.34
1989														.34	.34	.34	.34	.34
1990															.34	.34	.34	.34
1991																.34	.34	.34
1992																	.34	.34
1993																		.35

Source: Commerce Clearing House, *Standard Federal Tax Reporter* (Chicago, 1996), 1: ¶¶ 3265.0129–.0139.

Note: State tax rates have been ignored.

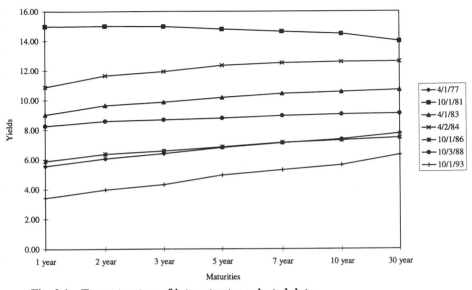

Fig. 2.1   Term structure of interest rates, selected dates
Source: Federal Reserve Board and authors' calculations.
Note: Average bond yields for various maturities, selected dates. Dates correspond to extrema in the 10-year yield.

years), we use a linear interpolation of the rates reported for the nearest adjacent maturities.

We calculate spot prices for policies written on 1 April and 1 October (more precisely, the first business days of the second and fourth quarters) each year. The applicable term structures are derived as simple averages of the term structures, compiled on a daily basis by the Federal Reserve Board, during the first and second halves of the year. Figure 2.1 shows the term structure at selected dates (the turning points in the 10-year yield in the constructed time series).

We use the notation $a(t)$ for the after-tax discount factor applied to a cash flow at time point t after the date of issue of a spot policy. These discount factors vary with the date of issue, in part because the term structure of before-tax interest rates varies and in part because the tax rates vary. The applicable tax rates for purposes of determining the break-even premium at any time are those anticipated at that time. Because the discrete payment profile that we use is an approximation to a continuous profile, the applicable tax rate is obtained by averaging over the interval from zero to the time midway to the next discrete payment point. So, for example, if $T = 6$, and the tax rate is 46 percent for the first year and 40 percent for the next five and a half years, the after-tax discount factor applicable to a cash flow at the six-year point is

$$a(6) = \exp\left[-r(6)\left(\frac{(1 - .46) + 5.5(1 - .40)}{6.5}\right)6\right].$$

Note that for this model we assume that the relevant tax rates are not the ones that actually prevailed in all instances. Rather, they are the tax rates that were expected to prevail at the date for which the after-tax discount factor is being derived.

Reserve Discount Factors

The reserve discount factors applied to undiscounted loss reserves for income tax purposes after 1986 are those promulgated by the Treasury in 1987 and 1992. The factors provided in 1992 are for the post-1989 definition of lines. For our analysis, we use five of the six lines for which data are available before 1989. For the post-1989 period we have aggregated the more narrowly defined lines into the same five broader lines (auto liability, etc.). The reserve discount factors applied in 1992 and thereafter are obtained by averaging the published IRS factors, using aggregate incurred losses in the disaggregated lines for the year as weights.

2.5.2   Calculated Spot Premiums, 1976–93

Tables 2.6 to 2.10 show the calculated break-even spot premiums in each line of insurance from 1976 through 1993 based on our model in section 2.4. The figures shown are simple averages of the 1 April and 1 October spot policy premiums that we use in the derivation of break-even standard and break-even earned premiums. The tables also show the break-even spot premiums that would have been implied based on statutory accounting (undiscounted loss reserves) and nominal economic income accounting for tax purposes throughout the series of years. For the years up to 1986, the applicable tax law is based on statutory accounting for loss reserves. After 1986, reserves are discounted for tax purposes. The special fresh-start rules applied in 1986. The column headed "Ratio of $P(\text{ATL})$ to $P(\text{NEI})$" indicates the influence on the break-even spot premiums of the deviation of the applicable tax law accounting from the nominal economic income accounting applied to ordinary borrowing and lending. After 1986, this ratio also indicates how closely the Treasury's rules replicated nominal economic income accounting. The column headed "Ratio of $P(\text{ATL})$ to $P(\text{SA})$" indicates the impact of the change in rules in 1986.

Referring to table 2.4, we see that the calculated break-even spot premiums have the expected relationship to the length of the tail in a line. In 1978, for example, the break-even premium under the applicable tax law was 0.91 in the farmowners, etc., line (the line with the shortest tail) and 0.55 in the medical malpractice line (the line with the longest tail). The differences were more pronounced in the early 1980s when interest rates were very high by historical standards. In 1981, the break-even price in the farmowners, etc., line was 0.85 and in the medical malpractice line was 0.36.

The difference between break-even prices under statutory accounting and applicable tax law accounting after 1986 also corresponds to the expectations based on the average length of the tails. As expected, the case where the difference is most pronounced is medical malpractice, where the change from undis-

Table 2.6 **Break-Even Spot Premiums for Auto Liability, 1976–93**

Year	P under Nominal Economic Income, P(NEI)	P under Applicable Tax Law, P(ATL)	Ratio of P(ATL) to P(NEI)	P under Statutory Accounting, P(SA)	Ratio of P(ATL) to P(SA)
1976	0.91	0.90	0.99	0.90	1.00
1977	0.91	0.90	0.99	0.90	1.00
1978	0.89	0.88	0.99	0.88	1.00
1979	0.87	0.86	0.99	0.86	1.00
1980	0.85	0.84	0.99	0.84	1.00
1981	0.82	0.80	0.98	0.80	1.00
1982	0.84	0.82	0.98	0.82	1.00
1983	0.86	0.85	0.99	0.85	1.00
1984	0.85	0.84	0.98	0.84	1.00
1985	0.87	0.86	0.99	0.86	1.00
1986	0.90	0.81	0.90	0.88	0.92
1987	0.90	0.90	1.00	0.88	1.02
1988	0.89	0.89	1.00	0.88	1.01
1989	0.88	0.88	1.00	0.88	1.01
1990	0.89	0.89	1.00	0.88	1.01
1991	0.91	0.91	1.00	0.90	1.01
1992	0.93	0.93	1.00	0.92	1.00
1993	0.94	0.94	1.00	0.93	1.00

Source: Authors' calculations.

Table 2.7 **Break-Even Spot Premiums for Other Liability, 1976–93**

Year	P under Nominal Economic Income, P(NEI)	P under Applicable Tax Law, P(ATL)	Ratio of P(ATL) to P(NEI)	P under Statutory Accounting, P(SA)	Ratio of P(ATL) to P(SA)
1976	0.76	0.73	0.96	0.73	1.00
1977	0.76	0.73	0.96	0.73	1.00
1978	0.73	0.68	0.93	0.68	1.00
1979	0.70	0.65	0.94	0.65	1.00
1980	0.66	0.60	0.91	0.60	1.00
1981	0.61	0.53	0.87	0.53	1.00
1982	0.63	0.56	0.89	0.56	1.00
1983	0.68	0.62	0.92	0.62	1.00
1984	0.65	0.58	0.90	0.58	1.00
1985	0.69	0.64	0.92	0.64	1.00
1986	0.76	0.55	0.73	0.68	0.81
1987	0.74	0.73	0.99	0.69	1.07
1988	0.73	0.72	1.00	0.70	1.04
1989	0.72	0.72	1.00	0.70	1.04
1990	0.73	0.73	1.00	0.70	1.04
1991	0.76	0.76	1.00	0.73	1.03
1992	0.79	0.79	1.00	0.77	1.02
1993	0.82	0.81	1.00	0.80	1.02

Source: Authors' calculations.

Table 2.8   **Break-Even Spot Premiums for Workers' Compensation, 1976–93**

Year	P under Nominal Economic Income, P(NEI)	P under Applicable Tax Law, P(ATL)	Ratio of P(ATL) to P(NEI)	P under Statutory Accounting, P(SA)	Ratio of P(ATL) to P(SA)
1976	0.83	0.81	0.97	0.81	1.00
1977	0.84	0.81	0.97	0.81	1.00
1978	0.81	0.78	0.96	0.78	1.00
1979	0.79	0.75	0.96	0.75	1.00
1980	0.76	0.72	0.94	0.72	1.00
1981	0.73	0.67	0.92	0.67	1.00
1982	0.75	0.69	0.93	0.69	1.00
1983	0.78	0.74	0.95	0.74	1.00
1984	0.76	0.71	0.94	0.71	1.00
1985	0.79	0.75	0.95	0.75	1.00
1986	0.83	0.67	0.81	0.78	0.86
1987	0.82	0.82	1.00	0.78	1.05
1988	0.81	0.81	1.00	0.79	1.02
1989	0.81	0.81	1.00	0.79	1.03
1990	0.81	0.81	1.00	0.79	1.03
1991	0.83	0.83	1.00	0.81	1.02
1992	0.86	0.86	1.00	0.84	1.02
1993	0.87	0.87	1.00	0.86	1.02

Source: Authors' calculations.

Table 2.9   **Break-Even Spot Premiums for Medical Malpractice, 1976–93**

Year	P under Nominal Economic Income, P(NEI)	P under Applicable Tax Law, P(ATL)	Ratio of P(ATL) to P(NEI)	P under Statutory Accounting, P(SA)	Ratio of P(ATL) to P(SA)
1976	0.66	0.61	0.92	0.61	1.00
1977	0.67	0.62	0.92	0.62	1.00
1978	0.63	0.55	0.88	0.55	1.00
1979	0.59	0.52	0.87	0.52	1.00
1980	0.55	0.45	0.82	0.45	1.00
1981	0.49	0.36	0.73	0.36	1.00
1982	0.51	0.40	0.77	0.40	1.00
1983	0.56	0.47	0.83	0.47	1.00
1984	0.53	0.42	0.79	0.42	1.00
1985	0.58	0.49	0.85	0.49	1.00
1986	0.66	0.39	0.59	0.55	0.71
1987	0.64	0.63	0.98	0.56	1.13
1988	0.62	0.62	0.99	0.58	1.07
1989	0.63	0.62	1.00	0.58	1.07
1990	0.63	0.63	1.00	0.58	1.07
1991	0.66	0.66	1.00	0.62	1.06
1992	0.69	0.69	1.00	0.66	1.05
1993	0.73	0.73	0.99	0.70	1.04

Source: Authors' calculations.

Table 2.10   **Break-Even Spot Premiums for Farmowners, etc., 1976–93**

Year	P under Nominal Economic Income, P(NEI)	P under Applicable Tax Law, P(ATL)	Ratio of P(ATL) to P(NEI)	P under Statutory Accounting, P(SA)	Ratio of P(ATL) to P(SA)
1976	0.93	0.93	1.00	0.93	1.00
1977	0.93	0.93	1.00	0.93	1.00
1978	0.92	0.91	0.99	0.91	1.00
1979	0.90	0.89	0.99	0.89	1.00
1980	0.89	0.88	0.99	0.88	1.00
1981	0.86	0.85	0.98	0.85	1.00
1982	0.88	0.87	0.99	0.87	1.00
1983	0.90	0.89	0.99	0.89	1.00
1984	0.89	0.88	0.99	0.88	1.00
1985	0.91	0.90	0.99	0.90	1.00
1986	0.93	0.84	0.91	0.91	0.92
1987	0.92	0.93	1.01	0.91	1.02
1988	0.92	0.92	1.00	0.91	1.01
1989	0.91	0.91	1.00	0.91	1.01
1990	0.92	0.92	1.00	0.91	1.01
1991	0.93	0.93	1.00	0.93	1.00
1992	0.95	0.95	1.00	0.94	1.00
1993	0.95	0.95	1.00	0.95	1.00

Source: Authors' calculations.

counted to discounted loss reserves accounts for a difference of 13 percent in the break-even price in 1987, declining to a roughly 4 percent difference in 1993. The impact of the fresh-start rules in 1986 (which gave an extra tax boost to loss reserves established in 1986 and earlier) meant that for that year the tax law change reduced the break-even price below what it would have been under statutory accounting. The particularly large effect of the tax law change in 1987 reflects in part the impact of the declining rate of tax from 1986 to 1988. Under statutory accounting for tax purposes, a declining rate of tax between the receipt of premium and the policy payout results in a lower break-even premium. The pattern of declines in the impact of tax reform on break-even premiums after 1987 presumably results from declining interest rates (at a zero rate of interest the two should be the same) since there were no major changes in the tax rates after that point.

Comparing the columns of break-even prices under nominal economic income accounting for tax purposes with the effect of the actual tax law in the period from 1987 onward (i.e., after the fresh-start rule had ceased to have any influence), we see that the two are very close. The ratios are essentially one throughout, for all lines, suggesting the Treasury succeeded in implementing the presumed objective of the 1986 shift to discounted loss reserves.

2.5.3   Calculated Standard Policy Premiums, 1976–93

In getting to the break-even earned premiums, we calculated break-even standard policy premiums in each line of insurance for 1 April and 1 October from 1976 through 1993. The difference between these premiums and the spot premiums presented above is that the standard policy premiums incorporate the effect of changes in the treatment of unearned premium reserves (a minor effect) and bring to an earlier time point the effect on premiums of changes in interest rates and tax rules. Thus a premium on a policy written on 1 October 1986, incorporates the effect of tax changes manifested in break-even spot premiums during most of 1987.

2.5.4   Predicted Break-Even Premiums versus Actual Earned Premiums, Accident Years 1977–93

Under competitive conditions, the opportunity for profit from all sources, including tax saving, will tend to be driven to zero. Thus we assume that the tax saving is "passed along" to the buyer of the policy in the form of a reduced premium. To make the comparison of the calculated break-even premiums with industry data, we make use of the break-even earned premium concept discussed above. Table 2.11 presents these premiums, for accident years 1977–93 (1976 is lost in the derivation of earned premiums), together with the unit earned premiums implicit in industry data for these accident years, interpreted as the inverse of the loss ratio reported at the end of each accident year. For each line of insurance, there are two columns, one showing the break-even earned premium ("B-E Earned P") calculated from our model and one showing the ratio of earned premiums per dollar of losses incurred ("1/Industry Loss Ratio") registered in data for the industry for the year in question. So, for example, our calculated average of the break-even premiums for the unit standard policies contributing to earned premiums in the other liability line in 1985 was 0.58. The ratio of earned premiums to losses incurred in that line in that year was 0.81. The observed average "price" was higher than would be predicted by our calculation.

In evaluating these figures, one needs to keep in mind that our calculations are highly stylized, neglecting risk premiums in the discount rates, for example. We would hope to see a relationship between the calculated and the observed prices, not necessarily equality. One important influence on the empirical ratios is the fact that industry data relate to premiums earned *gross* of the cost of acquiring the policies, whereas our calculations would apply to premiums net of acquisition costs. *Best's* reports the following figures for "other underwriting expenses" incurred, as a ratio to premiums earned, in the reporting years: 1990 (26.36 percent), 1989, (26.25 percent), 1988 (25.97 percent), 1987 (25.95 percent), and 1986 (26.77 percent). Data disaggregated by line, available for 1990, are shown in table 2.12.

To permit more ready comparison of the relationship between calculated

Table 2.11   Break-Even Earned Premiums and Observed Loss Ratios by Line, 1977–93

Accident Year	Auto Liability		Other Liability		Workers' Compensation		Medical Malpractice		Farmowners, etc.	
	B-E Earned P	1/Industry Loss Ratio	B-E Earned P	1/Industry Loss Ratio	B-E Earned P	1/Industry Loss Ratio	B-E Earned P	1/Industry Loss Ratio	B-E Earned P	1/Industry Loss Ratio
1977	0.87	1.36	0.70	1.50	0.78	1.30	0.59	1.19	0.90	1.70
1978	0.85	1.34	0.66	1.57	0.75	1.39	0.54	0.98	0.88	1.72
1979	0.82	1.29	0.62	1.45	0.72	1.41	0.49	0.82	0.85	1.52
1980	0.79	1.26	0.56	1.20	0.68	1.39	0.42	0.68	0.83	1.37
1981	0.76	1.18	0.51	1.01	0.64	1.37	0.35	0.60	0.80	1.43
1982	0.77	1.15	0.53	0.82	0.65	1.22	0.38	0.59	0.81	1.27
1983	0.80	1.09	0.58	0.68	0.69	1.08	0.43	0.58	0.84	1.20
1984	0.80	1.01	0.57	0.59	0.68	0.93	0.41	0.68	0.84	1.19
1985	0.81	1.02	0.58	0.81	0.69	0.96	0.43	0.83	0.84	1.25
1986	0.81	1.12	0.59	1.57	0.69	1.05	0.44	1.23	0.84	1.64
1987	0.86	1.15	0.69	1.77	0.77	1.10	0.57	1.39	0.89	1.73
1988	0.86	1.13	0.70	1.61	0.79	1.08	0.60	1.33	0.89	1.60
1989	0.85	1.10	0.69	1.44	0.77	1.06	0.60	1.23	0.88	1.31
1990	0.86	1.11	0.70	1.35	0.78	1.07	0.61	1.02	0.88	1.36
1991	0.88	1.16	0.73	1.30	0.80	1.12	0.63	0.89	0.90	1.27
1992	0.90	1.16	0.77	1.27	0.83	1.17	0.68	0.83	0.92	0.95
1993	0.92	1.12	0.80	1.23	0.86	1.23	0.71	0.80	0.94	1.25

Source: Authors' calculations and A. M. Best Company (various years).

Table 2.12   **Other Underwriting Expenses by Line, 1990**

Line	Ratio of "Other Underwriting Expenses" Incurred to Premiums Written in 1990	Premiums Written in 1990 (thousand $)	Other Underwriting Expenses (thousand $)
Auto	23.9	60,042,447	14,374,550
Other liability	26.3	17,217,566	4,528,220
Workers' compensation	17.6	30,957,411	5,448,504
Medical malpractice	15.5	4,014,622	622,266
Farmowners, etc.	34.1	44,032,383	15,002,167

Source: A. M. Best Company (1991).

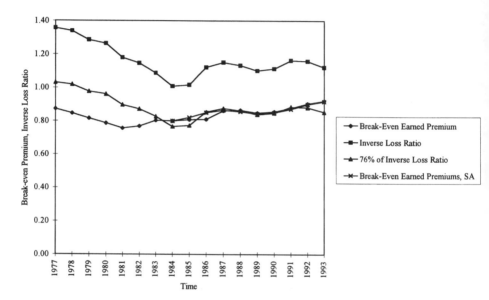

Fig. 2.2   Auto liability: break-even earned premium and inverse loss ratio, 1977–93
Source: Authors' calculations and A. M. Best Company (various years).

and empirical prices, we present in figures 2.2 to 2.6 plots of normalized break-even prices and unit earned premiums in the data for the five lines. For each line of insurance four lines are graphed, plotting the break-even earned premium ("Break-Even Earned Premium," our calculated amount), the break-even earned premium with statutory accounting ("Break-Even Earned Premium, SA," also calculated, showing what the break-even premium would have been under continuation of the pre-1986 tax law), the estimated average unit premium in the industry data ("Inverse Loss Ratio"), and the same average unit

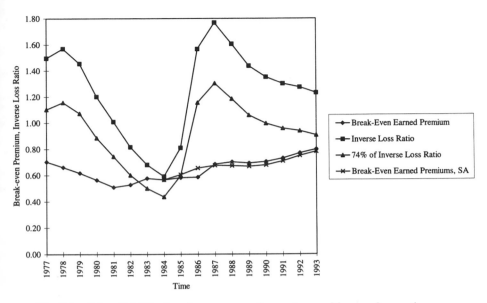

Fig. 2.3   Other liability: break-even earned premium and inverse loss ratio, 1977–93

Source: Authors' calculations and A. M. Best Company (various years).

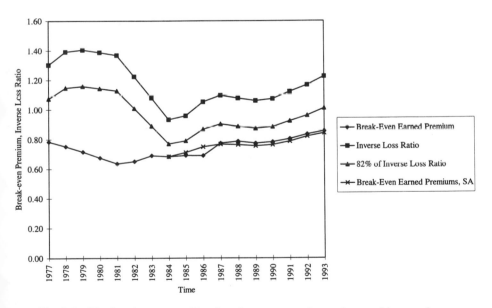

Fig. 2.4   Workers' compensation: break-even earned premium and inverse loss ratio, 1977–93

Source: Authors' calculations and A. M. Best Company (various years).

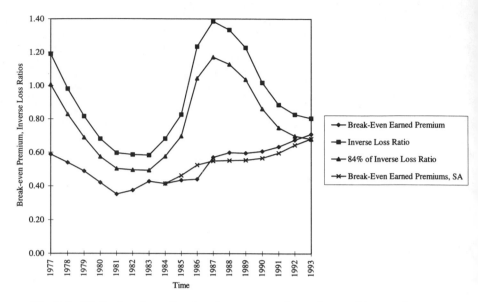

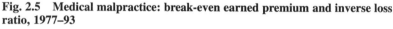

Fig. 2.5   Medical malpractice: break-even earned premium and inverse loss ratio, 1977–93
Source: Authors' calculations and A. M. Best Company (various years).

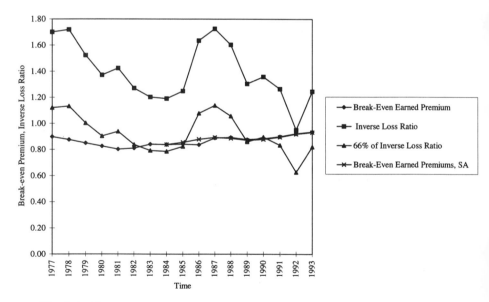

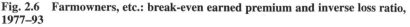

Fig. 2.6   Farmowners, etc.: break-even earned premium and inverse loss ratio, 1977–93
Source: Authors' calculations and A. M. Best Company (various years).

premium deflated by the acquisition cost, represented by the ratios of "other underwriting expenses" to premiums written in 1990, assumed constant throughout ("X% of Inverse Loss Ratio"). The two key graphs from the point of view of assessing the predictive power of the calculated break-even prices on the industry results are "Break-Even Earned Premium" and "X% of Inverse Loss Ratio." For the short-tailed lines (auto liability and farmowners, etc.), the two graphs arguably track reasonably closely. For the longer tailed lines, for which the discount rate is much more important, the industry data display large variation relative to the path of the calculated break-even prices and generally lie above the calculated levels. Taking the industry loss reserve data at face value, they reveal the highly risky nature of the long-tailed insurance lines. Except for the very longest tailed line, medical malpractice, the variation in the calculated prices (due, mainly, to variation in interest rates) is very small relative to the variation in the industry results.

Finally, the comparison of the two calculated price graphs ("Break-Even Earned Premium" and "Break-Even Earned Premium, SA") allows an assessment of the importance of changes in tax rules as an explanatory factor in the time series of industry results. The graphs suggest that the impact of the changes in tax law in 1986 was small relative to the other factors that influence the average level of industry prices.

2.6 Conclusion

One bottom-line conclusion of our investigation is that the effect of changes in tax law is small relative to the other forces that bear on variation in the average price of property-casualty insurance. The other major conclusion, taken from the tables of break-even spot premiums, is that the 1986 reforms could account for an increase in the predicted price of insurance ranging from next to nothing for the very short tailed lines to 5 or 6 percent in the longest tailed line, medical malpractice. If the 1986 reforms are understood as an excise tax increase on long-tailed property-casualty insurance, perhaps the size of the predicted price effect is not a negligible amount, even if it is not large relative to the annual variation in the industry's results.

Appendix A
Loss Reserve Discounting with Taxes

In the presence of taxes, the appropriate discount rate for the company to use in evaluating after-tax cash flows is the after-tax rate of interest in the market. This is because the after-tax rate of interest expresses the opportunity available to the company to exchange dollars in one period for dollars in another. The discount rate applied to the anticipated losses in deriving the reserves used in calculating nominal economic income is, however, the before-tax interest rate.

To explain why this is so, consider an analogy with a company's writing an insurance policy: floating a zero-coupon bond. The proceeds of the borrowing are analogous to the premium on the insurance policy. The single payment on the bond at maturity corresponds to the payoff on a single-payment insurance policy. The analogy of the sale of a policy by an insurance company with a loan from policyholder to the company has been noted by others (see, e.g., Cummins and Grace 1994).

The analogue to treating the premium as "gross income" of the insurance company would be treating the proceeds of the borrowing as gross income. There would, however, be an immediate deduction of the discounted value of the payment anticipated at maturity. Subsequently, as the time for the company to repay the loan approached, its liability, the discounted value of its repayment obligation, would grow. In the income calculation, this growth in liability would be allowed as a deduction (it is simply accruing interest). Finally, at maturity, the company would pay off the loan, taking a deduction for the amount paid, but taking into income the value of the liability, in equal amount, that it takes off its books at that point.

Keeping the analogy with the unit single-payment spot policy, let the face value of the discount bond be one, payable at time T after the date of issue, time 0. Let r be the rate of interest, and τ the tax rate. Finally, let A be the amount received by the issuing company. The cash flow of the company at the moment of issuing the bond consists of the proceeds received, A, less the tax on A, treated as gross income, and plus the tax saving due to the deduction of the discounted (at r) value of one, payable T years in the future. (Note: In general, in this paper we treat taxes as though assessed and paid continuously.) Subsequently, the company obtains a deduction for the growth in value of its repayment obligation under the bond, so there is a stream of tax savings. At maturity, the company pays one and takes a deduction of this amount in the calculation of income for tax purposes (corresponding to the inclusion as gross income of the premium). This deduction is, however, balanced by an equal inclusion in income of the elimination of the accrued value of the liability for payment, corresponding to the write-down of loss reserves in the insurance context. So there is no tax consequence of payoff at maturity. This three-part after-tax cash flow—a lump sum received (net of tax), a flow of tax savings, and a lump sum paid—will be discounted by the company at the after-tax interest rate. It remains to show that the break-even value of A is simply the payoff, one, discounted to time 0 at the *before-tax* rate of interest.

The break-even condition is that the stream of net after-tax cash flows have a discounted (at the *after-tax* rate of interest) value of zero:

$$(1 - \tau)A + \tau e^{-rT} + \tau \int_0^T r(e^{-(T-t)r})e^{-(1-\tau)rt}\, dt - e^{-(1-\tau)rT} = 0.$$

This simplifies to

$$(1 - \tau)A + \tau e^{-rT} + \tau r e^{-rT} \int_0^T e^{\tau rt} \, dt - e^{-(1-\tau)rT} = 0.$$

We can explicitly integrate to get

$$(1 - \tau)A + \tau e^{-rT} + \tau r e^{-rT} \left(\frac{e^{\tau rT} - 1}{\tau r} \right) - e^{-(1-\tau)rT} = 0.$$

This, in turn, simplifies to

$$(1 - \tau)A - (1 - \tau)e^{-rT} = 0,$$

or

$$A = e^{-rT}.$$

After a bit of work, we get the expected answer: under nominal economic income taxation, the value of a discount bond, taking into account tax effects, is obtained by discounting the cash flow, exclusive of taxes, at the before-tax interest rate.

Appendix B
Details of the Calculations

In this appendix we add details to the description in the body of the paper of the calculation of premiums for empirical implementation.

Calculating Break-Even Spot Prices

Break-Even Spot Prices under Nominal Economic Income Accounting

Under nominal economic income accounting, the tax rate does not enter the determination of break-even spot prices. The break-even spot premium is simply the discounted value of the loss payments, using the before-tax discount rate. So the break-even spot premium for a general policy with loss profile specified by the sequence, l_j, is given by

$$P(\{l_j\}) = \sum_j l_j e^{-r(t_j)t_j}.$$

Break-Even Spot Prices under Statutory Accounting for Tax Purposes (Pre-TRA86)

The break-even spot premium for a single-payment spot policy, with maturity T, in the pre-1986 tax regime is given by

$$(1 - \tau)P(T) + \tau = e^{-(1-\tau)r(T)T}$$

provided there is no anticipated change in the tax rate. If a change in tax rate is anticipated, the exponent in the discount factor on the right-hand side is modified, as discussed in the body of the paper.

The break-even spot premium for a general policy with loss profile specified by the sequence l_j (to simplify, again assuming no change in the applicable tax rate) is given by

$$(1 - \tau)P(\{l_j\}) + \tau = \sum_j l_j e^{-(1-\tau)r(t_j)t_j}.$$

Break-Even Spot Prices with Discounted Loss Reserves (Post-TRA86)

For policies written after 31 December 1986, prescribed reserve discount factors are applied to loss reserves at year end, the factors depending on the line of insurance. As we have done in the analysis of break-even prices with statutory accounting, we assume that tax liabilities are calculated continuously so that the gross premium income and initial loss reserve deductions are effectively realized immediately on writing a new spot policy. In the case of discounted loss reserves, there is a sequence of additions that result from the passing of time.

To illustrate the way the discount factors enter the break-even conditions, let the reserve discount factors applied at the moment of writing, on the first anniversary, and so on, be denoted f_0, f_1, f_2, etc. For a single-payment spot policy, the factors are increasing, as the undiscounted loss reserve remains constant until the moment of payment. The discount factors thus reflect the approach in time of the single payment. For a more general policy, the discount factors may decrease, as the effective length of the remaining tail of payments may increase as the early payments are realized. In the case of a unit single-payment spot policy with maturity T (taken to be an integer), assuming a constant tax rate, the break-even condition is

$$(1 - \tau)P(T) + \tau f_0 + \tau(f_1 - f_0)e^{-(1-\tau)r(1)} + \tau(f_2 - f_1)e^{-(1-\tau)r(2)2} + \cdots$$

$$+ \tau(f_{T-1} - f_{T-2})e^{-(1-\tau)r(T-1)(T-1)} + \tau(1 - f_{T-1})e^{-(1-\tau)r(T)T} = e^{-(1-\tau)r(T)T}.$$

On the left-hand side are included the tax savings due to the successive additions to loss reserves owing to the passing of time. The last term on the left is the tax saving due to any divergence of the last value of the discounted reserve from unity. On the right-hand side is the discounted loss payment.

If the tax rate is varying over time, the value of the deductions and the after-tax discount factors will be affected in the manner discussed in general terms above and spelled out in detail below.

Using Line-Specific Reserve Discount Factors

If we were provided with the appropriate discount factors for each possible single-payment policy, we could calculate the break-even premium for a general spot policy, with loss profile specified by a sequence of loss payments, by treating each separate payment as a single-payment spot policy, using the formula above, then adding the premiums together.

For our purposes, there are two problems with the discount factors provided by the IRS. First, they are designed to apply to an aggregation of policies over a one-year period, rather than spot policies. Second, they apply to a given line, rather than to single-payment spot policies.

The first reserve discount factor specified by the IRS is to be applied to the reserve in the relevant line on the company's books at the end of the initial accident year. Conceived of in terms of an aggregate of spot policies, this reserve includes amounts remaining to be paid on policies ranging in age from one year (written on 1 January) to zero years (written on 31 December). The IRS reserve discount factor is based on a spot policy written on 1 July. It is thus "too close" to the loss payout (i.e., too high) compared to the factor appropriate for the actual payout pattern associated with a newly written spot policy. Compared with the policy written a year earlier, the IRS factor is six months "too far" from the actual payouts (so, too low). As an approximation, we apply this factor to the undiscounted loss reserve (equal to one for a unit policy) associated with a newly written spot policy. That is, we allow an immediate deduction of this first factor at the time of writing a unit spot policy.

The development of the further reserve deductions, associated with the gradual increase in the reserve discount factor as the payout time approaches, is complicated by the fact that the IRS reserve discount factors are specified by line of insurance, rather than by timing of single payments. As will be discussed, because of the way cumulative loss data are reported, we approximate the loss profile in a given line as involving discrete loss payments at the three-month point from the date of writing a spot policy, followed by payouts on the anniversary dates. In our treatment of the payout profiles as known with certainty, an equal reduction in the (undiscounted) unpaid loss reserve corresponds to each loss payout.

The taxable income calculation brings *into* income the *decline* in discounted reserves during the year and allows a *deduction* of the loss payments during the year. Using the notation $L(t)$ for the cumulative payments up to and including t, the path of undiscounted reserves for a unit policy is given by $1, (1 - L(1))$, $(1 - L(2))$, etc., at the outset and at successive anniversaries. The path of discounted reserves is thus given by $f_0, f_1(1 - L(1)), f_2(1 - L(2))$, etc. The taxable income associated with a unit policy is thus $P - f_0$ at the moment of writing, $f_0 - f_1(1 - L(1)) - L(1)$ in the first year, $f_1(1 - L(1)) - f_2(1 - L(2)) - (L(2) - L(1))$ in the second year, and so on. In the last year, the taxable income will be $f_{T-1}(1 - L(T - 1)) - (1 - L(T - 1))$.

The IRS cumulative loss profiles specify amounts regarded as paid as of six months from the time of writing the policy in a line, 1.5 years, etc., through an assumed "last year." Let the cumulative amount paid out at these successive points be denoted F_0, F_1, etc., through F_T. For a unit policy, $F_T = 1$. We think of these cumulative payouts as derived from constant payout *rates* over the interval in question. So the rate of loss payout would start at $2F_0$ for the first six months of the policy life (the factor of two comes from the fact that the interval to the first cumulation point is just half a year). The loss payout would continue at the rate of $F_1 - F_0$ for the period from .5 years to 1.5 years, at the rate of $F_2 - F_3$ for the period from 1.5 years to 2.5 years, etc.

The constant rates are in turn converted to discrete payments at the midpoints of the various intervals. So the first loss payout is taken to be F_0 at the .25-year (three-month) point. The second payout is $F_1 - F_0$ at the midpoint between .5 years and 1.5 year, that is, at the one-year point. And so on. The last payout is $F_T - F_{T-1} = 1 - F_{T-1}$ at the T-year point.

The formulas above assume constant tax rates. In the calculations, as summarized in table 2B.1, the after-tax discount factors, $a(t)$, are based on the actual anticipated tax rates, which are also used to determine the projected tax consequences of future cash flows.

Break-Even Spot Prices after TRA86: The Transition

These descriptions apply to spot policies written in worlds governed entirely by either the pre- or post-TRA86 rules. It remains to determine the break-even price for a policy that crossed the boundary. Consider, for example, a single-payment spot policy written on 1 April 1986. An immediate deduction of the undiscounted loss reserve would apply at the moment of writing. Then, as of 1 January 1987, it would begin to accrue additional deductions for the accruing value of its *discounted* reserve as of that date. These deductions would continue until the maturity date, at which point, ideally, the discounted reserve would equal the payoff amount. The tax effect of the loss deduction would, as usual, be offset by the write-down of the reserve associated with the policy.

The fresh-start rule meant that, in effect, companies received tax deductions of more than 100 percent of the amount of the losses. For policies that had already been written, this meant a gain to the companies, but it had no incentive effect, no effect on the break-even prices. But to the extent a company could anticipate the fresh-start rule, there would be a downward effect on the break-even price.

For purposes of this exercise, we assume that the fresh-start rules were built into break-even premiums starting 1 January 1986. As will be discussed below, in application, we calculate spot prices as of the first day of the second and fourth quarters each year. So the fresh-start rules need to be taken into account for the two prices calculated for 1986.

For the single-payment spot policy with maturity T, written on 1 April 1986, the fresh-start rule meant an immediate deduction of one and then a stream of deductions, which we treat as occurring on the anniversary dates, along the lines just discussed for the policy entirely in the post-TRA86 regime. For the case of a constant tax rate, the break-even condition is then

Table 2B.1   Unit Spot Policy Cash Flows, Post-TRA86 Rules

Time (relative to issue date of spot policy)	Payments/Receipts Other Than Taxes	Taxable Income	Applicable Tax Rate	Applicable Discount Factor
0	P	$P - f_0$	$\tau(0)$	1
.25	$-F_0$	0	$\tau(.25)$	$a(.25)$
1	$-(F_1 - F_0)$	$f_0 - f_1(1 - F_1) - F_1$	$\tau(1)$	$a(1)$
2	$-(F_2 - F_1)$	$f_1(1 - F_1) - f_2(1 - F_2) - (F_2 - F_1)$	$\tau(2)$	$a(2)$
$\cdot$	$\cdot$	$\cdot$	$\cdot$	$\cdot$
$\cdot$	$\cdot$	$\cdot$	$\cdot$	$\cdot$
T	$-(1 - F_{T-1})$	$f_{T-1}(1 - F_{T-1}) - (1 - F_{T-1})$	$\tau(T)$	$a(T)$

$$(1 - \tau)P(T) + \tau + \tau(f_1 - f_0)e^{-(1-\tau)r(1)} + \tau(f_2 - f_1)e^{-(1-\tau)r(2)2} + \cdots$$
$$+ \tau(f_T - f_{T-1})e^{-(1-\tau)r(T)T} + \tau(1 - f_T)e^{-(1-\tau)r(T)T} = e^{-(1-\tau)r(T)T}.$$

The difference from the previous formula is that the first reserve deduction is worth τ, instead of τf_0.

Summing Up the Cases

In all we calculate break-even spot prices under three sets of assumptions about taxes: Under statutory accounting, the unit loss is deducted at the moment of writing the policy. In terms of table 2B.1, the effect is to set $f_i = 1$ for all i. Under applicable tax law, the same is true until 1986. From 1987 onward, the discount factors, f_i, prescribed by the IRS apply. For 1986, the same discount factors apply for cash flows in 1987 and later, but taxable income *in the 1986 year of writing the policy* (but not on the anniversary) is based on $f_0 = 1$. Under nominal economic income accounting the price is based on the cash flow of premium and payments only, without regard to taxes, using the discount factors based on *before-tax* interest rates.

Calculating Standard Policy Premiums

Accounting for the Time Structure of an Insurance Policy

In order to calculate break-even premiums to compare with data we need to take account of the fact that the usual insurance policy covers events that occur during a specified period, usually a year, commencing with the date of issue. The premium is generally payable at the beginning of the policy year. At the moment of writing, there will have been no losses incurred, and so no addition to the loss reserve. As time passes, losses accumulate, and the company books incurred losses, basing its accounts on actual information (e.g., claims actually filed) and experience with similar insurance policies in the past. At the moment of writing the policy the company does acquire an asset, the premium paid or receivable, to which corresponds the liability to provide coverage for the period covered. At the moment of writing, the coverage for which the premium is payment has yet to be delivered, so the liability to provide that coverage is carried on the books as an "unearned" premium reserve. By convention, the premium on a policy is treated as "earned" ratably over the policy period.

The significance of these accounting details is, in part, the necessity they reveal of dealing with the distinction between premiums written, which are taken into income for both tax and regulatory purposes, and the set-aside for premiums not yet earned, which is allowed for in tax and statutory accounting. The tax rules with respect to unearned premium reserves were changed in TRA86, and we need to incorporate this change into our calculations.

A second reason for undertaking an explicit analysis of the timing of premiums received and earned is that the premium determined in our calculations will actually be earned over a period of time that will generally include more than one taxable year. Since tax rules generally apply to whole calendar years, the price of a policy that will span 1 January will need to incorporate the changing rules on the income as well as the deduction (loss reserves) side.

A third reason is that industry data we examine relate to premiums earned, reported by accident year. Those premiums earned will be in part the playing out of policy years that began the year before the accident year in question and in part the initial phase of policies written during the accident year. If premiums were separately calculated and reported for coverage within a particular calendar year (so that a typical one-year policy written on 1 September 1987 would have a premium for the period through 31 December 1987 and a premium for the period 1 January through 31 August 1988), this would not create problems for us. But the convention that premiums are earned ratably over the policy period means that data on earned premiums may show a different pattern than year-by-year calculations would imply.

To illustrate, suppose that the theory tells us that in some isolated year, say 1983, the tax rules imply a very high spot premium relative to all other years. A company writing a one-year policy on 1 September 1982 could be thought of as writing two policies, a low-priced one for the last four months of 1982 and a high-priced one for January–August 1983. There will be just one price, however, intermediate between the two, which will be reported (and taxed) partly in 1982 and partly in 1983. Premiums earned for accident year 1982 will thus include some of the effect of the 1983 tax rule changes (and thus be higher than would be predicted based just on 1982 tax rules), while the premiums earned in the 1983 accident year will include a residual influence of the pre-1983 rules.

The analysis thus far of break-even spot premiums assumed that, at a given moment, the insurance company acquires a liability to make a known sequence of loss payments over time and inquired into the up-front payment that would make this a break-even proposition, taking into account the tax-implied tax payments. The fact that, in actuality, the company typically sells a whole year's worth of spot policies at once influences the way we need to interpret data on loss reserves and earned premiums and, because of details of the treatment of the premium payment under the tax law, it affects the break-even formulas as well.

For example, when an insurance company sells a medical malpractice policy for a term of one year commencing on 1 September 1988, it knows that on 1 September, with certain probabilities, an event will occur that will give rise to a claim and that the result will be a certain series of loss payments and expenses in the future. It knows the same for 2 September, and so on. The premium it charges for this one-year policy is to pay for these 365 one-day policies. For present purposes, we continue to dispense entirely with the risk aspect of this situation, and we imagine the company as taking on 365 known liabilities. Thus one of the liabilities, incorporated in the premium as of 1 September, is to provide a stream of payments, starting 6 December, with the characteristic medical malpractice profile.

In the absence of taxes, this nicety would not matter much. The one-year premium would simply be the discounted value of the 365 spot premiums on the daily policies. With taxes, the nicety could matter because the spot prices may themselves vary over the year as the result of variation in the interest rates or in the tax rules themselves. But the tax system, in effect, treats the spot price as uniform throughout the policy year. (The single annual premium is treated as "earned" in proportion to the fraction of the policy year that has elapsed.)

To explore this issue, consider the case of a loss payment profile on the spot policy whereby the first loss payment occurs .5 years after the covered day. After that, payments occur at one-year intervals. The loss reserve is set up on the date the policy is written. The new question to be considered is how tax law changes as of 1 January affect the analysis.

For a policy written after 1 July, the loss payments are shifted by one year, in terms of the applicable tax law, compared with the policy written before 1 July. So if interest rates are unchanged, for the case of spot premiums (implying no unearned premium problem) there will be one premium before 1 July and another one after 1 July. In going from the second half of one year to the first half of the next, there may be a difference in spot premium (even given constant interest rates), owing to the taxation of the premium, net of loss reserve. This is why we calculate two spot prices for each year, using the interest rate conditions as of the beginning of April and October.

Calculating Break-Even Standard Policy Prices

The break-even premium on a standard policy is the amount the company must receive to finance the flow of premiums on the embedded implicit spot policies over the year. So the starting point for calculating it is the calculation of spot premiums.

We assume that, looking forward from 1 April, the company correctly anticipates the spot premiums that will prevail on 1 October of the current year and on 1 April of the next year. Our calculated break-even standard premium on 1 April is based on the approximation of a single spot policy issued on 1 July of the current year and 1 January of the next year. The 1 July spot premium is the average of the spot premiums on 1 April and 1 October. The 1 January spot premium is the average of the 1 October spot premium and next year's 1 April spot premium. These hypothetical spot premiums (1 July and 1 January) are discounted to 1 April.

The analogous procedure is used to derive the 1 October standard premium each year.

The detail to be resolved is the discount rate to apply to these spot premiums in getting to the standard premiums.

Table 2B.2   **Discounting from Spot to Standard Premium before TRA86**

After-Tax Cash Flows	1 October 1983	30 September 1984
Up front	x	$-\tau(9/30/84)*x$
Spot		$y - \tau(9/30/84)*y$

Standard Policy Prices with No Taxes

In the absence of taxes, the break-even premium on a standard policy starting at a particular time would simply be the discounted (at the before-tax rate of interest) value of the flow of spot premiums over the year. In the case in which the unit spot premium is P and taxes and interest rates are constant, this will simply be

$$\int_0^1 Pe^{-rt} = P\left(\frac{1 - e^{-r}}{r}\right).$$

Typical values of the multiplicative factor are .975, .952, and .906 for $r = .05$, .10, and .20, respectively.

Standard Policy Prices before TRA86

Taxes complicate the story. Consider the question: what payment must the company receive on 1 October 1983 to deliver a commitment to provide a unit spot policy on 30 September 1984 (i.e., the last day of the policy year)? In the pre-TRA86 regime, the 1 October 1983 payment, regarded as gross income, would have been offset by an addition to the unearned premium reserve, so there would be no tax consequences at that point. On 30 September 1984, the unearned premium reserve would have been debited by the amount of the unearned premium reserve, resulting in an inclusion in taxable income. So if x is the 1 October 1983 payment and y is the 30 September 1984 spot premium, then the after-tax cash flows that need to be equated in value are summarized in table 2B.2.

Carrying out the calculation for equating the values of the two cash flows, using the after-tax discount rate, yields (assuming constant tax rate)

$$x(1 - \tau e^{-(1-\tau)r}) = y(1 - \tau)e^{-(1-\tau)r},$$

or

$$\frac{x}{y} = \frac{(1 - \tau)e^{-(1-\tau)r}}{1 - \tau e^{-(1-\tau)r}}.$$

The implicit discount from spot to the element of the standard premium that buys the last bit of spot coverage in the policy year is found by taking the negative of the natural logarithm of the right-hand side. For example, for $r = 10$ percent and $\tau = 40$ percent, the implicit discount rate is 9.8 percent.

Table 2B.3   **Discounting from Spot to Standard after 1986**

After-Tax Cash Flows	1 October 1988	30 September 1989
Up front	$x - \tau(10/1/88)*.2x$	$-\tau(9/30/89)*.8x$
Spot		$y - \tau(9/30/89)*y$

The example suggests that for the pre-TRA86 rules, one could safely derive standard premium prices from spot prices by discounting at the before-tax rate of return. We adopt this approximation.

Standard Policy Prices after 31 December 1986

In the post-TRA86 regime, the company would be allowed a deduction from the 1 October 1988 payment of only 80 percent of the addition to the unearned premium reserve account, so there would be taxable income at that point. On 30 September 1989, the reduction of the unearned premium reserve account by the amount of the spot premium would give rise to an inclusion in taxable income of 80 percent of that amount. So if x is the 1 October 1988 payment and y is the 30 September 1989 spot premium, then the after-tax cash flows that need to be equated in value are as shown in table 2B.3.

Using subscripts to indicate the timing of the tax rates, the value of x is given by

$$x(1 - .2\tau_1 - .8\tau_2 e^{-(1-\tau_2)r}) = y(1 - \tau_2)e^{-(1-\tau_2)r},$$

$$\frac{x}{y} = \frac{(1 - \tau_2)e^{-(1-\tau_2)r}}{1 - .2\tau_1 - .8\tau_2 e^{-(1-\tau_2)r}}.$$

As table 2B.4 shows, the effect of the TRA86 change was to reduce slightly the implicit discount rate applicable to the end-of-year spot premium in determining the beginning-of-year standard premium (i.e., raise the break-even standard premium). The effect was enhanced by the pattern of tax rate changes in effect in 1987 and 1988. (For calendar year taxpayers, the rate was 40 percent in 1987 and 34 percent in 1988.) As a simplification, we ignored the effect of the changed treatment of the unearned premium reserve except for 1987, when we based the discounting on one-half of the market rate.

Transition from Pre- to Post-TRA86 Rules

Just as special transition rules were enacted in connection with the change in the treatment of unpaid losses effected by TRA86, special rules also applied to the change in the treatment of the unearned premium reserve. As has just been discussed, according to TRA86, only 80 percent of the end-of-year stock of unearned premiums is allowed as a deduction. The effect is to exclude 20

Table 2B.4   **Implicit Discount from End-of-Year Spot to Beginning-of-Year Standard Premium, Post-TRA86 Rules**

τ_1 (%)	τ_2 (%)	r (%)	$\hat{r}$ (%)	Ratio of Implicit to Market Discount
34	34	5	4.6	0.93
34	34	10	9.2	0.92
34	34	20	18.2	0.91
46	40	5	2.6	0.52
46	40	10	7.1	0.71
46	40	20	16.0	0.80
40	34	5	2.8	0.56
40	34	10	7.4	0.74
40	34	20	16.4	0.82

Source: Authors' calculations.

percent of the beginning-of-year stock from taxable income. Applied at the transition, 1 January 1987, the new rule would have implied forgiveness of tax on 20 percent of the then-outstanding stock of unearned premiums. Under special transition rules, that 20 percent was brought into income over a six-year period, one-sixth each year.

Looking ahead from 1986, the transition treatment of unearned premiums for that year was actually more favorable than the preexisting regime since the return of unearned premiums to taxable income was slightly deferred and the tax rates at which the deferred premiums were included was lower than that at which they had been deducted. We decided to neglect this transitional effect in our calculations.

Modeling the Annual Statement Data on Earned Premiums

One more step is needed in getting to a break-even premium figure that can be compared to company or industry data on premiums earned during a particular year. Let $P(t)$, temporarily, stand for the total of standard policy premiums written (by a company or for the industry) at time t, representing prepayment of coverage over the next year, where the current year begins at time 0. $P(t)$ will give rise to a quantum $(1 - t)P(t)$ of premiums earned in the current year and $tP(t)$ in the next year. With a constant flow of new policies, an average of one-fourth of the new premiums written in the first half of the year will show up the next year. An average of three-fourths of the new premiums written in the second half of the year will show up the next year. If the premiums written in the successive halves of calendar years are P_1, P_2, P_3, and P_4, the premiums reported as earned in year 2 will be

$$\frac{P_1 + 3P_2 + 3P_3 + P_4}{4}.$$

This is motivation for what we term the *break-even earned premium*. The break-even earned premium is a weighted average of unit standard premiums. It corresponds to the level of premiums earned during an accident year in the case of a company writing policies at a constant rate. Reinterpret P_1, P_2, P_3, and P_4 as the unit standard premiums in the respective half-years (rather than totals of premiums written), thought of as centered in each half-year (1 April and 1 October). The normalized break-even earned premium in year 2 is then

$$\frac{P_1 + 3P_2 + 3P_3 + P_4}{8}.$$

This is the formula used in calculating the break-even earned premium.

References

A. M. Best Company. Various years. *Best's aggregates and averages: Property-casualty.* Oldwick, N.J.: A. M. Best Company.

Bradford, David F. 1981. Issues in the design of savings and investment incentives. In *Depreciation, inflation, and the taxation of income from capital,* ed. Charles R. Hulten, 13–47. Washington, D.C.: Urban Institute.

———. 1995. Fixing realization accounting: Symmetry, consistency and correctness in the taxation of financial instruments. *Tax Law Review* 50, no. 4 (summer): 731–85.

Bradford, David F., and Kyle D. Logue. 1997. The influence of income tax rules on insurance reserves. NBER Working Paper no. 5902. Cambridge, Mass.: National Bureau of Economic Research, January.

Butsic, Robert P. 1991. Determining the proper interest rate for loss reserve discounting. In *Managing the insolvency of insurance companies,* ed. J. David Cummins and Richard A. Derrig. Boston: Kluwer.

Cummins, J. David. 1990. Multi-period discounted cash flow ratemaking models in property-liability insurance. *Journal of Risk and Insurance* 57:79–109.

Cummins, J. David, and Elizabeth Grace. 1994. Tax management and investment strategies of property-liability insurers. *Journal of Banking and Finance* 17:43–72.

D'Arcy, Stephen P. 1988. Use of the CAPM to discount property-liability loss reserves. *Journal of Risk and Insurance* 55, no. 3 (September): 481–91.

General Accounting Office (GAO). 1995. Congress should consider changing federal income taxation of the property/casualty insurance industry. GAO/GGD-85-10. Washington, D.C.: General Accounting Office, 25 March.

Gordon, Roger H. 1985. Taxation of corporate capital income: Tax revenues versus tax distortions. *Quarterly Journal of Economics* 100 (February): 1–27.

Kraus, Alan, and Stephen A. Ross. 1982. The determination of fair profits for the property-liability insurance firm. *Journal of Finance* 37, no. 4 (September): 1015–28.

Logue, Kyle D. 1996. Toward a tax-based explanation of the liability insurance crisis. *Virginia Law Review* 82 (6): 895–959.

Miller, Merton H. 1977. Debt and taxes. *Journal of Finance* 32 (May): 261–75.

Mooney, Sean, and Larry Cohen. 1991. *Basic concepts of accounting and taxation of property/casualty companies.* New York: Insurance Information Institute Press.

Myers, Stewart C., and Richard A. Cohn. 1987. A discounted cash flow approach to property-liability insurance rate regulation. In *Fair rate of return in property-liability insurance,* ed. J. David Cummins and Scott E. Harrington, 55–78. Boston: Kluwer Nijhoff.

Troxel, Terrie E., and George E. Bouchie. 1990. *Accounting and finance,* 3d ed. Malvern, Pa.: American Institute for Property and Liability Underwriters.

U.S. Congress. Joint Committee on Taxation. 1984. *General explanation of the revenue provisions of the Deficit Reduction Act of 1984.* 98th Cong., 2d sess.

3 The Causes and Consequences of Rate Regulation in the Auto Insurance Industry

Dwight M. Jaffee and Thomas Russell

3.1 Introduction

The extent and detail of state regulatory control over the auto insurance industry has increased markedly in the past 10 years.[1] In many cases, this change in the regulatory environment has come about as a consequence of well-organized, grass-roots consumer activism. The passage of California's Proposition 103, a voter initiative that, among other provisions, enacted a rollback of insurance premium rates and a limit on the actuarial information that could be used in setting these rates, is a case in point. Proposition 103, however, is by no means unique; following its passage in November 1988, 44 states considered similar regulatory changes, and similar legislation passed in the states of Nevada, New Jersey, South Carolina, and Pennsylvania (see Rosenfield 1991).

These "populist" moves to regulate auto insurance rates are based on the view that the insurance industry uses "unfair and discriminatory pricing practices."[2] Two forms of regulation have been imposed. One form restricts the factors that insurance companies are allowed to use in defining *risk categories*—this is called *rate compression*. A second form restricts either the overall level of premiums or the rates applied to particular categories—this is called

Dwight M. Jaffee is professor of real estate and finance at the Haas School of Business, University of California, Berkeley. Thomas Russell is associate professor of economics at the Leavey School of Business, Santa Clara University, Santa Clara, California.

The authors thank the participants in seminars at which earlier versions of this paper were presented, particularly David Bradford, Georges Dionne, Patricia Danzon, Louis Eeckhoudt, Fred Furlong, and Sean Mooney, for their helpful comments. They also thank Ashok Bardhan for excellent research assistance.

1. A brief history of early developments with further references may be found in Kimball (1961).

2. In many states, the law directs the insurance commissioner to eliminate "unfair and discriminatory pricing practices." Dudey (1991) claims that "among the more severe criticisms of the insurance industry is the inequity of the ratings methods used, particularly, but by no means exclusively, in auto insurance."

rate suppression; see Harrington (1992) for a discussion of this term. We use the term *rate regulation* to refer to compression and suppression together.

Rate compression is illustrated by California's Proposition 103, which stipulates that, without the additional approval of the insurance commissioner, passenger automobile insurance rates may apply only the following three factors:

1. The insured's driving record
2. The number of miles driven annually
3. The number of years of driving experience

Such characteristics as the driver's place of residence, age, sex, and marital status could no longer be used without the approval of the insurance commissioner. These factors were frequently used by insurance companies prior to the passage of Proposition 103.[3]

Rate suppression is used in Massachusetts, where premiums in many categories are explicitly set below the actuarial cost—a system called *tempering.* Blackmon and Zeckhauser (1991) report that in Massachusetts, expected costs vary across drivers by a factor of 4.4, but premiums vary by only a factor of 3. Expected costs vary across territories by a factor of 2.7, but premiums vary by only a factor of 2.

Insurance companies, of course, have an incentive to reject customers who must be charged suppressed rates. Since auto insurance is mandatory in all states, rejected customers still need insurance, which is generally provided through *assigned risk pools.* Drivers who are denied auto policies are placed in the assigned risk pool and charged premiums that may be below the actuarial costs. Each auto insurance company in the state is then required to take a share of the assigned risk pool equal to its share of the overall market.[4]

Standard welfare economics provides no simple explanation for regulatory pressures in this market. There are two factors that may work in the direction of welfare enhancement. First, in a world of imperfect information and costly sorting, rate compression could work to curtail a tendency to form (socially) too many risk categories. Second, by lowering premiums, rate suppression could induce previously uninsured drivers to purchase coverage, thus eliminating externalities associated with uninsured motorists. On the other hand, as with any cross-subsidization scheme, there are obvious welfare losses associated with rate regulation. Drivers who are charged premiums above their true costs will underconsume driving, auto insurance, or both, and vice versa. The net welfare effect of regulation is thus far from clear.

Given this, we raise the question, Why has the auto insurance industry emerged as a primary target for increased regulation? The main goal of this paper is to try to answer this question by linking the possible sources and con-

---

3. A California Department of Insurance (1978) study noted that every insurance company in California that wrote automobile liability insurance in 1978 used place of residence in setting its rates.

4. Assigned risk plans differ across states in the details of their operation, but the general principal is that the companies operating in the standard market share the losses of the assigned risk pool.

sequences of rate regulation. The agenda of the paper is the following. Section 3.2 develops the economics of auto insurance for an unregulated industry. Section 3.3 outlines the details of Proposition 103. Section 3.4 explores the various sources of demand for rate regulation, including the populist sentiments already mentioned. Section 3.5 looks at the economic effects of rate regulation. Section 3.6 provides empirical results that evaluate the welfare effects of auto insurance regulation. Section 3.7 provides corresponding empirical results concerning the voting record on Proposition 103. Section 3.8 provides conclusions and topics for future consideration.

3.2   Structure of an Unregulated Insurance Industry

To understand the reasons for the success of the proregulation movement and to provide a benchmark from which to evaluate the consequences of regulation, it is useful to examine how the auto insurance industry in California operated before the passage of Proposition 103. Even before Proposition 103, the state insurance commissioner had the duty to ensure that insurance rates were "neither excessive nor inadequate," but as noted by Sugarman (1990), this price control authority was rarely used. Once the commissioner found that the market was competitive, the inquiry into excessive rates ended. Rather remarkably (at least for economists), Proposition 103 expressly states that with regard to excessive rates, "no consideration shall be given to the degree of competition." [5] Assume then that prior to the passage of Proposition 103, auto insurance in the state of California was, in essence, an unregulated competitive industry. How does such an industry operate?

In the first wave of economic analysis of this question, Arrow (1963), Borch (1990), and Malinvaud (1972) showed that if sellers of insurance have full information regarding the risk class of each insured, then a competitive industry, given zero administrative costs and a large number of risks in each risk class, would offer an array of insurance contracts, one for each risk class, the premium on each contract being set so that each contract earned zero profits on average. Buyers of insurance, given that they act to maximize expected utility, would then fully insure at the actuarially fair odds appropriate to their risk classes.

This early analysis was followed by the seminal contribution of Rothschild and Stiglitz (1976), who noted that the assumption of full information regarding individual risk does not hold in many insurance markets. Often the buyers of insurance have more information regarding the risk of loss than do the sellers. Rothschild and Stiglitz showed that in this case, the resulting adverse selection may prevent the market from having an equilibrium (in the Nash sense). When an equilibrium does exist it will separate the high-risk and low-risk buyers, with the low-risk buyers facing quantity rationing.

5. California Insurance Code #1861.05(a) (West Supp. 1990) as cited by Sugarman (1990).

The equilibrium concept was subsequently refined by Miyazaki (1977), Riley (1979), and Wilson (1977), who assumed that sellers anticipate the reactions of other sellers when adding or deleting new contracts. These models identify a set of reaction functions under which equilibrium always exists, and the equilibrium structure may have either separating contracts, as in Rothschild-Stiglitz, or a single pooled contract for all buyers.

These authors were all concerned with characterizing equilibrium in a one-period model of the industry. When the industry deals with customers in a multiperiod setting, there are a number of additional methods for dealing with the problem of adverse selection. Cooper and Hayes (1987), for example, noted that it is possible to design a contract pair (a single period contract and a multiperiod contract in which the premium falls over time) so that only low-risk individuals buy the multiperiod contract. Thus, this contract pair solves the adverse selection problem.

Kunreuther and Pauly (1985), on the other hand, note that over time an insurance company obtains private information regarding a driver's riskiness. Insurance companies may then underprice policies in the first year of a contract because this provides them the option to renew good customers at favorable rates in later years. In the following years, the companies may increase premiums even to those drivers whose records show them to be of low risk, given the transaction costs these drivers would face in switching companies. This model thus predicts the opposite dynamic pricing structure from that predicted by Cooper and Hayes, since here the insured faces a premium structure that is predicted to *rise* over time. See D'Arcy and Doherty (1990) for a fuller discussion of this issue.

The existence of equilibrium is also made problematic by the presence of moral hazard. In a monopolistic setting, multiperiod contracts designed by Radner (1985) to deal with moral hazard in labor markets and extended to insurance markets by Rubinstein and Yaari (1983) could deal with this problem. However, these contracts cannot be offered competitively. The issues of adverse selection and moral hazard are surveyed in Dionne and Doherty (1992).

Relative to the large body of theoretical work giving possible equilibrium structures for this industry, the amount of empirical work describing actual equilibrium is rather small. Dahlby (1983) provides evidence of adverse selection, and D'Arcy and Doherty (1990) provide evidence that seasoned customers generate quasi rents. More recently, Puelz and Snow (1994), in a study of contract structures offered by an insurance company in Georgia, demonstrated the existence of quantity rationing of good risks, and Dionne and Doherty (1994) used California data to test the commitment strategies of auto insurance companies. However, such features as quantity rationing of good risks, multiyear contracts, and price increases to good customers do not seem to be any part of the rhetoric of those who wish to limit market competition.

On the other hand, the industry does have a number of features that, as yet, have not received much attention from theorists. Since these features may be relevant to the industry's vulnerability to regulatory attacks, we now set out a stylized structure designed to capture the essence of the way in which the industry actually operated before regulation. We concentrate on four features of this stylized equilibrium.

1. Recognizing the fact that individuals belong to different risk classes, each firm in the industry set up a large number of information cells and collected data on the loss experience in each cell. These cells were largely standardized across the industry, with little variation from firm to firm. (An example of a cell might be a 50-year-old married man who drives a 1990 Volvo and lives in San Francisco.) The standardization of cells was coordinated through an industry data collection agency (such as the Insurance Service Office) and presumably arose as a consequence of economies of scale in data collection and analysis.

   Industry standardization of the classification scheme can be motivated by at least two factors. First, firms that attempt to introduce new rating classes will face the costs of obtaining and applying the new information. But they are unlikely to obtain a competitive edge from the innovation since other firms can costlessly observe and apply the innovator's premium structure. Second, standardization may be an important mechanism through which the industry helps protect itself against individual firms offering new contracts that attempt to "cream-skim" customers.

2. Since each cell had an associated loss experience, the insurance company could then statistically determine a loss relative for each cell and from this could determine a cell-specific premium. (A useful summary of the statistical methods used to determine loss relatives is given by Jee 1989). It is clear, however, that within any cell there are individuals whose risk is misclassified in the sense that their true risk of accident lies above or below the estimated risk for their cell. This was treated by each firm as a fact of life. In particular, direct quantity rationing was not used to induce individuals to self-select the appropriate risk cell.[6]

3. Although it is possible to associate a competitive risk premium with each cell, in fact firms did not write an insurance contract for each cell. Even before regulation of prices, firms in the insurance industry engaged in a system of voluntary rationing and "risk tiering." It is easiest to describe how this system worked by example.

   Suppose that an individual applied for auto insurance at a major automobile insurance company. Three events could occur:
   a. If the individual fell into a high enough loss ratio cell (say because of multiple moving violations), the insurance company simply refused to

---

6. Of course, insurance companies used deductible limits and other forms of nonlinear pricing, but it appears to us that these reflected cost considerations and were not used to induce individuals to self-select specific contracts.

write a policy and instead placed the individual in the involuntary assigned risk pool.

b. If the individual fell into a cell with a loss ratio below that which led to
outright rejection of the risk but was still at the high end of the loss ratio
(say because of one moving violation), the insurance company would
not write a policy in its own name but would issue a policy through a
wholly owned subsidiary that handled only high-risk drivers. This tier of
insurance is called "nonstandard insurance."

c. If the individual fell into a low enough risk cell, the insurance company
would then write a policy in its own name. This is called "standard insurance."

The existence of this three-tier structure is not easy to understand in
terms of standard economic theory. Risk tiering, however, has been observed in other industries (e.g., banks do not make high-risk consumer
loans), and in the case of credit markets Jaffee and Russell (1992) argue
that risk tiering is a market response to concerns of fairness. We will examine this question of fairness later when we examine the reasons for regulation.

4. Insurance companies, in general, did not issue multiyear contracts. There
was some limited experience rating, good drivers in some cases being given
discounts, but insurance contracts offering a menu of premium terms based
on the length of the contract do not seem to have been offered.

3.3   Regulation in California: Proposition 103

Proposition 103 was (narrowly) passed to regulate an industry with the
above structure. The immediate impetus for the initiative seems to have been
twofold, partly concern with the large rate of premium increases in the years
prior to 1988 and partly concern with the large disparity in premiums among
individuals with prima facie similar risk characteristics. (E.g., individuals liv-
ing on opposite sides of a street could have auto premiums that differed by a
factor of 2.0; see Williams 1992.)

With respect to the industry equilibrium, Proposition 103 required the following changes:

a. All insurance rates were to be rolled back 20 percent from the rates holding
on 8 November 1987.

b. All future rate changes were to be approved by the insurance commissioner,
who was now to be elected, not appointed.

c. Only very specific factors could be used in setting risk classes. These were
to be (in order of importance):
    i. The insured's driving record
    ii. The number of miles driven annually
    iii. The number of years of driving experience

Other factors could be used, if approved, but less weight must be given than to the first three factors.

d. Insurance companies were required to accept all "good drivers" who applied for insurance, where "good driver" was defined as a driver having no more than one moving violation in the past three years. In addition all "good drivers" were to be offered a "good driver" discount.

With many of these provisions now in place, it is no longer possible to view the insurance industry in California as providing a competitive solution to the problem of risk allocation. What was it about the competitive solution outlined above that so upset the California voters? We turn now to an analysis of the possible causes of insurance market regulation.

3.4   Why Insurance Contracts Provoke Regulatory Action

There are many possible reasons why auto insurance has become the target of consumer-based regulatory movements. Perceived self-interest, for example, may lead to a call for rollbacks and rate ceilings, since consumers may think that premium ceilings can create lower prices with unchanged supply.

Why insurance, though, and not, say, beer? The absence of a grass-roots consumer movement calling for a rollback in the price of beer (and most other goods) suggests that consumers recognize that the deadweight costs of price regulation generally exceed the benefits of such regulation. It thus remains an important question why automobile insurance has been singled out for such attention.

Our analysis considers three main sets of explanations for consumer initiatives that create rate regulation. The first set uses considerations of *distributional equity* to motivate rate regulation as a means of achieving risk sharing or income redistribution for risk-averse individuals. The second set is based on the *welfare enhancement* that may arise from rate regulation in insurance models such as the type developed by Rothschild and Stiglitz (1976) and its extensions. The third set is based on concepts of *fairness* in response to the perception of unfair and discriminatory practices in insurance premium setting.

3.4.1   Distributional Equity

In their recent study, Blackmon and Zeckhauser (1991; BZ) consider motives based on distributional equity that might cause risk-averse individuals to accept the deadweight losses created by rate regulation. We summarize here their arguments concerning the risk-sharing and income redistribution motives that would be relevant to risk-averse individuals.

Risk Sharing

Suppose, for simplicity, that each driver's risk of an auto accident belongs to one of two categories, a high-risk class or a low-risk class. At some initial date

($t = 0$), drivers are assumed to be in a Rawlsian state of ignorance about their true classes. At a later date ($t = 1$), insurance markets open and each driver's risk is revealed to both the driver and the market. In the absence of deadweight loss, all risk-averse drivers would vote at $t = 0$ to force insurance firms at $t = 1$ to charge only a single premium rate, reflecting the average risk of the population.

Using a similar argument, drivers might resist any form of categorization because it introduces a classification risk. That is, consumers may prefer to have premiums based on the community's average risk, instead of entering what they may think of as a classification lottery to determine whether they are to be treated as high risk or low risk. The argument is particularly forceful if consumers do not know their risk classes initially but are provided estimates of them through the categorization process.

BZ estimate the deadweight loss and compute the coefficient of risk aversion required to cause individuals to support single-class contracts in the face of this loss. They reject the risk-class uncertainty hypothesis on the basis of the unrealistically high risk aversion coefficient that is required to generate the amount of tempering observed in Massachusetts. However, we should recognize that Massachusetts has perhaps the greatest degree of tempering of auto insurance rates in the United States. Also BZ estimate a relatively high price elasticity of demand, which magnifies the deadweight loss of rate regulation.

On the other hand, the existence of bans on the use of certain immutable characteristics, for example, gender, in the setting of auto insurance rates provides support for the Rawlsian argument. In a Rawlsian state of ignorance, individuals would not know their genders, and the adoption of this moral reference point would explain their desire that insurance rates be blind to immutable characteristics.

Income Redistribution

Individuals may use rate suppression as a means to redistribute income. Obviously, if insurance is offered at the same rate to individuals with objectively different risks of accident, the high-risk individuals will be subsidized by the low-risk individuals. This in turn will generate income distribution from low-risk (presumably high-income) to high-risk (presumably low-income) drivers. Citizens could desire this income redistribution for its own sake.

BZ, however, again reject the income redistribution hypothesis on the basis of the high level of deadweight loss. It should be noted that in Massachusetts rate regulation was imposed by the insurance commissioner, who presumably was responsible for evaluating the trade-off between the income distribution benefits and the deadweight costs. In the context of voter initiative states such as California, however, it is not clear to what extent this deadweight loss enters the mind of individual voters when they pull the ballot lever.

3.4.2   Welfare Enhancement

It is possible that the move to regulate the insurance market was motivated by a desire to remove observed inefficiencies in the unregulated market. The consumer activists who pressed for regulation, however, did not document such inefficiencies, instead arguing that regulation was necessary to improve the fairness of the pricing structure.

Of course, it is still possible that as a "side effect" of fairness-led reform, the market could become more efficient. Since welfare enhancement was not the primary motive for regulation, however, we postpone a discussion of the efficiency aspects of rate regulation to the section dealing with the consequences of regulation. We turn now to the central argument used by the proregulation camp, the view that auto insurance rates were unfair.

3.4.3   Fairness

Kahneman, Knetsch, and Thaler (1986) have documented that consumers have a well-developed sense of when a price is or is not fair. As a consequence, these authors argue that considerations of fairness will limit price dispersion when the price dispersion has no obvious basis in differential costs.[7]

This argument clearly has relevance to the types of regulation that we observe in auto insurance. Suppose perceived costs to a buyer of insurance are gauged by actual accident costs. Since most insurance buyers have no accidents in any given year, most buyers will perceive themselves as imposing the same costs on insurance companies. Yet drivers in different risk classes may face very different prices.

For example, in Los Angeles County, in the five-year period 1983–88, the frequency of claims for bodily injury liability was 2.4 times the statewide average for these claims (National Association of Independent Insurers 1988). Yet in this five-year period, the actual total of incurred claims in Los Angeles County was 71,890 on an "installed base" of 1,464,079 autos. Thus 95 percent of all insured automobiles in Los Angeles County had no claims in five years. Nevertheless, these Los Angeles County drivers faced insurance premiums about 2.4 times as high as the state average.

The inherent concerns for fairness raised by the pricing structure of a competitive insurance industry are exacerbated by the following considerations:

1. In the years before Proposition 103, private passenger auto insurance rates in the state grew very fast (National Association of Insurance Commissioners 1988):[8]

---

7. When we use the word "fairness" we should stress that we mean "perceived fairness." As economists, we are not endorsing these reported dimensions of fairness as being in any welfare sense fair or just.

8. Rapid growth in auto insurance fraud may be one explanation for the rapidly rising premiums. It has been suggested that the companies took action to control fraud following the passage of Proposition 103, with the result that their claim losses fell.

Year	Growth Rate of Auto Insurance Premiums (%)
1982	+9
1983	+8
1984	+12
1985	+20
1986	+22
1987	+13
1988	+13

To the extent that consumers use a historical premium as a reference point for calculating a fair premium, and again remembering that most drivers would have no claims in this six-year period, this doubling of premiums seems likely to contribute to the sense of unfairness.

2. Returning to the question of fairness across risk categories, in any risk cell there will be some drivers who are misclassified simply because statistical procedures are designed to classify risk on average. Again remembering that a small difference in loss relative, say 1.2 rather than 1, translates into a 20 percent difference in premium, misclassified drivers may well feel aggrieved.

3. In addition to objectively legitimate concerns about misclassification, there is also the Lake Wobegone effect. Recall that in mythical Lake Wobegone every student is above average. If every driver believes himself to be above average, he will vote to be placed in a lower risk pool, and this can lead to rate compression.

4. Classification based on immutable characteristics or characteristics that are correlated but not causative will also increase concern. Individuals may feel that immutable characteristics such as gender ought not to be used as criteria for price discrimination. Similarly, when the classification factor is correlative but not causative, for example, zip code as opposed to years of driving experience, concerns about fairness may be heightened.

Further evidence on consumers' views of the fairness of insurance premiums is given by a Gallup Organization poll of 1,000 consumers conducted in 1990. The results of this poll are shown in table 3.1.

As can be seen, in this poll, which focused specifically on the fairness of premiums, 65 percent of consumers thought that property-casualty insurance companies overcharged, and 61 percent of consumers thought that property-casualty insurance companies were more profitable than companies in other industries. This suggests that issues of fairness in the Kahneman et al. (1986) sense could easily contribute to an explanation of both the rollback and rate compression features of Proposition 103. Whatever the motivation, of course, once these regulations are in place they will have more standard welfare implications. We turn now to an examination of these welfare effects.

Table 3.1   **Consumer Sentiment and the Auto Insurance Industry**

The insurance industry achieves its profits by . . .	Total (n = 1,000)
Overcharging for premiums	65%
Charging fair and adequate premiums and investing and managing this money wisely	26
Undercharging for premiums but making up the difference through investments	4
Don't know	5

Companies that sell auto, homeowners, and business insurance are . . .	Total (n = 1,000)	Male (n = 490)	Female (n = 510)
Just as profitable as the companies in most other industries	28%	21%	34%
Less profitable than the companies in most other industries	5	5	5
More profitable than the companies in most other industries	61	71	52
Don't know	6	3	9

Insurance companies that sell auto, homeowners, and business insurance . . .	Total (n = 1,000)				
	Strongly Agree	Agree	Disagree	Strongly Disagree	Mean Rating[a]
Make a killing, but pretend they are not making money	5%	32%	25%	5%	2.99
Make a fair profit after expenses and loss payments	22	48	16	11	2.84
Make very little because their losses are always going up	2	8	48	39	1.73

Source: Best's Review: Property-Casualty Insurance Edition 91, no. 1 (May 1990): 16.
[a]4 = strongly agree, 3 = agree, 2 = disagree, 1 = strongly disagree.

3.5   Rate Regulation, Efficiency, and Welfare

The welfare economics literature for insurance markets has expanded greatly in recent years, partly reflecting fundamental advances in information economics, and partly reflecting attempts to apply economic analysis to the current political issues in insurance markets. Our primary goal is to identify the results that are applicable to auto insurance markets.

In most competitive industries,[9] regulation of prices or quantities reduces efficiency. The auto insurance industry, however, has at least two special features requiring special attention.

1. By its nature, the automobile insurance industry uses actuarial information to sort individuals into risk classes. Since Spence (1973), it has been

9. Because so many features of the automobile insurance industry seem compatible with competition, we will proceed on this premise.

known that private and social incentives to sort do not always coincide. There is thus room for rate compression to be welfare enhancing.

2. In many states a large number of drivers do not purchase auto insurance. (E.g., some estimates suggest that as many as 30 percent of the drivers in California do not insure.) If price rollbacks induce noninsured motorists to buy insurance, rate suppression may be welfare enhancing (see Smith and Wright 1992). We now discuss each of these cases in turn.

3.5.1   Categorization in Auto Insurance Markets

There is now an extensive literature dealing with the welfare economics of risk classification in insurance markets. Important contributions include Bond and Crocker (1991), Crocker and Snow (1986), Hoy (1989), Puelz and Kemmsies (1993), and Rea (1992). There are also excellent summaries by Borenstein (1989) and Harrington (1993).

Rather than discuss this literature in detail, we simply state the fundamental conclusion. In a competitive market, the decision whether to introduce a new risk class is based solely on a calculation of the costs and benefits to the potential members of this new class. A proper accounting for social welfare, however, should take into account not just the welfare of the members of the new class but also the welfare of the remainder of the population who do not join the new class. It is very easy, see Borenstein (1989), to construct examples of costly sorting in which introducing a new risk class increases the welfare of its members slightly (after they pay the cost of the sorting) but decreases substantially the welfare of the rest of society so that net social welfare is reduced.

In the case of costless sorting, however (and this may be the more common case in auto insurance), restrictions on categories will normally reduce welfare. The magnitude of this welfare loss is positively related to the level of the premium elasticities. In section 3.6 we provide estimates of these elasticities.

3.5.2   Uninsured Motorists

The presence of uninsured drivers generates an externality that can be corrected by appropriate intervention. To see this we present here a simplified version of the models of Keeton and Kwerel (1984) and Smith and Wright (1992), in which a competitive market equilibrium with uninsured motorists is Pareto dominated by a regulated market with appropriate income transfers.

Suppose that in a group of drivers the probability of an accident is p and that when an accident occurs the total damage in dollars is $2L$, L to each driver. Suppose that the legal system assigns 100 percent fault to one of the drivers in every accident and that in this case the driver at fault is responsible for the total loss ($2L$) up to the value of initial wealth, W. Assume that the probability that any given driver will be involved in an accident in which he is at fault is $p/2$.

The actuarially fair (collision) insurance premium for each driver is thus

$p/2$ dollars per dollar of insurance. Expected-utility-maximizing drivers with sufficient wealth will fully insure by purchasing $2L$ of collision insurance at this premium. If all drivers fully insure, the resulting equilibrium is Pareto efficient.

Suppose, however, that drivers fall into two classes based on initial wealth. Assume that q percent of the population have a level of initial wealth W_{low}, which is such that it is expected utility maximizing to purchase zero collision insurance. Let the remaining $1 - q$ percent have a wealth level W_{high}, which is such that they fully insure at a fair premium.

The presence of uninsured motorists sets up a demand for a new form of insurance that pays in the event that a driver is involved in an accident in which an uninsured motorist is at fault. Assuming that the probability of an accident between an uninsured and an insured motorist only reflects the proportions of these two types in the total population, the actuarially fair premium for this uninsured motorist coverage is clearly $qp/2$ per dollar of insurance. Drivers who are rich enough to fully insure will fully insure this risk too, but in this case they will buy coverage L, the value of their own loss.

Market equilibrium in this case has high-income drivers paying a premium of pL for full collision insurance and $q(p/2)L$ for uninsured motorist insurance, and low-income drivers buying zero insurance of either type.

To generate a Pareto improvement on this equilibrium, suppose we require each uninsured driver to buy full collision insurance at a cost of pL. Note that if each uninsured motorist were risk neutral, the income transfer necessary to compensate for purchasing full collision insurance would be

$$pL - [(p/2)L + q(p/2)L] = (1 - q)(p/2)L.$$

The first term in the square bracket is the uninsured motorist's own expected collision loss when the accident is his own fault. The second term is the expected loss to an uninsured driver resulting from being in an accident caused by another uninsured driver. We subtract these terms since they are no longer borne by an uninsured motorist if he fully insures.

Now suppose we tax each fully insured motorist $q(p/2)L$, the cost of uninsured motorist coverage. Since insured motorists make up $1 - q$ percent of the population, this tax would enable us to give each uninsured motorist (with uninsured motorists making up q percent of the population) an income transfer of $(1 - q)q(p/2)L/q = (1 - q)(p/2)L$. As we have just seen, however, this is precisely the amount needed to compensate a risk-neutral uninsured motorist for buying full collision coverage. A fortiori, if the uninsured motorist is risk averse, we could give him less income and still leave him as well off as when he was uninsured.

Furthermore, once the uninsured motorists buy full coverage there is no reason for the insured drivers to buy $q(p/2)L$ of uninsured motorist insurance. Thus this income transfer leaves the rich drivers as well off as before and increases the welfare of the poor drivers, so the scheme is Pareto improving.[10] This, of course, merely demonstrates the *possibility* of a welfare improvement. Proposition 103 did not require an income transfer from the insured to the uninsured. Indeed, the retroactive premium rollback is more directly a transfer of income from the stockholders of the insurance companies to those already buying insurance.

To this extent, the price rollbacks of Proposition 103 seem more consistent with explanations based on fairness rather than with explanations based on efficiency. Nevertheless, the possibility remains open to design a cross-subsidization scheme that causes all drivers to fully insure, and this would be welfare enhancing. In designing such a scheme it is again crucial to know the value of the elasticity of demand for insurance.

3.5.3   Rate Suppression

In discussing categorization, it was assumed that insurance firms were allowed to charge whatever premiums they desire for a given category. Only the factors available for categorization were regulated. Now we consider matters the other way around. We take as given the available categories but consider what happens if regulations impose ceilings on the premiums charged certain categories.

If the industry is competitive, as we have been assuming, and no restrictions are placed on categories, then insurance firms should refuse to write policies for categories with suppressed prices. In other words, we should observe that policies are granted to all customers in categories where rates are not suppressed. We should also observe that policies are granted to no customers in categories where rates are suppressed.

The experience in California sheds light on the issue of rate suppression. One of the features of Proposition 103 is that risk rating of bad drivers is to be encouraged, suggesting that firms should be able to price this risk fully and then provide insurance to these customers. However, many companies have opted not to provide insurance to "unsafe drivers." This would suggest either that the companies believe the premiums for this category are likely to be suppressed or that they are reluctant to file rates that consumers may consider unfair.

The experience in Massachusetts also sheds light on the issue of rate suppression. In Massachusetts, all rates are regulated with an explicit degree of tempering. We would expect to find no voluntary policies in the underpriced cells and no rejections in the overpriced cells. In fact, as reported by BZ, many cells feature partial acceptance and partial rejection. This suggests that firms

10. Again, note that we are assuming that the probability of an insured motorist's being in an accident with an uninsured motorist reflects only the proportions of the two types of drivers. If uninsured motorists have a higher tendency to have accidents with each other, then our conclusion need not follow.

are using factors not included in the standard cell structure, perhaps including factors that were otherwise prohibited.

Rate suppression leads to a form of insurance rationing, comparable in some respects to credit rationing in the loan market. Auto insurance, however, is mandatory, and therefore the government must ensure that all drivers can obtain coverage. This creates the assigned risk pools, to which firms send drivers whom they have rejected for insurance.

In many ways, the assigned risk pool represents a very peculiar system. First, when assigned risk pool premiums are suppressed, the plan subsidizes the objectively worst risks among drivers. What basis can there be for giving this group subsidies? Second, when assigned risk pool premiums are not suppressed, as is increasingly the case, there should be little need for an assigned risk pool. In a competitive market, voluntary insurance companies should be serving these customers.

We might expect rate suppression to create additional effects in terms of industry exit. Exit appears to occur only in the most egregious cases, and even then in limited amounts; for example, in Massachusetts, BZ report that 18 percent of insurance firms left the state. There are reasons, however, why exit may not occur, including the expectation that regulation is temporary or that the industry is earning quasi rents.

We might also expect rate suppression to create reductions in quality. Quality reductions, however, are not widely evident, perhaps because other factors such as reputation, fear of lawsuits, and expectations that lower quality will create further pressure for lower premiums all mitigate the incentive for lower quality (see Harrington 1992).

3.6   Welfare Effects of Auto Insurance: Empirical Evidence

Rate regulations influence welfare by distorting the relationship between premiums and costs. This causes individuals to drive too much (or too little) or to buy too much (or too little) auto insurance. The size of this welfare loss depends on two elasticities, the elasticity of demand for automobiles and, given that a car has been purchased, the elasticity of demand for insurance. In this part, we develop estimates for these elasticities.

3.6.1   Blackmon and Zeckhauser Estimates

In some states, the distinction between the drive/not drive decision and the insure/not insure decision is of little consequence since the percentage of uninsured motorists is quite small. In Massachusetts, for example, less than 6 percent of motorists drive uninsured (see table 3.2). Therefore, BZ, in their study of the welfare costs of regulation in Massachusetts, calculate the deadweight loss by estimating the demand for insured vehicles. The number of insured cars per household I_h is regressed against household income Y_h, auto insurance

Table 3.2   **Percentage of All Vehicles That Are Uninsured (based on uninsured motorist claim frequencies for 1985)**

State Rank	State	Percentage Uninsured
1	Colorado	30.3
2	Florida	29.7
3	Alabama	24.8
4	*California*	*23.3*
5	Tennessee	22.2
46	New York	6.2
47	South Dakota	5.9
48	*Massachusetts*	*5.8*
49	Vermont	5.1
50	North Carolina	4.6

Source: All-Industry Research Advisory Council (1989).

Table 3.3   **Demand for Insured Cars, Blackmon and Zeckhauser Specification**

Equation	State	C	Y_h	D	P	R^2
3.1	Massachusetts		.48	−.04	−.57	.59
			(10.8)	(4.0)	(4.8)	
3.2	California	1.0	.31	.003	−.63	.26
		(0.9)	(2.5)	(0.2)	(3.6)	

Sources: For Massachusetts data sources, see Blackmon and Zeckhauser (1991). For California symbol definitions and data sources, see the data appendix.

Notes: Dependent variable is log (insured cars per household) = log I_h. Estimation is by ordinary least squares, all variables in log. Numbers in parentheses are absolute values of *t*-statistics.

premiums P, and household density D (a measure of congestion costs). The observations consist of 294 Massachusetts towns in 1988, with the insurance premium measured as the average price of a standard package of coverage. Their estimated equation using ordinary least squares is shown as equation (3.1) in table 3.3. The variables all have the expected signs and are statistically significant. The insurance premium elasticity of −0.57 is the key factor for evaluating the welfare consequences of rate regulation. A higher elasticity indicates that demand for autos is more sensitive to insurance premiums, thus increasing the deadweight costs of mispricing insurance through rate regulation. As already discussed above, BZ find that the deadweight costs based on this equation are higher than the risk-sharing or income redistribution benefits that rate regulation might confer.

We have estimated a comparable equation for California data, where the observations consist of 58 California counties in 1990. The insurance premium variable available to us for California is not the same variable used in the Massachusetts study by BZ. The BZ insurance premium refers to a standard package of coverage, whereas the California insurance premium variable measures the *average effective premium*—the total auto premiums paid in each county divided by the number of insured cars.[11] The estimated equation using ordinary least squares is shown as equation (3.2) in table 3.3.

The California equation confirms the BZ conclusion regarding the insurance premium elasticity. Specifically, the insurance premium elasticity is of the same order of magnitude in California (−0.63) as in Massachusetts (−0.57), suggesting that the deadweight costs of auto premium regulation may also be of the same order of magnitude in the two states.[12] The income elasticity in California is lower than in Massachusetts (0.31 vs. 0.48) but remains statistically significant. The density variable (congestion cost) in California has an unexpected positive sign and is not statistically significant. This difference in congestion cost results between California and Massachusetts may depend on, among other factors, variations in the supply of public transportation across the two states.

In California, it is not enough to know how premiums affect the demand for insurance, because a large fraction of the population of drivers choose not to buy insurance (over 23 percent in 1985 [table 3.2] and over 24 percent in our 1990 data set). We therefore must estimate separate elasticities for the demand for registered cars and the demand for insured cars. To assist in the interpretation of these elasticities, we provide a simple model of driver/insurance choice.

3.6.2 Effects of Insurance Premiums on Uninsured Motorists

Consider a specific motorist i. There will be a reservation premium P_i^* below which the motorist will buy insurance; call this status I. In other words, for a given market premium P, if $P < P_i^*$, then $i \in I$. The reservation premium P_i^* will vary among drivers, depending on individual characteristics.

When the market premium P rises to or above P_i^*, the motorist will stop buying insurance. There are then two choices. He or she may no longer drive; call this status W (for walker). Or he or she may drive uninsured; call this status U. The choice between W and U will be determined by the relative costs of W (the inconvenience of walking) and U (the expected costs of driving uninsured), with individual drivers making different choices depending on their circumstances. However, whatever the choice made at $P = P_i^*$, the same choice will be made at $P > P_i^*$, assuming that the factors determining the choice between W and U do not depend on P.

The demand for insured cars per capita, I, will depend on, among other

---

11. The insurance premium data for California counties in 1990 were obtained from the California Department of Insurance. The premiums include three components, liability coverage for bodily injury and property damage, uninsured motorist coverage, and comprehensive coverage. The liability component is a weighted average of the premium paid in the voluntary insurance market and for the assigned risk pool.

12. The slightly higher estimated elasticity in California may arise because insurance premiums (California) vary less than standard coverage premiums (Massachusetts).

things, the premium P relative to the distribution of the reservation premiums P_i^* over the population. The higher the market premium P, the lower I, since more drivers will find that P exceeds their reservation premium. This determines the elasticity of demand for insured cars per capita (variables are all in logs):

(1) $I = a_0 - a_1 P, \quad a_1 > 0 .$

A comparable argument holds for the demand for uninsured cars per capita, U. The higher the market insurance premium, the higher the demand for uninsured cars. U will also depend on other factors that determine the choice between driving uninsured and not driving at all. The dependence of U on P can be written

(2) $U = b_0 + b_1 P, \quad b_1 > 0 .$

We should have $b_1 < a_1$, since as individuals leave status I, some enter status U but others enter status W.

The total demand for registered cars per capita, R, is identically equal to the sum of I and U. (In our data set, all cars are assumed to be registered.) The relationship between R and the market premium P can then be determined by combining equations (1) and (2):

(3) $R = I + U = (a_0 + b_0) - (a_1 - b_1)P = c_0 - c_1 P, \quad c_1 > 0 .$

Thus the registered car premium elasticity c_1 based on equation (3) should be lower than the insured car premium elasticity a_1 based on equation (1).

The total insurance premium P does not take into account the additional information provided by the disaggregation of the premium into its component parts. Indeed our data set includes three insurance components: liability coverage for bodily injury and property damage P_L, comprehensive coverage P_C, and uninsured motorist coverage P_U. For insured drivers, each component should have a negative effect on the decision to drive a car, and the liability component P_L should be the most important since (1) the risk of loss is greatest for this component and (2) a minimum amount of liability coverage is legally required.

For uninsured drivers, the liability and comprehensive components should also have negative effects on the decision to drive because the premiums are a signal of the accident rate in each county and uninsured drivers should respond in the same way as insured drivers since the premiums represent the real risk of driving. The uninsured motorist premium, however, has two effects on the decision to drive, one positive and one negative. The negative effect arises because the uninsured motorist premium is a signal of accident costs just as it is for insured drivers. The positive effect arises because the uninsured motorist premium represents the expected value of liability claims that are avoided on average because uninsured drivers are "judgment proof" (see Shavell 1986). Consequently, the combined effect for insured and uninsured drivers of the

Table 3.4   **Demand for Autos and Auto Insurance in California**

Equation	Estimation	Dependent Variable	C	Y	T	P	R^2
4.1	TSLS	Registered R	4.8	.51	−.04	−.51	.53
			(4.4)	(6.1)	(2.2)	(3.1)	
4.2	OLS	Insured I	5.7	.59	−.01	−.83	.45
			(4.1)	(4.9)	(0.5)	(5.1)	
4.3	TSLS	Uninsured U	1.2	.23	−.10	.29	.13
			(0.4)	(1.0)	(2.1)	(0.6)	
4.4	TSLS	Log odds U:	−4.4	−.36	−.09	1.1	.17
		$\dfrac{\mu}{(1-\mu)}$	(1.1)	(1.2)	(1.4)	(1.8)	

Sources: See data appendix for symbol definitions and data sources.

Note: Observations for 58 California counties in 1990. All variables in log. Numbers in parentheses are absolute values of *t*-statistics.

uninsured motorist premium on the demand for registered cars should be smaller than for the other two insurance components.

3.6.3   Estimates of the Demand for Registered Cars

We now consider empirical estimates of the above model. As the starting point, we have made two revisions in the California version of the BZ equation, which was shown above as equation (3.2). First, we now use population instead of households as the scaling variable for insured cars and income. Population data are likely to be more accurate than household data, and there is no obvious theoretical basis for preferring households to population as the scaling variable. Second, we replace the BZ congestion variable D, which was estimated with the wrong sign for California data, with a measure of the percentage of the population using public transportation, denoted as T.

There is potential for simultaneous equation bias in estimating this model since registered cars include uninsured cars and larger numbers of uninsured cars may create higher insurance premiums (through the uninsured motorist coverage component). To correct for the correlation that might therefore exist between the error term and the insurance premium, we have estimated those equations in which the dependent variable is the demand for registered cars or uninsured cars with two-stage least squares (TSLS). The supply-side variables used as instruments include average miles driven per vehicle (MILES), accidents per capita (ACC), and the population density (D).

Equation (4.1) in table 3.4 provides empirical estimates of equation (3) for the number of registered cars per capita. The constant, income Y, and public transportation T terms correspond to the coefficient c_0 in equation (3). Compared with the specification in equation (3.2), the insurance premium elasticity (−0.51) is slightly lower, the income elasticity (0.51) is somewhat higher, and the goodness of fit ($R^2 = .53$) is substantially better. Furthermore, the public

Table 3.5   Correlation Matrix for Insurance Premium Components (58 California counties in 1990)

	P	P_L	P_U	P_C
Total premium P	1.00	.99	.94	.83
Liability coverage P_L	.99	1.00	.92	.75
Uninsured motorist P_U	.94	.92	1.00	.77
Comprehensive P_C	.83	.75	.77	1.00

Source: California Department of Insurance.

transportation variable T, which replaces the density variable D in equation (3.2), is now statistically significant and has the expected negative coefficient, indicating that greater use of public transportation reduces the demand for registered autos.

The insurance premium P used in equation (4.1) can be separated into its three coverage components, liability for bodily injury and property damage P_L, uninsured motorist P_U, and comprehensive P_C. Unfortunately, it proved impossible to estimate stable effects from the separate components because they are extremely highly correlated, as shown by the correlation matrix in table 3.5. Consequently, we have been unable to test hypotheses concerning the individual premium components.

3.6.4   Estimates of the Demand for Insured and Uninsured Cars

We next consider how car owners decide whether to be insured or uninsured drivers. We have carried this out in two forms. First, we have estimated the demand for insured and uninsured cars per capita, directly following the theoretical equations (1) and (2). Second, we have estimated the insured/uninsured decision using a logit estimator. The results are shown in table 3.4.

Equation (4.2) in table 3.4 provides empirical estimates of the number of insured cars per capita I, the empirical version of equation (1) (where the constant, income Y, and public transportation T terms correspond to the coefficient a_0). The equation is estimated using ordinary least squares because the simultaneity bias is only present when the left-hand-side variable includes uninsured drivers. The income elasticity (0.59) and the insurance premium elasticity (-0.83) are both larger than the corresponding estimates in equation (4.1) for registered cars, in accord with the discussion of equations (1) and (3).

Equation (4.3) in table 3.4 provides empirical estimates of the number of uninsured cars per capita U, the empirical version of equation (2). The number of uninsured cars in each California county is computed as the difference between the number of registered cars and the number of insured cars.[13] The

---

13. This measure will miss uninsured vehicles that are also unregistered. This becomes a serious problem, however, only if the percentage of all vehicles that are uninsured and unregistered varies significantly across counties.

point estimate of the insurance premium elasticity is 0.29; thus, as expected, the insurance premium elasticity is positive and smaller than the absolute value of the elasticity in equation (4.2) for insured drivers. The estimated coefficient, however, is not statistically significant, leaving open the possibility that the effect of insurance premiums on uninsured drivers is small or even zero. (In contrast, the effect on *insured* drivers is *negative* and significant.)

Since the number of registered cars is identically the sum of insured cars and uninsured cars, the premium elasticity in equation (4.1) for registered cars is close to the algebraic sum of the elasticities in equations (4.2) for insured cars and (4.3) for uninsured cars. If the estimated equations (4.1), (4.2), and (4.3) were linear, instead of log linear, then the elasticity condition would be exactly satisfied.

A logit estimator provides an alternative functional form in which this adding up constraint is exactly met (the log-odds specification):

(4) $$\log\left(\frac{\mu}{1 - \mu}\right) = a_0 + a_1 Y - a_2 T + a_3 P,$$

where $\mu = U/R$ (= the ratio of uninsured cars to registered cars). The estimated coefficients using TSLS are shown as equation (4.4) in table 3.4.[14] The income and public transportation elasticities are both negative, indicating that counties with either higher income or more public transportation have a lower ratio of uninsured drivers (although neither coefficient is statistically significant). The insurance premium coefficient is positive, large (1.1), and significant at the 10 percent level. When this premium coefficient is transformed at the point of the sample means to the form of an elasticity for the number of uninsured cars per capita, the result is 0.33, very close to the directly estimated elasticity of 0.29 in equation (4.3). Our conclusion is that there is a positive relationship between the level of insurance premiums and the number of uninsured drivers, although the moderate statistical significance of the logit estimate and the insignificant direct estimate suggest that the point estimate is not well determined.[15] (An equivalent equation can be estimated for the log odds of insured drivers, but the magnitude and statistical significance of the coefficients will be identical to those in eq. [4.4] with the algebraic signs switched, since the log odds of uninsured drivers and the log odds of insured drivers sum identically to zero.)

3.6.5 Effects of Insurance Premiums on the Assigned Risk Pool

We next consider how insured car owners decide whether to purchase insurance through the voluntary market or the assigned risk pool. This decision was

14. The general conditions discussed in Pindyck and Rubinfeld (1981, 289–95) under which reliable coefficient estimates of logit specifications can be obtained without maximum likelihood estimators are satisfied in our application.

15. The number of uninsured motorists is, no doubt, the least accurate of our data. This may be the reason for the lack of statistical significance in the insurance premium coefficient here.

Table 3.6   Demand for Insured Autos in California by Insurance Class

Equation	Estimation	Dependent Variable	C	Y	T	$P_{V/A}$	P_V	P_A	R^2
6.1	OLS	Voluntary	−7.5	.63	−.02	−.72			.50
		V	(6.0)	(5.1)	(0.8)	(5.8)			
6.2	OLS	Assigned	−9.9	.74	.02	2.3			.78
		risk A	(2.9)	(2.2)	(0.3)	(6.9)			
6.3	OLS	Voluntary	−4.8	.64	−.01		−.84	.42	.51
		V	(1.8)	(5.1)	(0.4)		(5.0)	(1.5)	
6.4	OLS	Assigned	−13.5	.74	.01		2.5	−1.9	.78
		risk A	(1.9)	(2.2)	(0.1)		(5.4)	(2.4)	
6.5	OLS	Log odds A: $\dfrac{v}{(1-v)}$	−2.4 (0.8)	.11 (0.4)	.03 (0.7)	3.0 (10.5)			.86
6.6	OLS	Log odds A: $\dfrac{v}{(1-v)}$	−8.7 (1.4)	.10 (0.3)	.02 (0.3)		3.3 (8.5)	−2.3 (3.5)	.86

Sources: See data appendix for symbol definitions and data sources.

Notes: Observations for 58 California counties in 1990. All variables in log. Numbers in parentheses are absolute values of *t*-statistics.

particularly important in California in the early 1990s because assigned risk pool premiums had been significantly suppressed during the late 1980s, creating a situation in which many drivers found the assigned risk pool premium to be lower than the corresponding premium in the voluntary market. (This situation was later rectified, resulting in a dramatic decline in the size of California's assigned risk pool during the early 1990s.) We thus expect the ratio of the voluntary market premium to the assigned risk premium to have a significant effect on the choice of market in which to purchase insurance.

We have carried out this estimation in two forms. First, we have estimated equations for the per capita number of cars insured through the voluntary market V and through the assigned risk pool A, respectively. Second, we have estimated the voluntary market/assigned risk pool decision using a logit estimator. The results are shown in table 3.6.

Equations (6.1) and (6.2) show per capita demand estimates for cars with voluntary insurance V and assigned risk pool insurance A, where $V + A = I$ (total insured cars per capita). The insurance premium $P_{V/A}$ is the ratio of the effective voluntary market premium for liability coverage P_V to the effective assigned risk pool premium for liability coverage P_A.[16] The income and public

16. We could obtain reliable estimates for the effective insurance premiums in the assigned risk pool by California counties only for bodily injury and property damage liability coverage. Consequently, the premiums P_V and P_A and their ratio are based only on this component of auto insurance coverage.

transportation elasticities in both equations parallel the results for total insured cars in equation (4.2). The new factor here is the insurance premium ratio $P_{V/A}$, which, as expected, has a large, negative (−0.72), and significant effect on voluntary market cars per capita and has a corresponding large positive (2.3) and significant effect on assigned risk pool cars per capita.

Equations (6.3) and (6.4) estimate a similar specification for voluntary market and assigned risk insured cars per capita, respectively, with the insurance variables for the voluntary market P_V and assigned risk pool P_A treated separately. In both cases, as expected, the own premium has a negative elasticity and the cross premium has a positive elasticity. Furthermore, the voluntary market premium coefficient is larger in absolute value than the assigned risk pool premium coefficient in both equations, indicating that a 1 percent suppression in both premiums would reduce the assigned risk pool by 0.6 percent and increase the voluntary market by 0.4 percent. However, F-tests at the 5 percent level indicate that we cannot reject the null hypothesis of equal elasticities for P_V and P_A in both equations (6.3) and (6.4).

A logit estimator provides an alternative functional form in which to estimate the choice between voluntary market and assigned risk insurance:

(5)
$$\log\left(\frac{v}{1 - v}\right) = a_0 + a_1 Y - a_2 T + a_3 \frac{P_V}{P_A},$$

where $v = A/I$ (= the ratio of assigned risk pool cars to total insured cars). The estimated coefficients are shown as equation (6.5) in table 3.6. The income and public transportation elasticities are relatively small and not significant, indicating that these factors do not play an important role in the choice between the two forms of insurance. The insurance premium ratio, however, has a large and highly significant coefficient, in line with the results in equations (6.1) to (6.4). Equation (6.6) estimates a similar log-odds specification, with the two insurance premium terms separated. As in equations (6.3) and (6.4), the voluntary market premium P_V has a larger effect than the assigned risk pool premium P_A, but F-tests cannot reject the null hypothesis of equal coefficients at the 5 percent level. In both equations (6.5) and (6.6), the implied insurance premium elasticities for the number of drivers insured per capita in the voluntary market and in the assigned risk pool are very close to the corresponding elasticities in equations (6.1) to (6.4).

3.6.6   Summary of the Effects of Insurance Premiums

In summary, our estimates for California auto insurance premium elasticities, based on a cross section of California's 58 counties, show large and significant effects along a variety of dimensions. At the most aggregated level, equation (4.1) indicates an insurance premium elasticity of −0.51 for total registered cars. This is very close to the premium elasticity (−0.57) estimated in equation (3.1) by BZ for Massachusetts, where they used insured autos as the dependent variable. This raises the question of what BZ would have found if they had used registered autos, instead of insured autos, as their dependent variable. It seems, however, this would not have changed their results in a substantive way because uninsured motorists are not important in Massachusetts (see table 3.2).

In California, it is important to decompose registered cars into insured and uninsured cars. For insured cars per capita, equation (4.2) indicates a premium elasticity of −0.83; whereas, for uninsured cars per capita, the estimated elasticities are positive (0.29 in eq. [4.3] and 0.33 in eq. [4.4]), although of limited statistical significance.

Insured cars in California can be further decomposed into voluntary market and assigned risk pool insurance. Using the ratio of the voluntary market premium to the assigned risk pool premium, equation (6.1) indicates an insurance premium elasticity of −0.72 for voluntary market insured cars, and equation (6.2) an elasticity of 2.3 for assigned risk pool cars. When the voluntary market premium and the assigned risk pool premium are estimated separately, (eqs. [6.3] and [6.4]), the voluntary market premium receives a larger coefficient in absolute terms, although in each case an F-test fails to reject the null hypothesis that the two insurance premium coefficients are equal in absolute value.

These results can be used to evaluate public policies that would suppress insurance. One such policy would be to suppress (reduce) both voluntary market and assigned risk pool premiums. As summarized in equations (4.2) to (4.4), lower premiums will reduce the number of uninsured drivers per capita and raise the number of insured drivers per capita. At the same time, lower premiums may either leave the mix between voluntary market insurance and the assigned risk pool unchanged (eq. [6.5]) or create a shift away from the assigned risk pool (eq. [6.6]).

The results can also be used to evaluate public policies in which only one or the other of the insurance premiums is suppressed. Suppressing either premium will reduce the number of uninsured drivers per capita and raise the number of insured drivers per capita, with the quantitative effect depending on the initial mix between voluntary market and assigned risk pool insurance. At the same time, suppressing the voluntary market premium alone will shift the mix away from the assigned risk pool, while suppressing the assigned risk pool premium alone will shift the mix toward the assigned risk pool.

The overall implication is that insurance regulation that suppresses premiums reduces the number of uninsured cars and possibly reduces the number of cars in the assigned risk pool. A reduction in the number of uninsured cars can be welfare enhancing for two reasons. First, the premiums or costs paid by insured motorists for losses created by uninsured motorists will fall. Second, those uninsured motorists who become insured motorists enjoy a welfare gain because the decision to adopt insurance reveals their preference for the insured status.[17] These benefits could be offset by a tendency for drivers to take less care when they switch from uninsured to insured status, although the evidence indicates that uninsured motorists actually have a higher accident frequency on average than insured motorists.[18] A reduction in the assigned risk pool may be welfare enhancing due to the principal agent inefficiencies that arise in such pools.

Overall, our estimates of the response of uninsured motorists to insurance premiums lend support to the view that insurance premium regulation, such as contained in Proposition 103, can be welfare enhancing. On the other hand, as with all regulation, the resulting deadweight losses have to be weighed against the possible benefits.

3.7   Proposition 103

We next consider the voting pattern on Proposition 103, the California voter referendum creating insurance regulation in California. Three special interest groups faced off in the campaign for auto insurance regulation: consumer activists, insurance companies, and trial lawyers. Each group had least one auto insurance referendum on the ballot:

Proposition 100 by the California Trial Lawyers

Proposition 101 by Coastal Insurance Company

Proposition 103 by Ralph Nader and Voter Revolt

Proposition 104 by the insurance industry (to create no-fault)

Proposition 106 by the insurance industry (to limit legal fees)

Campaigning for and against these propositions approached an intensity not seen since California's property tax initiative Proposition 13, which had occurred 10 years earlier. A poll of California attitudes with respect to the insurance propositions, taken several months before the election (see Field Institute 1988), asked the following:

"Overall, do you feel that the amount of money that the average person like yourself pays for automobile insurance is much too high, somewhat high or about right?"

If much too high or somewhat high: "Why do you think rates are so high?" (May indicate more than one category)

---

17. The welfare benefits of decreasing the percentage of uninsured motorists are discussed at greater length in Smith and Wright (1992).

18. The statistics tabulated in Kuan and Peck (1981) found that compared to the average California driver, the uninsured driver had (1) a much worse prior accident record and (2) a much worse prior traffic conviction record. Of course, this does not necessarily mean that driving habits change when a driver changes his or her status from uninsured to insured.

Table 3.7   Proposition 103 Voting

Equation	Dependent Variable	C	Y	P	I	R^2
7.1	VOTE	−3.4	.36	.58		.62
		(4.4)	(3.5)	(4.5)		
7.2	VOTE	−6.2	.10	.98	.45	.71
		(6.2)	(0.9)	(6.3)	(3.9)	
7.3	Log odds VOTE: $\dfrac{\tau}{(1-\tau)}$	−12.8	.61	1.1		.67
		(10.3)	(3.7)	(5.0)		
7.4	Log odds VOTE: $\dfrac{\tau}{(1-\tau)}$	−17.1	.22	1.7	.68	.73
		(10.2)	(1.2)	(6.5)	(3.5)	

Sources: See data appendix for variable definitions and data sources.
Notes: Observations for 58 California counties. Estimation is by ordinary least squares, all variables in log. Numbers in parentheses are absolute values of *t*-statistics.

Auto insurance was thought "much too high" by 77 percent, "somewhat high" by 17 percent, and "about right" by only 4 percent. The blame for high insurance rates was placed on the insurance industry by 45 percent,[19] lawyers or the legal system by 36 percent, and California drivers by 38 percent.

To explore the motives of California voters further, we estimated regression equations to explain the voting record on Proposition 103 across California counties. In equation (7.1) of table 3.7, the dependent variable is the log of the percentage voting yes (VOTE) on Proposition 103, and the independent variables are per capita income (Y) and the effective insurance premium (P), the same variables used in equation (4.1). There is a significant and positive relationship by county between higher insurance premiums and a yes vote on Proposition 103. The income relationship in equation (7.1), however, may just reflect the larger percentage of voters who own cars in high-income counties, a relationship already confirmed in equation (4.1). Equation (7.2) verifies this hypothesis, since the number of insured cars per capita I is significant while income is no longer significant.

A logit estimator provides an alternative functional form in which to estimate the voting choice:

$$(6) \qquad \log\left(\frac{\tau}{1-\tau}\right) = a_0 + a_1 Y + a_2 P,$$

where τ = the percentage voting yes. The estimates are shown in equation (7.3) in table 3.7 and in equation (7.4) with the number of insured cars per capita added as an additional right-hand-side variable. The estimated coefficients re-

19. Specific responses included "Insurance companies are greedy" (22 percent), "Insurance companies are unregulated" (13 percent), and "Insurance companies make too much money" (12 percent).

flect the same pattern evident in equations (7.1) and (7.2). When the premium coefficients are transformed at the point of the sample means to the form of an elasticity for the percentage voting yes on Proposition 103, the resulting elasticities are 0.63 for equation (7.3) and 0.98 for equation (7.4), both somewhat higher than the corresponding elasticities estimated in equations (7.1) and (7.2).

These results confirm the importance of high auto insurance premiums as a primary determinant of voting yes on Proposition 103. This leaves open, however, the question of whether this voting behavior simply reflects self-interest (voters in high-premium counties hoped Proposition 103 would lower their premiums) or a sentiment of fairness (voters sensed that their premiums were unfair relative to some reference standard). The fairness hypothesis receives some support from the fact that even in low-premium counties, which stood to lose from premium compression, Proposition 103 received a substantial number of yes votes. On the other hand, Proposition 103 restructured premium setting and the administration of premium regulation in a number of other ways as well, so even voters in low-premium counties may have expected to receive lower premiums as a result of Proposition 103.

In conclusion, we briefly comment on some of the directly observed effects of Proposition 103 since it was enacted five years ago. In the first place, the second tier of risk, the so-called nonstandard insurance contract has been eliminated. The fact that "take all comer" laws eliminate the second tier of contracts has been noted in a number of other states, for example, Hawaii, Massachusetts, New Hampshire, North Carolina, and South Carolina (see Sloan and Githens 1994). This, of course, raises the question of what happens to those customers who were previously in the second tier.

Second, although the intent of Proposition 103 was to limit risk classification to the three factors named in the proposition, this has not happened and a number of other factors have been approved for use. Among these is zip code, though now zip code is used in contiguous clusters, rather than the individual zip codes used previously. Obviously, this does not eliminate the possibility that by crossing a street one's insurance rates could double, but it does reduce the number of boundaries at which this can occur.

What has changed, however, is the methodology used to calculate loss relatives. Insurance companies now estimate loss relatives sequentially, starting with a univariate estimation based on the driver's safety record, then adding number of miles driven, and so on. Details of this procedure are sketchy, and how this affects premiums in specific cases is not yet known.

3.8 Conclusions

We have confirmed the Blackmon and Zeckhauser result that the demand for registered cars is highly premium elastic. In the context of Massachusetts's rate tempering, BZ concluded that this high premium elasticity leads to welfare losses. In the case of rate compression, as in California, the high estimated premium elasticity also leads to welfare losses, at least when categorization is costless.

We have found evidence of a positive relationship between insurance premiums and the number of uninsured drivers. This implies that insurance premium regulation, such as Proposition 103, may be welfare enhancing to the extent that it causes the percentage of uninsured motorists to decline. There is, however, an alternative strategy for lowering the percentage of uninsured motorists: the "pay at the pump" initiative that is likely to be forthcoming soon as a California referendum proposition. With pay-at-the-pump, insurance premiums are collected primarily as fees included in gasoline purchases. Since gasoline is needed to drive, pay-at-the-pump eliminates all uninsured motorists. Pay-at-the-pump may thus provide the same welfare benefit as suppressed insurance premiums in reducing the number of uninsured drivers, but at a lower dead-weight cost.

Our results also point to the potentially important role of "fairness" with regard to insurance premium regulation. References to unfair insurance premiums were common in the campaign to pass Proposition 103. These references to fairness were successful because insurance companies find it difficult to document that high premiums reflect high expected costs, especially for drivers who rarely or never create accidents. It remains unclear, however, whether the importance of high insurance premiums as a determinant of yes votes on Proposition 103 reflects simple self-interest or true voter concern for fairness.

Although we have concentrated here on auto insurance, similar rate regulation questions arise in other areas of property-casualty insurance. For example, recent attempts by insurance companies to charge higher premiums for hurricane insurance written on properties with close proximity to the ocean has met with strong consumer opposition. This practice is now widely called "shorelining" by obvious analogy with "redlining" in loan markets. Legislation against shoreline pricing will have the same effects on the availability of hurricane insurance that the legislation against territory-based pricing has had on the availability of auto insurance.

Earthquake insurance has recently become another area of major concern for casualty insurance companies in California. The Los Angeles (Northridge) earthquake caused these companies and their reinsurance partners to reevaluate the expected costs of such insurance; some companies, in fact, now consider earthquake risks uninsurable (see Jaffee and Russell 1997 for details). The result is that a quasi-governmental agency has been created—the California Earthquake Authority—at the request of the insurance companies to provide earthquake insurance. It is intriguing that in this case the insurance companies have chosen not to provide earthquake insurance because they fear that earthquake insurance premiums that would be high enough to protect the companies financially would be viewed by consumers as unfair. Thus, in this line of business also, questions of perceived fairness are preventing firms from offering contracts at the break-even price, leading to a search for regulatory alternatives to the market.

Data Appendix

All variables relate to the cross section of California's 58 counties and to the year 1990, unless otherwise noted. The variables I, R, U, A, and V are stated on a per capita basis; Source of county population data is California Department of Finance (1991). In table 3.3, all of the variables are stated on a per household basis; the number of California households comes from California Department of Finance (1991).

A	Number of insured cars (per capita, full-year-equivalent policies) in the assigned risk pool, from California Department of Insurance
ACC	California car accidents in 1989, from California Counties Foundation (1991)
C	Constant
D	Population/miles^2, from California Department of Finance (1991)
I	Number of insured passenger vehicles (per capita, full-year-equivalent policies), from California Department of Insurance
MILES	Annual miles of travel per vehicle, from California Counties Foundation (1991)
P_V	Effective insurance premium, voluntary insurance companies, from California Department of Insurance
P_A	Effective insurance premium, assigned risk pool, from California Department of Insurance
$P_{V/A}$	P_V/P_A
P	Effective insurance premium; weighted average of P_V and P_A, where the weights reflect the percentage of total insured cars in each category
R	$I + U$; includes all registered cars and 68 percent of registered trucks and light commercial vehicles (the percentage used for personal purposes)
T	Percentage of residents journeying to work by public transportation, by California metropolitan area, divided into counties for 1985 (latest year available); counties without any indicated public transportation are set equal to the minimum value across the listed counties; from U.S. Department of Commerce, Bureau of Census, *State and Metropolitan Area Data Book 1986* (Washington, D.C., 1986)

U	Number of uninsured vehicles (per capita), from California Department of Insurance
V	Number of insured cars (per capita, full-year-equivalent policies) in the voluntary insurance market, from California Department of Insurance
Y	Per capita income, from California Department of Finance (1991)
VOTE	Percentage of yes votes on Proposition 103, from California Secretary of State (1988)
μ	U/R
ν	A/I

References

All-Industry Research Advisory Council. 1989. *Uninsured motorists.* Oak Brook, Ill.: All-Industry Research Advisory Council.

Arrow, K. J. 1963. *Essays in the theory of risk-bearing.* Amsterdam: North-Holland.

Blackmon, B. Glenn, and Richard Zeckhauser. 1991. Mispriced equity: Regulated rates for auto insurance in Massachusetts. *American Economic Review* 81 (2): 65–69.

Bond, Eric, and Keith Crocker. 1991. Smoking, skydiving and knitting: The endogenous categorization of risks in insurance markets with asymmetric information. *Journal of Political Economy* 99 (1): 177–99.

Borch, K. 1990. *The economics of insurance.* Amsterdam: North-Holland.

Borenstein, Severin. 1989. The economics of costly risk sorting in competitive insurance markets. *International Review of Law and Economics* 9:25–39.

California Counties Foundation. 1991. *1991–1992 California county fact book.* Sacramento: California Counties Foundation Research Division.

California Department of Finance. 1991. *California statistical abstract.* Sacramento: California Department of Finance.

California Department of Insurance. Rate Regulation Division. 1978. *Study of California driving performance by zip code (phase 1).* Sacramento: California Department of Insurance, Rate Regulation Division.

California Secretary of State. 1988. *Supplement to statement of vote, November 1988.* Sacramento: California Secretary of State.

California State Association of Counties. 1991–92. *County fact book, 1991–1992 California.* Sacramento: California State Association of Counties.

Cooper, R., and B. Hayes. 1987. Multiperiod insurance contracts. *International Journal of Industrial Organization* 5:211–31.

Crocker, Keith, and Arthur Snow. 1986. The efficiency effects of categorical discrimination in the insurance industry. *Journal of Political Economy* 94 (2): 321–44.

Dahlby, G. B. 1983. Adverse selection and statistical discrimination. *Journal of Public Economics* 20:121–30.

D'Arcy, Stephen, P., and Neil A. Doherty. 1990. Adverse selection, private information, and lowballing in insurance markets. *Journal of Business* 63 (2): 145–64.

Dionne, Georges, and Neil Doherty. 1992. Adverse selection in insurance markets: A selected survey. In *Contributions to insurance economics,* ed. G. Dionne. Boston: Kluwer.

————. 1994. Adverse selection, Commitment, and renegotiation: Extension to and evidence from insurance markets. *Journal of Political Economy* 102 (2): 209–35.

Dudey, Paul O. 1991. History of consumer activism as respects the insurance industry. In *The impact of consumer activism on the insurance industry.* Malvern, Pa.: Society of CPCU.

Field Institute. 1988. The California poll. Statistical Release no. 1450.

Harrington, Scott E. 1992. Rate suppression. *Journal of Risk and Insurance* 59:185–202.

————. 1993. The economics and politics of automobile insurance rate classification. *Journal of Risk and Insurance* 60 (1): 59–84.

Hoy, Michael. 1989. The value of screening mechanisms under alternative insurance possibilities. *Journal of Public Economics* 39:177–206.

Jaffee, D. M., and T. Russell. 1992. Fairness, credit rationing, and loan market structure. Working Paper Series, no. 7. Princeton, N.J.: Princeton University, Center for Economic Policy Studies.

————. 1997. Catastrophe insurance, capital markets, and uninsurable risks. *Journal of Risk and Insurance* 64 (2): 205–30.

Jee, B. 1989. A comparative analysis of alternative pure premium models in the automobile risk classification system. *Journal of Risk and Insurance* 56:434–59.

Kahnemann, D., J. Knetsch, and R. Thaler. 1986. Fairness as a constraint on profit seeking entitlements in the market. *American Economic Review* 76:728–41.

Keeton, William, and Evan Kwerel. 1984. Externalities in automobile insurance and the underinsured driver problem. *Journal of Law and Economics* 27 (April): 149–79.

Kimball, S. W. 1961. The purpose of insurance regulation: A preliminary inquiry in the theory of insurance law. *Minnesota Law Review* 45:471–524.

Kuan, Jensen, and Raymond Peck. 1981. A profile of uninsured motorists in California. Sacramento: California Division of Motor Vehicles.

Kunreuther, H., and M. Pauly. 1985. Market equilibrium with private knowledge: An example. *Journal of Public Economics* 26:269–88.

Malinvaud, E. 1972. The allocation of individual risks in large markets. *Journal of Economic Theory* 5:312–28.

Miyazaki, H. 1977. The rat race and internal labor markets. *Bell Journal of Economics* 8:394–418.

National Association of Independent Insurers. Insurance Services Office. 1988. *Factors affecting urban auto insurance costs.* New York: Insurance Services Office.

National Association of Insurance Commissioners. 1988. *Report on profitability by line by state, 1981–1988.* Kansas City, Mo.: NAIC Publications.

Pindyck, Robert, and Daniel Rubinfeld. 1981. *Econometric models and economic forecasts,* 2d ed. New York: McGraw-Hill.

Puelz, Robert, and Walter Kemmsies. 1993. Implications for unisex statutes and risk-pooling: The costs of gender and underwriting attributes in the automobile insurance market. *Journal of Regulatory Economics* 5:289–301.

Puelz, Robert, and Arthur Snow. 1994. Evidence on adverse selection: Equilibrium signaling and cross-subsidization in the insurance market. *Journal of Political Economy* 102 (2): 236–57.

Radner, R. 1985. Repeated principal-agent games with discounting. *Econometrica* 53:1173–99.

Rea, Samuel A., Jr. 1992. Insurance classifications and social welfare. In *Contributions to insurance economics,* ed. Georges Dionne, 377–96. Boston: Kluwer.

Riley, J. 1979. Informational equilibrium. *Econometrica* 47:331–60.

Rosenfield, Harvey. 1991. Proposition 103: The consumer's viewpoint. In *The impact of consumer activism on the insurance industry.* Malvern, Pa.: Society of CPCU.

Rothschild, M., and J. Stiglitz. 1976. Equilibrium in competitive insurance markets. *Quarterly Journal of Economics* 90:629–49.

Rubinstein, A., and M. E. Yaari. 1983. Repeated insurance contracts and moral hazard. *Journal of Economic Theory* 30:74–97.

Shavell, S. 1986. The judgment proof problem. *International Review of Law and Economics* 6:45–58.

Sloan, F., and P. B. Githens. 1994. Drinking, driving, and the price of automobile insurance. *Journal of Risk and Insurance* 61:33–58.

Smith, Eric, and Randall Wright. 1992. Why is automobile insurance in Philadelphia so damn expensive? *American Economic Review* 82 (4): 756–72.

Spence, Michael. 1973. Job market signaling. *Quarterly Journal of Economics* 87:355–74.

Sugarman, Stephen D. 1990. California insurance regulation revolution: The first two years of Proposition 103. *San Diego Law Review* 27:683–714.

———. 1993. *"Pay at the pump": Auto insurance.* Berkeley: University of California, Institute of Governmental Studies Press.

Williams, G. 1992. "The wrong side of the tracks": Territorial rating and the setting of automobile liability insurance rates in California. *Hastings Constitutional Law Quarterly* 19:846–909.

Wilson, C. 1977. A model of insurance markets with incomplete information. *Journal of Economic Theory* 16:167–207.

4   Rate Regulation and the Industrial Organization of Automobile Insurance

Susan J. Suponcic and Sharon Tennyson

4.1 Introduction

Property-liability insurance markets, especially those for personal coverages such as automobile insurance, have traditionally been closely regulated. Areas of government oversight include the imposition of licensing and capital requirements, the monitoring of solvency and liquidation of insolvent firms, and, in some cases, direct regulation of insurance rates. Under the provisions of the McCarran Ferguson Act of 1945, this regulation is undertaken by the individual state governments rather than at the federal level. As a result, the extent of regulatory intervention and enforcement differs across locations.

A primary area of state differences in regulation is the degree to which rates for private passenger automobile insurance are regulated. Just over half of the states intervene directly in the rate-making process for automobile insurance. The most common method of rate regulation is the *prior approval* system, under which each insurer's rates must be approved by the state insurance commissioner prior to their introduction into the market. A few states instead require all insurers to charge rates that are set by the insurance commissioner, or by an industry rating bureau. The remaining states allow rates to be competitively determined, although most require that insurers file rate changes with the state commissioner.

The effects of rate regulation on insurers' underwriting margins have been

Susan J. Suponcic is a Ph.D. candidate in the Department of Public Policy and Management at the Wharton School of the University of Pennsylvania. Sharon Tennyson is assistant professor of insurance at the Wharton School of the University of Pennsylvania.

The authors thank Kip Viscusi and other conference participants for useful comments on the paper. Financial support from the University of Pennsylvania Research Foundation is gratefully acknowledged.

113

the subject of numerous analyses.[1] Most studies assess underwriting results by the *unit price* of insurance, the ratio of premium revenue received to losses incurred by the insurer. This ratio is a measure of the average price paid by insureds per dollar of benefits (loss payments) received. Early studies tended to find that regulation raised unit prices for automobile insurance, suggesting that regulation promoted collusive pricing or inhibited price competition (Joskow 1973; Ippolito 1979; Frech and Samprone 1980). However, these studies examined the time period from the late 1960s to early 1970s, a period when virtually all states regulated rate setting and deregulation was a very recent phenomenon. Later studies, availed of greater variability in regulatory regimes and longer time horizons for comparison, have consistently found the opposite result: lower unit prices for automobile insurance in states that regulate rates (Pauly, Kunreuther, and Kleindorfer 1986; Harrington 1987; Grabowski et al. 1989). Thus, at least since the mid-1970s, rate regulation has had the effect of reducing insurers' premium revenues relative to insured losses, thereby lowering the average unit price of insurance.

The magnitude of unit price reductions under regulation has been shown to be relatively small on average, decreasing unit prices by 0.03 to 0.07. The price-decreasing effects of regulation are significantly larger in a few selected states, however (Harrington 1987; Grabowski et al. 1989). These findings have raised concerns about potential distortionary effects of rate regulation on insurance markets. Pauly et al. (1986) present indirect evidence, based on the estimation of cost functions, that rate regulation may lower quality or service provision by insurers. Grabowski et al. (1989) demonstrate that stringent rate regulation reduces insurance availability, where availability is assessed by the fraction of drivers able to purchase insurance in the voluntary insurance market.[2] Kramer (1992) investigates the effects of rate regulation on insurance company financial health and finds evidence of a relationship between stringent regulation of rates and increased risk of insurer insolvency.

This paper investigates the hypothesis that rate regulation distorts the industrial structure of state automobile insurance markets. As noted by Harrington (1992), insurers will be reluctant to commit resources to regulated states if current regulation is excessively stringent or if the regulator cannot commit to an established level of regulation in future periods. More generally, restrictive regulation may affect the operating decisions of insurers in the state. Our analysis focuses on how differences across insurers in costs, size, production technology, and market position will lead to different responses to regulation,

---

1. See Harrington (1984) and Grabowski, Viscusi, and Evans (1989) for comprehensive reviews of the literature.

2. Residual market pools exist in all states to provide insurance to drivers unable to obtain coverage in the open market. Regulation that holds prices below the competitive level will increase the fraction of drivers insured in the residual market, due to rationing in the voluntary market sector. The findings of Grabowski et al. (1989) are consistent with this view of regulation for several highly regulated states.

thereby distorting the industrial structure of the market. If the net effect of regulation is to lower the relative market presence of the lowest cost insurance providers, insurance market efficiency will be adversely affected.

The paper is organized as follows. Section 4.2 describes the industrial structure of automobile insurance markets. Section 4.3 discusses how differences in insurer organization and market position will lead to different responses to regulation. The remaining sections investigate the empirical content of these arguments. Section 4.4 compares the structure of automobile insurance markets in regulated and unregulated states. Sections 4.5 and 4.6 provide more controlled investigations of the effects of rate regulation, using multivariate analysis of regulatory effects on state insurance market structure. The final section of the paper summarizes our findings and suggests future research avenues.

4.2   The Industrial Organization of Automobile Insurance

Automobile insurance industry statistics for 1989 are presented in table 4.1. We use 1989 as the basis for our cross-sectional analysis because it is a year

Table 4.1   **Private Passenger Automobile Insurance Market Statistics, 1989**

Statistic	National Market	State Markets Mean	State Markets S.D.
Total premiums ($)	74,399,743,314	1,485,019,174	1,930,625,557
Unit price	1.33	1.37	0.13
Number of firms			
Total	526	103.38	26.00
Direct writers	101	27.88	6.71
National firms	78	62.64	7.89
National direct writers	21	18.62	2.47
Auto specialists	233	34.18	11.40
National auto specialists	20	16.98	2.39
Big Four	4	3.54	0.50
Market share			
Direct writers	0.646	0.642	0.117
National firms	0.697	0.701	0.125
National direct writers	0.476	0.481	0.139
Auto specialists	0.677	0.654	0.119
National auto specialists	0.432	0.431	0.113
Big Four	0.410	0.424	0.134
Measure of concentration			
C4	0.417	0.540	0.086
HHI	659	1,043	311.66

Source: Authors' calculations based on A. M. Best Company data tapes for Best's Executive Data Service.

Note: For definitions, see section 4.2.1 of the text.

of calm in the insurance business cycle, and it is the most recent year before major changes began in the insurance regulatory environment: 1989 was the last year that the major insurance rating bureaus issued advisory rates to their members, and the passage of California's Proposition 103 in late 1988 prompted consideration of regulatory initiatives in other states in subsequent years. These changes could differentially affect the competitive strategies or capabilities of different types of insurers, thereby affecting market structure.

4.2.1   The National Automobile Insurance Market

A. M. Best Company identifies 526 different groups and independent single companies writing positive auto insurance premiums in the United States in 1989.[3] In keeping with the large number of firms in the market, traditional measures of concentration are relatively low in the industry: the four-firm concentration ratio (C4) is 42 percent, and the Herfindahl-Hirschman Index (HHI) for the market is 659, based on direct premiums written. These values are not large in comparison to other industries (Klein 1989), and an HHI of under 1,000 falls into the range defined as "unconcentrated" by U.S. Department of Justice merger guidelines.

The variation in insurer size is considerable. The largest four writers in the market (known in the trade press as the "Big Four") obtain market shares of 20 percent (State Farm), 12 percent (Allstate), 5 percent (Farmers), and 4 percent (Nationwide), respectively, and only 13 other firms write over 1 percent of the market. Yet the largest 50 firms write over 80 percent of all auto insurance premiums. Fully 90 percent of auto insurance premiums are written by only 90 firms. To put this into perspective, this means that 436 firms share only 10 percent of the private passenger auto insurance market.

Insurers also differ greatly in the extent of geographic areas served. For example, only 78 of the 526 firms in the market write auto insurance in all nine census divisions in the country. The remainder sell in only some regions of the country, and 191 firms sell in only a single state. Hence a vast majority of firms in the market have operations that are concentrated in particular geographic areas. While the national firms (those that sell in all nine census divisions)[4] make up only 15 percent of insurance providers by number, these firms write 70 percent of total private passenger auto insurance premium volume. This implies that insurance markets are highly segmented by geographic location— with relatively few firms writing the bulk of premiums nationally and a much

---

3. Best Company lists a total of 570 groups and independent sellers of private passenger automobile insurance; however, some of these firms reported zero or negative premiums for this line and are omitted from the analysis.

4. Under the standard categorization popularized by Best Company reports, 40 firms are known as "national" insurance writers. However, this categorization is not based on automobile insurance writings: not all of these carriers sell auto insurance nationally, and there are a significant number of insurers categorized by Best as "regional" who do write nationally. We feel that our definition of national sellers is superior for purposes of analyzing the auto insurance market.

larger number of local or regional firms writing the balance of the market in their particular area.

The data also reveal significant differences in the market presence of firms using different organizational forms. There are two major systems of distribution used in the industry. Some insurers ("direct writers") use sales agents who sell exclusively the products of that specific firm. Other firms utilize the more traditional independent agency system, under which each agent may sell the policies of a number of insurance companies. Numerous empirical studies have shown direct writers to be lower cost sellers of automobile insurance than independent agency firms (Joskow 1973; Cummins and VanDerhei 1979; Barrese and Nelson 1992). Yet direct writing entails larger investment in firm-specific assets and greater sunk costs of entry than independent agency because the degree of integration and centralization is greater.

In accordance with their operating cost advantage, direct writers dominate the auto insurance market, achieving a nearly 65 percent market share in 1989. However, consistent with the higher fixed costs of direct writing, there are fewer firms employing this system than the independent agency system. Of the 526 firms in the market only 101 are direct writers; the remaining 425 are independent agency writers. This fact, in conjunction with the statistics on market shares, implies that on average direct writers are much larger than independent agency writers. There are substantial size differences among direct writers, however; a few extremely large firms, such as State Farm and Allstate, significantly influence averages for the group. While the 10 largest direct writers in the industry each write well over $1 billion in auto insurance premiums, the median-sized direct writer has premium revenue of only $39 million. Nonetheless, this is significantly greater than the median premium volume of $10.5 million for independent agency writers.

In addition to differences in market shares, there are also great differences in specialization across firms.[5] Of the 526 firms writing in the market, 88 firms (16.3 percent of all firms) write over 90 percent of their insurance premiums in private passenger automobile lines, and 233 firms (44.3 percent of firms) write at least 50 percent of their business in auto insurance. Since private passenger auto insurance makes up only 35 percent of total property-liability insurance premiums nationally, we classify these latter insurers as "auto specialists." This group contains several high-profile automobile insurers, including State Farm and Allstate, as well as a large number of relatively small specialist firms. At the other extreme from the auto specialists, 94 firms (17.9 percent of firms) write under 10 percent of their business in private passenger auto insurance. This latter category of firms includes a number of well-known brand-

---

5. These differences are likely to be related to differences in organizational structure because of the resulting differences in cost structures and production technologies. For empirical evidence on the relationship between insurer organizational structure and market positioning, see Mayers and Smith (1988), Marvel (1982), and Regan and Tennyson (1996).

name insurance writers, including Chubb, Firemans' Fund, and CIGNA. Although these firms may write substantial premium volume in private passenger auto insurance, their relative focus on these lines is limited.

This brief portrait of the national automobile insurance market highlights the great variation across firms in terms of size, geographic focus, and relative specialization in automobile insurance. These differences and differences in insurer organizational form are likely to reflect underlying differences in production and cost technologies. The data also show that a comparatively small number of firms, relative to the total number in the market, serve the vast majority of the market at the national level. This suggests that a relatively small number of large producers may possess a cost or technological advantage over the remainder of the producers in the market. This point of view is supported by comparisons of insurer expense data: the Big Four, national auto specialists, and direct writers all exhibit significantly lower expense ratios (underwriting expenses as a percentage of premium volume) than other automobile insurers (Tennyson 1996).

4.2.2   State Automobile Insurance Markets

In the national automobile insurance market, we observe a great deal of market segmentation by geographic location, as evidenced by the relatively small number of firms that sell nationally. This implies that auto insurance markets may differ substantially across states and that state markets may look very different from what is suggested by national market statistics. Closer examination of state insurance markets reveals evidence of both of these features in the data.

For comparison to the national market statistics, the second and third columns of table 4.1 present means and standard deviations of the industrial characteristics of state automobile insurance markets. The number of sellers in each state varies from 33 to 151, with a mean value of 103, much lower than the national total of 526 firms. State-level values for C4 vary from 33.2 percent to 80.4 percent, with a mean of 54 percent; the HHI by state ranges from 503 to 2,220, with a mean of 1,043. Thus, market concentration varies a great deal across states and is generally greater than at the national level.

The numbers and market shares of different types of sellers also vary across states. For example, the number of direct writers per state varies from 8 to 40, with a mean value of 28; direct writer market share by state ranges from 28 to 88 percent, with a mean value of 64 percent. The number of national writers ranges from 30 to 73 across states, with a mean of 63, and their state market share varies from 41 to 99 percent, with a mean of 70 percent. The number of auto specialists per state ranges from 7 to 60, with a mean of 34, and their market share ranges from 33 to 82 percent, with a mean of 65 percent.

These differences across states in the numbers of firms and their relative market shares suggest that the effects of rate regulation on market structure may vary greatly across states. It is also possible that this diversity in fact reflects the effects of regulation, if regulation distorts firms' entry and output decisions. The remaining sections of the paper further develop and explore the hypothesis that differences in state insurance market structure are related to differences in regulatory stringency.

4.3   Insurer Responses to Stringent Regulation

This section of the paper considers how insurers' choices regarding capacity allocation and output may respond to restrictive regulation of rates in a state insurance market. Consistent with the evidence presented in the previous section, and with previous characterizations of automobile insurance markets (Joskow 1973), we assume that a relatively small number of firms enjoy a persistent cost advantage over the remaining firms in the market. Firms engage in Bertrand competition over prices, but limited capacity prevents the large firms from meeting the entire market demand. Entry barriers, perhaps due to scarce managerial inputs or to increasing returns to scale, protect this segment of the industry from vigorous entry. These features imply that the large, low-cost firms can earn greater rates of return than the fringe firms in unregulated markets.

In analyzing the effects of regulation, it is important to keep in mind that rate regulation does not impose a uniform price constraint on insurers. Under the prior approval system, each insurer's rate proposal is supported by data on its loss and expense experience; the proposed rates are then evaluated with respect to some measure of a fair rate of return for the insurer. Hence, rates can and do vary across insurers; regulation simply limits the profitability of business written. The implications of profit regulation will differ from those of a regulatory price ceiling. In particular, limits on rates of return will be most binding for low-cost insurance providers, whereas a price ceiling will be most binding for high-cost providers.

Market structure is determined by both the market entry and exit decisions of firms and the output decisions of the firms that choose to sell in the market. We consider first the effects of regulation on insurer entry and exit decisions. To the extent that regulation reduces insurer returns below those available in other markets, firms will choose not to enter regulated markets. Concerns about future regulatory stringency may also deter entry if insurers must incur sunk investments to enter the market (Harrington 1992). Sunk investments required of insurers include investments in distribution and claims-handling networks, advertising in local markets, and costs of regulatory compliance in the state. The more stringent is regulation, and the larger are the necessary sunk investments, the greater will be the distortions to entry.

Incumbent firms in a market must decide whether to exit in response to stringent regulation. Empirical evidence from the 1960s through the early 1980s suggests that the nature and stringency of rate regulation has changed over time from profit increasing to profit reducing (Pauly et al. 1986; Grabowski et al. 1989). More recent evidence suggests that the trend toward more restrictive rate regulation may be continuing: in 1988 the state of California passed legislation that mandated rate rollbacks for all insurers, and at least 14 other states have since considered similar measures. This increased regulatory stringency may drive incumbent firms out of the market.

Withdrawal from regulated markets may be inhibited, however, by the existence of fixed, state-specific inputs to production. Important inputs into insurance production are labor, real capital, and financial capital. In the short run, labor inputs may be variable, but capital inputs are generally fixed. What we term real capital includes investments in distribution networks and claims-handling facilities, which are fixed in the short run. Financial capital incorporates surplus funds to bolster solvency and is also fixed. Unlike real capital, however, financial capital is not tied to any one line of business or state market even in the short run. Thus, to the extent that labor and real capital inputs are in place, insurers can quickly and costlessly reallocate capacity across insurance markets by a simple reallocation of financial resources. Insurers may nevertheless be slow to withdraw entirely from a regulated market because real capital resources are not mobile across markets in the short run.

There are also other factors at work that imply that insurers' response to rate regulation may be to reduce market share rather than to exit the market. Regulators in many states have the ability to force insurers to pay explicit or implicit exit ransoms. For example, the courts have consistently upheld the ability of regulators to withdraw licenses for all business in the state if an insurer wishes to withdraw from a heavily regulated line such as automobile insurance. Some states also force withdrawing insurers to continue contributions to the residual market deficit for a period of time after withdrawal from the state (Cummins and Tennyson 1992). These actions will significantly raise exit costs for insurers in regulated markets, which may discourage or slow the pace of exit (Harrington 1992). Firms that operate in more than one line of insurance may be especially slow to exit the regulated line as this could threaten licenses to write in other lines in the state.

One hypothesis that can be drawn from this discussion is that, all else equal, fewer firms will choose to operate in regulated states, since entry is relatively unattractive and exit is relatively attractive in these markets. Predictions regarding the relative numbers of different types of firms are less clear-cut, however. We might expect the number of direct writers in regulated insurance markets to be relatively lower than the number of independent agency writers because direct writing requires greater sunk investments in the market and hence direct writer entry into regulated environments will be discouraged. However, once these investments have been made they will inhibit exit if the regulatory environment worsens, implying that direct writers could be more prevalent under regulation. On the other hand, firms using the independent agency system tend to be less specialized in automobile insurance than direct writers (Regan and Tennyson 1996). This may slow their rate of exit from unfavorable market environments since their lack of specialization implies greater costs of exit in terms of profits forgone in unregulated lines of insurance.

National firms, especially those specializing in automobile insurance, may be quick to exit unprofitable auto insurance markets because their costs of exit may be lower due to their existing distribution networks elsewhere. However, market exit implies dismantling state distribution networks, and reentry at a later date would involve additional start-up costs. These firms may thus find it less costly to reduce market share than to exit, since they can easily reallocate financial resources to the most profitable state markets.

If regulation is not sufficiently stringent to induce market exit, regulatory profit restrictions will nonetheless lead to reductions in output in the regulated lines of business. The relative reliance on state-specific real capital inputs and alternative opportunities for the use of financial capital will determine differences in output reductions across insurers in response to regulation. This reasoning yields definitive predictions about the relative effects of restrictive rate regulation on the market shares of different types of firms.

Low-cost producers, especially those with existing distribution systems in other less stringently regulated states, should reduce output the most in the face of rate regulation. This reflects the ability of firms with lower production costs to achieve higher rates of return than other firms in the absence of regulation. These producers thus have higher opportunity costs of devoting resources to a regulated market for which rates of return are held below those achievable elsewhere. A national distribution system also lowers the cost to a firm of reducing market share in a regulated state since the firm can reallocate financial resources to other state markets without new investments in real capital inputs.

The (opportunity) costs of capacity reallocation may vary with the output mix of the insurer, however. Greater diversity of exposures across lines of business in a state may increase the costs of reducing auto insurance market share if this adversely affects the insurer's reputation or relationships with sales agents. Hence, market share reductions under regulation may be most observable in national firms that specialize in automobile insurance. This reasoning also implies that direct writers should have lower market shares in regulated states since these firms tend to be low-cost producers of automobile insurance. This should be especially true for direct writers that operate nationally.

4.4   Market Structure in Regulated and Unregulated States

The theoretical discussion above suggests a number of dimensions along which automobile insurance market structure may be affected by rate regulation. The remaining sections of the paper investigate the extent to which these distortions occur in practice, by examining differences in insurance market structure across regulated and unregulated states.

In this section of the paper we examine data on the mean values of the number of firms and firm market shares in regulated and unregulated states for the year 1989. The analysis is undertaken at the level of state aggregates, for all private passenger automobile insurance coverages combined. States are first grouped into two basic categories—regulated and unregulated. Consistent with previous studies, states that employ prior approval regulation, state-made rates, or mandatory bureau rates are considered regulated; states that primarily require insurers to file rates rather than to seek approval of rates are considered unregulated. The regulatory system employed in each state was determined from information obtained from the National Association of Insurance Commissioners and the Alliance of American Insurers.

The state of California is omitted from this portion of the analysis because of the passage of Proposition 103 in late 1988. This controversial legislation introduced prior approval regulation of insurance rates, along with a number of other controls on the practices of insurers in that state. Due to the lags inherent in implementation of these regulations and to the continuing challenges of the legislation by insurers, it is unclear whether California should be considered regulated or unregulated in 1989. Our sample thus contains 25 regulated states and 24 unregulated states.[6]

To further differentiate those states that are the most heavily regulated, we also classify five states that have extremely large residual markets for automobile insurance as states with "stringent" regulation. All states operate residual markets for automobile insurance, which are designed to provide at least minimal coverage to those individuals unable to obtain insurance in the private market. Previous studies have documented that stringent regulation of insurance rates is associated with large fractions of the population insured through these residual mechanisms (Grabowski et al. 1989). The five stringently regulated states in our sample are Massachusetts, New Hampshire, New Jersey, North Carolina, and South Carolina. In each of these states at least 20 percent of drivers were insured in the residual market throughout the 1980s.[7]

Table 4.2 compares summary measures of market structure for unregulated states, regulated states, and stringently regulated states. We first note that, consistent with intuition, the average number of firms selling automobile insurance is lower in regulated and stringently regulated states than in the unregulated states. This difference is significant at the 10 percent confidence level for regulated versus unregulated states, and significant at the 1 percent confidence level for stringently regulated versus unregulated states. This comparison is particularly meaningful since the table also shows no significant differences in the average size of the auto insurance market across these sets of states, where

6. Including California in either state category significantly affects the results of the comparison of mean values.

7. By comparison, unregulated states insured only an average of 1.2 percent of drivers in the residual market, and other regulated states insured on average 2.3 percent of drivers in the residual market, over the time period 1980–90. However, two regulated states (New York and Rhode Island) insured between 10 and 15 percent of drivers in the residual market for at least some portion of this time period.

Table 4.2   Private Passenger Automobile Insurance Statistics by State Regulatory Status, 1989

	Unregulated		Regulated		Stringent	
Statistic	Mean	S.D.	Mean	S.D.	Mean	S.D.
Total premiums (thousand $)	1,087,895	863,030	1,474,385	1,575,869	1,429,383	791,093
Unit price	1.39	0.13	1.34	0.14	1.23*	0.18
Number of firms						
Total	108.24	22.56	96.71*	27.80	83.00***	12.73
Direct writers	30.60	5.28	24.75***	6.81	19.80***	2.39
National firms	64.44	4.73	60.38**	9.82	56.40**	5.81
National direct writers	19.40	1.41	17.75***	3.07	16.20***	1.48
Auto specialists	37.20	9.55	30.46**	12.22	23.20***	4.27
National auto specialists	17.72	1.54	16.13***	2.85	14.20***	1.79
Big Four	3.76	0.44	3.29***	0.46	3.00***	0.00
Market share						
Direct writers	0.679	0.084	0.599***	0.133	0.520**	0.150
National firms	0.670	0.107	0.741**	0.159	0.732**	0.043
National direct writers	0.476	0.100	0.491	0.150	0.465	0.116
Auto specialists	0.711	0.069	0.588***	0.126	0.541***	0.095
National auto specialists	0.440	0.092	0.424	0.134	0.375	0.155
Big Four	0.459	0.100	0.386**	0.157	0.279**	0.167
Measure of concentration						
C4	0.562	0.058	0.518**	0.106	0.454**	0.087
HHI	1,111.57	221.33	977.19*	380.95	756.47***	219.97

*Significantly different from unregulated states at the 10 percent confidence level, one-sided test.
**Significantly different from unregulated states at the 5 percent confidence level, one-sided test.
***Significantly different from unregulated states at the 1 percent confidence level, one-sided test.

market size is measured by total written premium volume.[8] Hence, the fact that there are fewer firms writing in regulated state markets is not attributable to differences in market size. The same result holds for each specific type of insurance seller: in every category of firm examined, there are fewer firms operating in regulated and stringently regulated states than in unregulated states. This is what we would expect if rate regulation affects firms' incentives for market entry and exit.

The largest percentage reductions in number of firms are for direct writers and for auto specialists. Relative to unregulated states, on average there are 19 percent fewer direct writers and 18 percent fewer auto specialists in regulated states, and 35 percent fewer direct writers and 37 percent fewer auto specialists in stringently regulated states. This compares to an 11 percent reduction in the total number of firms in regulated states, and a 23 percent reduction in the number of firms in stringently regulated states, relative to the unregulated state average. These results are consistent with the hypothesis that firms with relatively high proportions of business in the regulated line will be less likely to enter and more likely to exit when faced with profit restrictions. The results for direct writers may also reflect the effects on entry of greater sunk investments required for direct writers to enter a market.

The numbers of firms in the various "national" categories included in the table are reduced significantly by regulation and stringent regulation, but by less in percentage terms than the reduction in the total number of firms. This may reflect a greater tendency by these firms to reduce market share in relatively unprofitable markets rather than to exit. It may also be a consequence of the definition of national firm in our study, however, which requires that the firm sell auto insurance in a substantial number of states. This latter interpretation is supported by the fact that the number of Big Four auto insurers (State Farm, Allstate, Nationwide, and Farmers) is lower in regulated and stringently regulated states, and by a greater percentage than the reduction in the total number of firms.[9]

Similar to the findings on numbers of firms, direct writers also exhibit lower market shares in regulated and stringently regulated states. The largest market share reductions are for auto specialists and the Big Four, however. This is consistent with the hypothesis that low-cost producers have the greatest incentive to shift resources out of a market in response to regulatory profit restrictions.

Interestingly, the national categories of firms do not exhibit significantly

---

8. The same is true if market size is measured by the number of car years insured or the number of automobiles registered in the state.

9. This is due largely to the fact that Farmers writes auto insurance only in 32 states, spanning six census divisions; thus, by our definition, Farmers is not a national auto insurer. Farmers does not write in many eastern states, and these states are more likely to be regulated than those in other regions. This leaves open the question of whether Farmers' entry decisions are motivated by regional issues or by regulation; this is addressed further in the regression analysis below.

lower market shares in regulated states, and national firms as a group actually have a significantly larger market share in regulated and stringently regulated states than in unregulated states. This result at first appears to contradict our theory, since a national distribution system should make it easy to reduce market share in response to regulation. However, many of the national firms (57 of 78) use the independent agency system of selling, and these firms tend to be high-cost producers of automobile insurance. Expense ratio evidence also shows that national firms on the whole are not low-cost producers of automobile insurance (Tennyson 1996). Hence, national firms may have less incentive than other firms to reduce market share in response to profit restrictions. In addition, many independent agency firms write a significant fraction of their business in lines other than automobile insurance and hence may be constrained to offer auto insurance as a condition of keeping customers and agents satisfied. Nonetheless, neither national direct writers nor national auto specialists exhibit significantly lower market shares in regulated states.

4.5   The Effect of Regulation on Market Structure

This section of the paper uses regression analysis to further investigate the effects of rate regulation on insurance market structure. This approach allows us to more precisely isolate regulatory effects by controlling for other features of the state that might be related to market structure. In addition, it allows us to pool data over several years in order to estimate the effect of regulation on average over time rather than using data for a single year. This may be important if there is noise in the data in any given year, or if there are systematic effects on market structure by year (e.g., the insurance cycle) that may imply that a single year is unrepresentative of true regulatory effects. The regression analysis is undertaken using annual data for all 50 states over the time period 1987–92.[10]

As in the previous section, several different features of market structure are analyzed. The basic hypothesis that regulation reduces incentives to sell in the state is tested by examining the total number of firms writing automobile insurance in the state. We also estimate the effects of regulation on both the numbers and the market shares of several different types of firms to investigate the effects of regulation on the relative incentives to operate in the market. We estimate models for the numbers and market shares of national firms, direct writers, national direct writers, national auto specialists, and the Big Four auto insurers.

To test for regulatory effects on market structure, we define a regulation dummy variable that is equal to one if the state uses prior approval regulation,

---

10. We treat California as a regulated state beginning in 1989. The estimation results are not sensitive to changing the effective date of regulation in this state or to the elimination of California from the sample. The results are also similar if only those states that maintained consistent regulatory regimes throughout the sample period are included in the sample.

state-made rates, or mandatory bureau rates. To test whether there are differences in regulatory effects between regulated states in general and those most stringently regulated, we include a dummy variable equal to one if a state has stringent regulation of rates.[11] Stringent regulation is defined as in the previous section to include those states for which the residual market constituted more than 20 percent of the total insurance market throughout the decade of the 1980s.

In addition to other control variables, discussed in more detail below, each regression model includes dummy variables for eight of the nine census divisions in the country to control for potentially omitted regional influences on insurance market structure. Of particular concern is the possibility that regional differences in the tendency of states to regulate insurance markets, coupled with locational factors that may influence firms' entry decisions (e.g., distance from the firms' headquarters), may lead to spurious inferences regarding the effects of regulation on insurance markets. Including the regional variables in the model assures that the estimated regulatory effects are net of such locational influences. The models also include dummy variables for the years 1988–92, to allow for year-specific fixed effects on insurance market structure. Summary statistics for all of the variables included in the regression analysis are reported in the data appendix.

4.5.1   The Effect of Regulation on the Number of Sellers

We first estimate the effect of regulation on the total number of firms, and on the numbers of firms of several specific types, operating in the state automobile insurance market. Several variables other than rate regulation are included in the models to control for insurance market characteristics that may affect the number of firms operating. Key among these is the size of the automobile insurance market. All else equal, we expect to observe a larger number of firms writing in larger insurance markets. The potential size of the automobile insurance market in a state is measured by the natural logarithm of the number of registered automobiles in the state.

The percentage of the population that moved into the state during the decade of the 1980s is included in the model as an indicator of state growth and economic dynamism. We expect this variable to be positively related to the number of firms in the market since high growth should attract entrants into the market. State per capita income is included as a measure of the demand for insurance and insurance services in the state. Income should be positively related to insurance demand and hence to the number of insurers in the market.

---

11. In an earlier version of the paper we also tried a continuous index of regulatory stringency, based on Conning and Company surveys of insurance and regulatory executives that assign an index number of competitive freedom to each state insurance market (Suponcic and Tennyson 1995). Previous analysis has shown this index to be highly correlated with indicators of the type of regulatory system in a state (Suponcic 1994). The estimation results using this alternative measure of regulation are similar to those using the two regulation dummy variables.

However, previous studies have argued that the demand for insurance services will vary with income (Pauly et al. 1986), and this could have confounding effects on the number of firms if there are scale economies in service provision. We therefore have no strong priors about the effect of this variable.

The degree of market segmentation by risk categories may also influence market structure. The primary rating factor used for automobile insurance is the geographic location of the insured vehicle, with different locations in the state assigned to different rating territories. We therefore include the number of standard rating territories per registered car in the state (territory density) as a measure of market segmentation. We expect to observe more insurance firms operating in more segmented markets, implying a positive coefficient on the territory density variable. The relative locational density of the consuming population in the state may also help to determine the number of sellers in the market; this possibility is controlled for by including each state's population density, defined as resident population divided by land area, in the regression model. This variable should also be positively related to the number of firms in the market since greater customer density should support greater numbers of firms.

The ordinary least squares estimation results are reported in table 4.3. As hypothesized, the total number of firms operating is significantly lower in regulated states, and lower still in stringently regulated states. The marginal effect of regulation is to lower the number of firms in the market by 3.8; in stringently regulated states the average reduction in the number of firms is 29.6. This amounts to a 3.5 percent reduction in the number of firms in regulated states, and a 27.3 percent reduction in stringently regulated states, relative to the unregulated state average.

Regulation also significantly reduces the number of each distinct type of firm in the market, and as expected, the reductions are much larger in stringently regulated states. The effects of regulation are greatest for national auto specialists, relative to the mean number of these firms writing in unregulated states. After controlling for other market features, on average there are 6.2 percent fewer national specialist firms in regulated markets, and 23.9 percent fewer in stringently regulated states, relative to the unregulated state average. The magnitude of regulatory effects on the numbers of firms are similar for national direct writers, national firms overall, and direct writers overall. The results for the Big Four are of only marginal statistical significance and of economically insignificant magnitude, presumably because of the small number of firms in this category.

4.5.2 The Effect of Regulation on Market Shares

The effect of regulation on the number of firms in the market reflects regulatory effects on firms' entry and exit decisions. As argued earlier, however, reductions in output are the more likely short-run response to regulatory profit restrictions, as they are less costly and easier to implement than market exit

Table 4.3   Number of Firms, 1987–92 Data by State (ordinary least squares estimation)

Variable	Total Firms	Direct Writers	National Firms	National Direct Writers	National Auto Specialists	Big Four
Intercept	-230.5620***	-36.2962***	-30.7778***	0.0496	-1.8279	1.7264***
	(14.4840)	(4.7576)	(5.9068)	(2.2310)	(2.1041)	(0.3774)
Log registered autos	23.3443***	4.6129***	6.5034***	1.3929***	1.4549***	0.1533***
	(0.9697)	(0.3185)	(0.3954)	(0.1494)	(0.1409)	(0.0253)
Per capita income	-0.0026***	-0.0005***	-0.0008***	-0.0003***	-0.0004***	-3.0E-5***
	(0.0005)	(0.0001)	(0.0002)	(0.0000)	(0.0001)	(1.2E-5)
Population density	11.3278**	2.5141	4.7095**	1.5297**	0.9874	0.0943
	(5.0084)	(1.6451)	(2.0425)	(0.7714)	(0.7276)	(0.1305)
Territory density	120.9282***	32.8396***	34.4123***	13.1611***	10.5495***	1.1220*
	(25.4305)	(8.3531)	(10.3709)	(3.9170)	(3.6942)	(0.6626)
Percent movers	1.1734***	0.1355*	0.1947**	0.0239	0.0857***	0.0062
	(0.2375)	(0.0780)	(0.0969)	(0.0366)	(0.0345)	(0.0062)
Rate regulation	-3.7808**	-1.1983**	-2.9247***	-1.0332***	-1.0933***	-0.0717*
	(1.6908)	(0.5554)	(0.6895)	(0.2604)	(0.2456)	(0.0441)
Stringent regulation	-25.8056***	-5.7404***	-10.6182***	-3.2061***	-3.1360***	-0.1234**
	(2.4537)	(0.8060)	(1.0007)	(0.3779)	(0.3564)	(0.0639)
Adjusted R^2	0.8135	0.7069	0.7046	0.5206	0.5674	0.7158

Notes: Numbers in parentheses are standard errors. The model also includes year and census division dummy variables not reported here.

*Significantly different from zero at the 10 percent confidence level, two-sided test.

**Significantly different from zero at the 5 percent confidence level, two-sided test.

***Significantly different from zero at the 1 percent confidence level, two-sided test.

decisions. Accordingly, this section of the paper examines the effect of rate regulation on the state market shares of large, national and low-cost automobile insurance producers. As in previous sections, we focus on direct writers, national writers, national direct writers, national auto specialists, and the Big Four. The market share of each category of firm is measured as the percentage of total state automobile insurance premiums written by firms included in that category. Because market shares of necessity lie between zero and one, the dependent variables used here are the log-odds ratios of market shares ln(share/(1 − share)) for each category of firm. This transformation ensures that the predicted values of market shares from the least squares regressions lie between zero and one.

Our empirical models of the determinants of the state market shares are similar to those for the numbers of firms operating in the state. The control variables included in the market share models are state per capita income, state population density, the proportion of the population that moved into the state between 1980 and 1990, and the ratio of automobile bodily injury claims to property damage claims in the state.

To the extent that higher per capita income indicates a higher level of insurance demand, income should be positively related to the market shares of low-cost firms since they should devote more resources to relatively attractive markets; however, if the demand for services increases with income, low-price, low-service firms may have lower market shares in high-income states (Pauly et al. 1986). Population density and the percentage of the population that recently moved into the state may be negatively related to market shares since these variables positively affect the number of firms in the market. Alternatively, higher population density and a more mobile population may give direct writer and national insurers a marketing advantage since these firms are more likely to use mass advertising to obtain customers.[12]

The bodily injury claims variable is added to this set of models as a measure of the relative riskiness of auto insurance in the state. Since bodily injury liability claims are the most expensive and unpredictable component of auto insurance claims, a higher rate of bodily injury claims may lead insurers to reduce their exposure in the market. The impact of these claims on relative output levels across insurers will depend on their relative expertise in underwriting and settling these claims. This makes strong predictions difficult at the level of aggregation in this study. However, if there are economies of scale with respect to underwriting and settlement of liability claims this would imply that the market shares of the largest firms should be positively related to the rate of bodily injury claims.

The parameter estimates from ordinary least squares estimation are reported in table 4.4. The results indicate relatively weak effects of regulation on the

---

12. See Marvel (1982) for a theoretical analysis of why direct writers are more likely to use mass advertising than are independent agency writers.

Table 4.4   **Log-Odds Market Shares, 1987–92 Data by State (ordinary least squares estimation)**

Variable	Direct Writers	National Firms	National Direct Writers	National Auto Specialists	Big Four
Intercept	−0.2057	−0.1509	−0.5150**	−0.6676***	−0.4321***
	(0.2176)	(0.4048)	(0.2540)	(0.2430)	(0.0358)
Per capita income	3.2E-5***	8.0E-5***	1.2E-5	1.1E-5	−5.2E-7
	(1.2E-5)	(2.3E-5)	(1.5E-5)	(1.4E-5)	(2.1E-6)
Population density	0.0622	−0.0259	0.1817	−0.0732	−0.0610***
	(0.1378)	(0.2564)	(0.1609)	(0.1539)	(0.0227)
Percent movers	0.0262***	0.0344***	0.0325***	0.0344***	0.0030***
	(0.0064)	(0.0119)	(0.0074)	(0.0071)	(0.0010)
Bodily injury claims	0.4587***	−0.5457**	−0.1949	−0.1678	−0.0133
	(0.1396)	(0.2598)	(0.1630)	(0.1559)	(0.0230)
Rate regulation	−0.1095**	0.2366***	−0.0296	−0.0456	−0.0059
	(0.0516)	(0.0960)	(0.0603)	(0.0576)	(0.0085)
Stringent regulation	−0.3080***	−0.8069***	−0.4097***	−0.4090***	−0.0675***
	(0.0747)	(0.1391)	(0.0873)	(0.0835)	(0.0123)
Adjusted R^2	0.6270	0.5388	0.5298	0.4695	0.6880

Notes: Numbers in parentheses are standard errors. The model also includes year and census division dummy variables not reported here.

*Significantly different from zero at the 10 percent confidence level, two-sided test.

**Significantly different from zero at the 5 percent confidence level, two-sided test.

***Significantly different from zero at the 1 percent confidence level, two-sided test.

market shares of the five groups of firms studied. The regulatory dummy variable is not significantly related to the market shares of national direct writers, national auto specialists, or the Big Four. For national firms as a group, the regulation dummy variable has the opposite sign from that expected. This latter finding may be due to the fact that most of the national insurers market through independent agents. Thus, we expect that their reduction in output in response to regulation will be lower than that of direct writers or other low-cost producers. This implies an increase in net market share in regulated states for these firms.

All five groups of firms exhibit significantly lower market shares in the most stringently regulated states, as expected. The estimated magnitude of market share reduction in these states is similar for national firms, national direct writers, and national auto specialists. These estimates range from 20 percent for national firms to 24 percent for national auto specialists, relative to their respective average market shares in unregulated states. These results are consistent with the argument that insurers with national distribution systems will respond to profit-reducing regulation by reducing output in the state.

These findings notwithstanding, there are two unexpected results in the table. First, the results for the Big Four are not entirely consistent with our theory. While these firms' aggregate market share is significantly reduced under stringent regulation, they exhibit the smallest percentage reduction in market share (4 percent) of all the categories of firms examined. In addition, direct writers are the only firms with a significantly lower market share in all regulated states. This latter finding is consistent with previous studies and may reflect other features of regulation that place direct writers at a disadvantage (e.g., Pauly et al. 1986; Gron 1995).

Alternatively, these results may reflect problems with interpreting the effects of regulation in a static analysis if insurance market structure influences a state's choice of regulatory regime. For example, if states with higher automobile insurance premiums are more likely to enact rate regulation, then the regulatory regime and insurance market structure are likely to be jointly determined.[13] To provide stronger evidence that rate regulation influences the structure of the insurance market rather than the reverse, the next section of the paper examines the impact of rate regulation on changes in insurance market structure over time.[14]

13. Cummins, Phillips, and Tennyson (1997) find that states with higher auto accident rates, higher auto claims severity, and higher proportions of young drivers are more likely to regulate auto insurance rates. However, they find no independent effect of a state's average unit price for auto insurance on the propensity to regulate.

14. Previous empirical work supports the view that both the choice of regulatory regime and the stringency of rate regulation in regulated states are affected by variables measuring the potential political influence of the insurance industry in the state (Cummins et al. 1997). We attempted two-stage least squares analysis of market shares, treating rate regulation and stringent rate regulation as endogenous. However, the results were extremely sensitive to model specification and yielded poor statistical fit overall. Nevertheless, these models usually produced results similar to those found in the first-differences regressions presented in the next section.

Table 4.5   **Private Passenger Automobile Insurance Market Structure Changes by State Regulatory Status, 1987–92 (percentage change)**

Statistic	Unregulated Mean	Unregulated S.D.	Regulated Mean	Regulated S.D.	Stringent Mean	Stringent S.D.
Total premiums	43.1	9.4	47.5	22.7	50.8	43.6
Number of firms						
Total	−3.9	6.6	−8.0**	6.9	−10.5	10.7
Direct writers	−10.6	8.8	−8.3	13.1	−3.9*	8.8
National firms	−1.4	5.0	−5.8**	7.8	−11.0*	10.9
National direct writers	1.5	9.5	0.3	11.6	2.7	12.3
National auto specialists	−1.1	6.6	−4.0	9.7	−8.0*	9.4
Big Four	1.7	11.0	−4.2*	10.8	−6.7	14.9
Market shares						
Direct writers	7.7	5.3	8.8	10.3	6.5	16.7
National firms	0.8	4.5	−0.4	8.8	−6.0	16.3
National direct writers	9.3	6.6	10.6	9.8	7.3	15.9
National auto specialists	13.3	8.0	16.5	11.0	11.0	11.8
Big Four	8.6	7.0	6.1	23.7	−4.1	49.3

*Significantly different from unregulated states at the 10 percent confidence level, one-sided test.
**Significantly different from unregulated states at the 5 percent confidence level, one-sided test.
***Significantly different from unregulated states at the 1 percent confidence level, one-sided test.

4.6   Regulation and Market Structure Change

Our theoretical argument is that persistently restricted rates of return should cause large, low-cost insurance sellers to reduce their market presence relative to that which would occur in an unregulated market environment. The strongest test of this argument rests on the dynamic implications of regulation for insurance market structure. If regulation affects the output choices of firms in the manner hypothesized, we should observe that the market presence of large, low-cost firms has declined, or has grown less rapidly, in regulated states than in unregulated states.

Table 4.5 presents summary statistics on the net percentage changes in our measures of market structure over the period 1987–92 for unregulated, regulated, and stringently regulated states. To preserve comparability of statistics across years, and to avoid picking up transitional effects of regulatory regime change, this analysis excludes several states that changed regulatory regimes during or just prior to our sample period. The table shows that the changes in market structure over the period are very similar for regulated and unregulated states overall. Except for a greater decline in the total number of firms and in the number of national firms and the Big Four in regulated states, there are no statistically significant differences in market trends across regulated and unregulated states. Both groups of states exhibit consolidation of the insurance market: the average number of firms declined over the period, but the aggregate market shares of direct writers and national sellers increased.

There are also few statistically significant differences in market trends between stringently regulated states and unregulated states. However, this is due to the large variance in the experiences of stringently regulated states. There are some noticeable differences in the patterns of change for these states. The percentage decline in the number of firms overall is much greater than that in unregulated states, as is the decline in the number of national firms, national auto specialists, and the Big Four. The mean percentage change in market shares for national firms and the Big Four are also different in stringently regulated states, where these two sets of firms actually lost market share over the time period.

The patterns of market structure change in stringently regulated states are not inconsistent with the hypothesis that national insurance sellers have decreased their market presence in response to regulation. However, the generally mixed findings and the lack of statistical significance make the relationship between stringent regulation and market structure difficult to ascertain. To control for other features of state insurance markets that might influence changes in market structure, table 4.6 presents a regression analysis of annual changes in market structure for the years 1988–92. Because annual changes in the number of firms and market shares are relatively small, the dependent variables used in the analysis are annual change in premium volume for each category of firm.[15] The premium data are transformed into logarithms to reduce heteroscedasticity. The control variables included in the regression model are those in the market share models estimated previously, along with the annual change in the (logarithm of) statewide automobile insurance premiums.

The regression results are generally consistent with the results obtained in the static analysis of market shares. There are no significant effects of regulation overall, but stringent rate regulation is negatively and significantly related to annual changes in premium volume for national direct writers, national auto specialists, and the Big Four. This confirms that our earlier findings are not simply an artifact of states' endogenous choices of regulatory regime.

Relative to overall state auto insurance premium growth, the table shows that the Big Four and national auto specialists have increased their market presence over time, once other factors are controlled for. The market shares of direct writers, national firms as a whole, and national direct writers are declining. The findings for stringently regulated states thus mean that the writings of the Big Four and national auto specialists have increased less over time, relative to the growth in state automobile insurance premiums, in states that stringently regulate automobile insurance rates. The writings of national firms and

---

15. The models were also run on market share changes, with similar results. The models for changes in the numbers of firms showed no significant effects, and the overall fit was very poor.

Table 4.6   First-Difference of Log Premiums, 1988–92 Data by State (ordinary least squares estimation)

Variable	Direct Writers	National Firms	National Direct Writers	National Auto Specialists	Big Four
Intercept	0.0046	0.0438**	0.0104	0.0052	-0.0639
	(0.0211)	(0.0197)	(0.0204)	(0.0348)	(0.0801)
First-difference of log state auto premiums	0.9649***	0.9535***	0.9473***	1.0755***	1.4393***
	(0.0440)	(0.0412)	(0.0426)	(0.0727)	(0.1671)
Per capita income	4.4E-7	-1.4E-6	4.3E-7	1.3E-7	-1.6E-7
	(1.1E-6)	(1.1E-6)	(1.1E-6)	(1.9E-6)	(4.3E-6)
Population density	-0.0367***	-0.0075	-0.0379***	-0.0284	-0.1253***
	(0.0128)	(0.0120)	(0.0124)	(0.0212)	(0.0488)
Percent movers	9.6E-5	0.0006	7.2E-5	-0.0005	0.0031
	(0.0006)	(0.0005)	(0.0006)	(0.0010)	(0.0022)
Bodily injury claims	0.0185	-0.0034	0.0311***	0.0357*	0.1218***
	(0.0127)	(0.0119)	(0.0123)	(0.0210)	(0.0483)
Rate regulation	0.0046	0.0033	0.0050	0.0066	0.0043
	(0.0049)	(0.0045)	(0.0047)	(0.0080)	(0.0184)
Stringent regulation	-0.0104	-0.0010*	-0.0120*	-0.0222**	-0.0852***
	(0.0069)	(0.0064)	(0.0067)	(0.0114)	(0.0261)
Adjusted R^2	0.6728	0.7326	0.6741	0.4843	0.2848

Notes: Numbers in parentheses are standard errors. The model also includes year and census division dummy variables not reported here.

*Significantly different from zero at the 10 percent confidence level, two-sided test.
**Significantly different from zero at the 5 percent confidence level, two-sided test.
***Significantly different from zero at the 1 percent confidence level, two-sided test.

national direct writers in stringently regulated states have decreased more rapidly, relative to the growth in state automobile insurance premiums, than in other states.

Unlike in previous regressions, the most significant effects are observed for the Big Four automobile insurance writers, and the largest percentage effects on premium volume changes are for the Big Four and national auto specialists. Rate regulation, even stringent rate regulation, is not significantly related to changes in premium volume for direct writers.[16] These findings are consistent with our theoretical predictions that low-cost firms with national distribution systems will have the greatest incentives to reduce output in regulated states.

4.7 Conclusion

This paper has argued that restrictive regulation of automobile insurance rates will distort the industrial structure of the market through its effects on insurers' entry and output decisions. The empirical evidence presented in the paper suggests that these effects are very weak in most regulated states. However, in those states that most stringently regulate automobile insurance rates, the empirical results are consistent with our theory. We find that stringent rate regulation lowers the number of firms selling in the market and lowers the numbers, market shares, and output growth of low-cost and national producers in the market. These results hold even after controlling for other factors that may influence the relative prevalence of these firms in the market, such as market size, density and growth, consumer income, and regional effects.

While normative assessments of regulatory policies lie beyond the scope of this analysis, our findings suggest that regulation could have adverse unintended effects on consumer welfare. If firms that achieve the largest size or that specialize most heavily in automobile insurance are the lowest cost producers of this insurance, then the decline in their relative market presence under regulation may raise the average price of insurance paid by consumers.

Much remains to be done to fully understand the effects of regulation on the industrial structure of auto insurance markets. One potentially fruitful approach would be to examine changes in market structure in the aftermath of changes in regulatory stringency. Further insights into the causes and consequences of market structure differences across regulated and unregulated states could also be garnered from analyzing entry, exit, and market share changes at the firm or group level. Use of this more detailed data would allow for controls related to the specific characteristics of each firm, rather than the average characteristics of generic categories of insurers. Given the great variation in size and specialization across firms identified in this paper, examining data at the

16. Interestingly, the contrast between these results and the results of the static market share analysis suggests that a larger direct writer market share reduces the probability that a state enacts rate regulation, while a larger market share for the Big Four increases the probability that a state enacts regulation.

firm level may be particularly important for assessing regulatory effects on insurance markets.

Data Appendix

This appendix provides the precise definition of and documents the data source used to obtain each explanatory variable used in the regression analysis. It also reports the mean and standard deviation of each variable over the sample period 1987–92 (see table 4A.1). All dependent variables used in the analysis were obtained from A. M. Best Company data tapes for Best's Executive Data Service. The other variable definitions and sources are as follows.

Number of registered autos: Number of privately owned motor vehicles registered in the state. Source: U.S. Department of Transportation, *Highway Statistics.*

Per capita income: Total income per capita in the state. Source: U.S. Department of Commerce, *Statistical Abstract of the United States.*

Population density: Resident population per square mile of land area in the state. Source: U.S. Department of Commerce, *Statistical Abstract of the United States.*

Table 4A.1   Summary Statistics for Regression Variables, 1987–92 Data by State

Variable	Mean	S.D.	N
Number of firms			
Total	99.52	24.89	300
Direct writers	27.25	6.52	300
National firms	660.52	8.07	300
National direct writers	18.57	2.39	300
National auto specialists	16.28	2.37	300
Big Four	3.54	0.525	300
Market share			
Direct writers	0.650	0.118	300
National firms	0.697	0.140	300
National direct writers	0.484	0.126	300
National auto specialists	0.442	0.114	300
Big Four	0.426	0.134	300
Other variables			
log (Registered autos)	14.36	1.03	300
Per capita income	16,993	3,107	300
Population density	0.162	0.229	300
Territory density	7.8E-6	3.8E-6	50
Percent movers 1980–90	11.36	4.68	50
Bodily injury claims	0.404	0.165	300
Rate regulation	0.493	0.501	300
Stringent regulation	0.100	0.301	300

Territory density: Number of rating territories employed by the major statistical rating agency in the state divided by the number of registered automobiles in the state. Source for rating territories: Insurance Research Council, *Trends in Auto Bodily Injury Claims* (Oak Brook, Ill., 1990).

Percent movers: Fraction of the state's resident population in 1990 who lived in a different state in 1980. Source: U.S. Department of Commerce, *Statistical Abstract of the United States.*

Bodily injury claims: Number of automobile bodily injury liability insurance claims incurred in the state divided by the number of automobile property damage liability insurance claims paid in the state. Source: National Association of Independent Insurers, FastTrack Monitoring System database.

References

Barrese, James, and Jack M. Nelson. 1992. Independent and exclusive agency insurers: A reexamination of the cost differential. *Journal of Risk and Insurance* 59:375–97.

Cummins, J. David, Richard Phillips, and Sharon Tennyson. 1997. Regulation, political influence and the price of automobile insurance. Working paper. Philadelphia: University of Pennsylvania.

Cummins, J. David, and Sharon Tennyson. 1992. Controlling automobile insurance costs. *Journal of Economic Perspectives* 6:95–115.

Cummins, J. David, and Jack VanDerhei. 1979. A note on the relative efficiency of property-liability insurance distribution systems. *Bell Journal of Economics* 10:709–19.

Frech, H., and J. Samprone. 1980. The welfare loss of excess nonprice competition: The case of property-liability insurance regulation. *Journal of Law and Economics* 23:429–40.

Grabowski, Henry, W. Kip Viscusi, and William N. Evans. 1989. The price and availability Trade-offs of automobile insurance regulation. *Journal of Risk and Insurance* 56:275–99.

Gron, Anne. 1995. Regulation and insurer competition: Did insurers use rate regulation to reduce competition? *Journal of Risk and Uncertainty* 11:87–111.

Harrington, Scott. 1984. The impact of rate regulation on prices and underwriting results in property-liability insurance: A survey. *Journal of Risk and Insurance* 51:577–623.

———. 1987. The impact of rate regulation on auto insurance loss ratios: Some new evidence. *Journal of Insurance Regulation* 5:182–202.

———. 1992. Rate suppression. *Journal of Risk and Insurance* 59:185–202.

Ippolito, Richard. 1979. The effects of price regulation in the automobile insurance industry. *Journal of Law and Economics* 22:55–89.

Joskow, Paul. 1973. Cartels, competition and regulation in the property-liability insurance industry. *Bell Journal of Economics and Management Science* 4:375–427.

Klein, Robert. 1989. Competition in private passenger automobile insurance: A report to the NAIC Personal Lines Committee. Internal report. Kansas City, Mo.: National Association of Insurance Commissioners.

Kramer, Orin. 1992. Rate suppression, rate-of-return regulation, and solvency. *Journal of Insurance Regulation* 10:523–63.

Marvel, Howard. 1982. Exclusive dealing. *Journal of Law and Economics* 25:1–25.

Mayers, David, and Clifford W. Smith. 1988. Ownership structure across lines of property-casualty insurance. *Journal of Law and Economics* 31:351–78.

Pauly, Mark, Howard Kunreuther, and Paul Kleindorfer. 1986. Regulation and quality competition in the U.S. insurance market. In *The economics of insurance regulation,* ed. Jorg Finsanger and Mark Pauly. New York: St. Martin's.

Regan, Laureen, and Sharon Tennyson. 1996. Agent discretion and the choice of insurance marketing system. *Journal of Law and Economics* 39:637–66.

Suponcic, Susan J. 1994. Regulatory stringency in automobile insurance. Working paper. Philadelphia: University of Pennsylvania.

Suponcic, Susan J., and Sharon Tennyson. 1995. Rate regulation and the industrial organization of automobile insurance. NBER Working Paper. Cambridge, Mass.: National Bureau of Economic Research.

Tennyson, Sharon. 1996. The impact of rate regulation on state automobile insurance markets. *Journal of Insurance Regulation* 15:502–23.

5   The Costs of Insurance Company Failures

James G. Bohn and Brian J. Hall

5.1   Introduction

In the event of a property-casualty (P&C) insurance company failure, the losses suffered by the insured are protected by state guarantee funds (or solvency funds). Guarantee funds pay the claims of policyholders of the failed firm, making up any shortfall between the failed firm's assets and the cost of these claims by levying assessments on the premiums collected by solvent insurers in that state. In recent years state guarantee funds have come under increasing pressure as more P&C insurance companies failed. As shown in figure 5.1, both the number of insolvencies and the costs to state guarantee funds have increased sharply since the mid-1980s. In 1993, the net costs to state guarantee funds was a record high of $800 million.

Some have argued that the dramatic increase in the number of insolvencies in the mid-1980s was caused by price cutting by liability insurers during the early 1980s (U.S. Congress 1990). In addition, some observers have noted a marked increase in the expected value and variance of claims cost distributions at this time (Clarke et al. 1988). Regardless of the reason for the wave of insolvencies, P&C insurance companies and policymakers have been concerned about the rising level of the assessments and the potential for much higher assessments should there be an even larger wave of insolvencies.

These facts raise a series of important issues about the solvency fund system, many of which have not been addressed in the academic literature. First, to what extent does the solvency fund system create perverse incentives? Because

James G. Bohn is an economist at the Board of Governors of the Federal Reserve System. Brian J. Hall is associate professor of business administration at the Harvard Business School and a faculty research fellow of the National Bureau of Economic Research.

The authors thank John Campbell, Richard Caves, Martin Feldstein, Paul Gulko, Louis Kaplow, Deborah Lucas, and Sean Mooney for their helpful comments and the National Conference of Insurance Guarantee Funds for providing much of the data used in this paper.

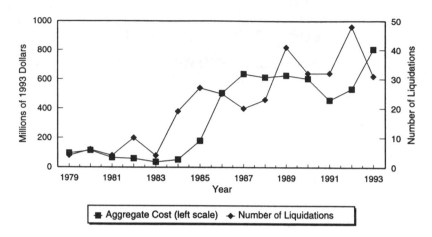

Fig. 5.1 Guarantee fund activity
Sources: NCIGF and A. M. Best Company (various years).

healthy firms are required to make (indirect) payments to the claimants of insolvent firms, the P&C solvency fund system is like a tax and social insurance
system. The mandatory nature of the assessments means that they can be viewed
as a tax on healthy firms. The assessments (taxes), which are not risk rated, are
the price that companies are forced to pay in order to purchase second-level insurance against the possibility of failure and the inability to pay claims.

In addition to any distortions created by mandatory assessments/taxes, this
social insurance scheme may create substantial moral hazard problems. This is
particularly true for insurance companies that are insolvent or near insolvent.
Such companies have the same incentive problems ("heads I win, tails some-
body else loses") that were faced by the savings and loans (S&Ls). Cash-poor
and near-bankrupt P&C companies have the incentive to undercut competitors'
prices, write more (potentially risky) policies, and increase cash flow, just as
S&Ls had the incentive to offer attractive deposit rates in order to increase
deposits and make risky loans. Note that this moral hazard problem would be
mitigated or even eliminated if P&C companies paid assessments that were
related to their riskiness. The difficulty, of course, is determining how to measure their riskiness.

A second important issue concerns the exposure of the solvency fund system. That is, how "exposed" are state guarantee funds to various shocks (e.g.,
natural disasters) that cause insolvencies? What scenarios would cause solvency fund assessments to reach their maximum level (typically 1 or 2 percent
of premiums per year)? How exposed is the system to a very large shock or set
of shocks that would create an S&L-like problem in the P&C insurance industry?

The first step toward answering any of these questions is to understand the
magnitude, nature, and determinants of the costs of resolving P&C insolvenc-

ies. The adequacy of guarantee funds depends on both the number of insolvencies and the net costs to the fund per insolvency. For the most part, previous studies of insolvencies in the P&C industry have involved estimating hazard models to predict the number or likelihood of insolvencies. In contrast, we focus on the cost dimension of P&C company insolvencies.

We have several major goals in this study. First, we estimate the total net costs of resolving insurance company insolvencies. While a number of studies have estimated insolvency costs for the banking industry, there have been no studies that have produced such an estimate for insurance companies. Second, since resolution of a given insolvency typically takes many years, we estimate the typical time path of the guarantee payments (and net costs) and analyze how these time paths differ with the composition of the firm's book of business. Third, we examine the determinants of the size of losses associated with insurance company insolvencies.

The results of our analysis should be of practical importance to regulators who seek to design prudent safeguards against insurance company failures. A better understanding of the magnitude and determinants of the costs of resolving insurance company failures will allow more informed regulation of insurer solvency. Research in this area is particularly necessary in light of the current interest in restructuring the guarantee fund system.[1]

This paper proceeds as follows. Section 5.2 discusses the organization and administration of the guarantee fund system. In section 5.3 we describe the data and produce estimates of the time path of resolution costs. In section 5.4 we use these time paths to produce estimates of the costs to the solvency funds of an "average" insolvency. In section 5.5 we regress insolvency costs on various firm characteristics to examine the determinants of insolvency costs. We discuss potential reasons for our finding that insolvency costs are quite high in section 5.6. Section 5.7 concludes.

5.2   The Guarantee Fund System: Background

In this section, we provide background information on the organization and administration of the guarantee fund system.[2] The current guarantee fund system was a response to a federal initiative in the late 1960s to establish a guarantee system for insurance that would function like the FDIC. As a result of the

---

1. There have been a number of recent proposals to reform the guarantee system. Hiestand (1986) discusses in depth problems that arise due to administration of solvency funds at the state level. In 1992, the NAIC's Focus Group issued a report calling for a uniform national receivership system. Alternative proposals include Hall and Hall's (1993) proposal to develop an insurer-run guarantee system and Schacht and Gallanis's (1993) modification of the current system to facilitate greater interstate cooperation. There is also ongoing interest in designing a system of risk-based assessments on premiums (see Cummins 1988). Risk-based capital guidelines have recently been adopted in some states.

2. Much of the discussion in the section is drawn from Epton and Bixby (1976), Duncan (1987), and NCIGF (1993a).

threat of federal intrusion into an industry theretofore regulated by the states, the National Association of Insurance Commissioners (NAIC) proposed model legislation for the establishment of guarantee funds at the state level. By 1971, 35 states had adopted guarantee fund provisions based on the NAIC's model act, and by 1982, every state had adopted some form of guarantee fund legislation. In most cases, the organization of the fund closely resembles that outlined in the model act.

The model act calls for the formation of a not-for-profit association consisting of all companies licensed to write insurance within a state in lines covered by the guarantee fund. Membership in the association is compulsory. The association is an entity distinct from the state insurance department. It is governed by a board composed of representatives of member firms and the state insurance commissioner's office. When a company becomes insolvent, the guarantee fund services and pays the claims of policyholders of the failed insurer in the same way that payments would be provided by a solvent insurance company. Each state's guarantee fund pays only for the claims of the insured residing in that state. Thus, the failure of a multistate insurer triggers action on the part of several guarantee associations.

Guarantee funds typically pay the full amount of an insured's claims up to a certain cap, except for a small deductible.[3] Any shortfall between the assets of the failed insurer and the obligations of the fund is covered by levying assessments against healthy firms doing business in the same state as the insolvent firm. Assessments of member firms are directly proportional to their shares of direct premiums written within a state in lines covered by the fund.[4] Thus assessments are not based on any measure of risk. Assessments are also made to cover the administrative, legal, and other expenses associated with the operation of the state guarantee funds. Thus the total costs of resolving insolvencies include the administrative costs of managing the guarantee funds.

In 49 states, funds operate on a postassessment basis. The funds maintain no reserves and only assess member insurers after an insolvency occurs.[5] Assessments are typically capped at 2 percent of premiums written, although some states maintain lower caps. All states have some provision that enables companies to partially offset amounts assessed by the fund. In most states, insurers are allowed to include the cost of assessments as a factor in determining premiums. Some states allow insurers to recover a portion of their assess-

3. The caps on the funds' liability per claim are typically $300,000 to $500,000. Some states maintain caps as low as $100,000. As a practical consideration, the upper limits are high enough that they are rarely binding in the claims administration process. Deductibles range from nothing to $200; however, most funds have a deductible of $100.

4. Guarantee funds are typically organized into separate accounts covering broad lines of insurance. The most common form of organization has three separate accounts—workers' compensation, automobile, and "all other" types of insurance. However, different states operate as few as one or as many as six accounts.

5. The exception is New York State, which adopted guarantee fund legislation in 1947. Unlike other funds, New York's operates on a preassessment basis. The state maintains a fund of $150 to $200 million for the resolution of insurance failures. Firms writing insurance in the state are assessed whenever the fund balance falls below the lower bound.

ments with credits against their premium tax liability, which shifts a portion of the costs of the insolvency to the state.

Guarantee funds are not responsible for the detection or prevention of insurer insolvencies. The typical sequence of events in an insurance insolvency begins with the filing of a petition in state court by the insurance commissioner in the company's state of domicile. If the court finds the insurer to be insolvent, insurance regulators take over the management of the firm. In most cases, regulators begin to liquidate the assets of the failed insurer and turn the file containing the claims over to the managers of the guarantee fund. The guarantee fund pays the claims of the insureds from the assessments levied on healthy insurers and the proceeds of the sale of assets of the failed insurer. Since policyholders cannot be paid by the guarantee fund before an order of liquidation has been approved by the court, regulators typically file a petition to liquidate the firm soon after the company has been found to be insolvent. Action by the guarantee fund is terminated once all claims against the estate of the failed insurer have been paid. This may take over a decade if the failed firm was involved in liability or compensation insurance.[6]

5.3   The Time Path of Resolution Costs

In the next section, we use data obtained from the National Conference of Insurance Guarantee Funds (NCIGF) to estimate the net costs to guarantee funds per insolvency. However, because the amount of time it takes to resolve an insolvency is typically long, we first estimate the typical time paths of these costs and analyze how these time paths differ with the composition of the failed insurer's business. Although our time-path estimates may be of independent interest to regulators, our main reason for analyzing the time paths is because it is a necessary first step (as will be explained later) to estimating total costs per insolvency.

Guarantee payments are the sum of all expenditures by the guarantee fund, including legal costs, operating expenses, and paid claims to those who were insured by the insolvent company. It should be emphasized that these payments are costs to the fund over and above the proceeds from the liquidation of assets of the insolvent company. On occasion, the fund receives cash inflows, called recoveries, from the (typically late) liquidation of assets of the failed company. Net costs to the fund are the difference between fund payments and recoveries.

5.3.1   Data Description

Our initial list of insolvencies was obtained from the 1992 and 1993 editions of the NCIGF's *Assessment and Financial Information Report* (1992, 1993b), which provides annual and cumulative payments, recoveries, and net cost data

---

6. Alternatively, the regulator may take actions to restore the financial health of the insolvent insurer. These rehabilitations are quite rare. Failures have been successfully resolved by rehabilitation in about a dozen cases (NCIGF 1993b).

for all insolvencies that necessitated guarantee fund payments. The NCIGF's 1993 report provided this data for 356 firms. Action on the part of guarantee funds is triggered by an order to liquidate the failed insurer. We searched *Best's Insurance Reports* (A. M. Best Company, various years), *Best's Solvency Study* (A. M. Best Company 1991), and documents provided by the NCIGF to determine the liquidation date and the date that each insurer became insolvent. We were able to determine the date of liquidation of 328 (92 percent) of these firms. The 28 firms for which liquidation dates were unavailable were very small. Collectively, they accounted for less than 1 percent of total fund payments. Data on annual fund payments and net costs (payments minus recoveries) for each firm were obtained from the 1992 and 1993 issues of the NCIGF's annual report. Due to differences in reporting practices, comparable annual data at the firm level were not available prior to 1992.

Financial data for each firm were obtained from the NAIC's Annual Statement Database. Financial data on the firm were drawn from the annual statement filed by the firm in the year before the firm became insolvent. We omit firms that were inactive or in runoff by excluding firms with direct premium writings less than or equal to zero. A firm was also excluded from our sample if we could not determine the year in which the firm became insolvent. Because machine-readable financial statement data are not available prior to 1984, we confined our analysis to the set of firms that were liquidated in the period between 1986 and 1993. Of the 214 liquidations involving fund activity in that period, we were able to obtain complete financial information on 141 firms (66 percent of the total). Firms included in the sample accounted for 80 percent of fund payments. We made an adjustment for inflation using the CPI so that all financial statement information and fund activity data are in real 1993 dollars. Since New York is the lone preassessment solvency fund and is not included in the NCIGF data, we do not include New York in our sample. For firms that operate in multiple states that include New York, we scaled the size (measured by assets) of these firms down by the percentage of premiums written in New York.[7] Our results are not sensitive to our scaling procedure.

5.3.2   The Time Path of Payments and Costs

Because of typically long resolution times, the majority of P&C insolvencies were not fully resolved as of 1993. Our approach, therefore, is to estimate "typical" paths of costs and then use these paths, along with the data that we do have on to-date cumulative costs, to determine the total costs for each (typically unresolved) insolvency. We used the annual payment and cost data from 1992 and 1993 so that each insolvency produced two observations in our data set. Time period $t = 1$ is defined as the year the liquidation order was issued.

---

7. There was one firm that operated entirely within New York State in the year prior to insolvency. However, it had written a small amount of business outside of New York in previous years, and thus its failure prompted a small amount of fund payments. We dropped this firm from our sample. The percentage of premiums written in New York State averaged only 2 percent in the remaining companies.

For example, if a firm was liquidated in 1989, the 1993 payments and net costs would form an observation in the $t = 5$ cohort while the 1992 results would be an observation in the $t = 4$ cohort. We begin with the year of liquidation because guarantee funds typically do not make payments to claimants until an order of liquidation has been obtained. We estimated the following equation, which we will refer to as specification 1:

$$\text{Payments}_{it} = \beta_t * \text{Premiums}_{it_0} + \varepsilon_{it},$$

for each of the eight cohorts ($t = 1, \ldots, 8$). Payments$_{it}$ is payments by the guarantee funds to policyholders of firm i in year t, and Premiums$_{it_0}$ is direct premiums written by firm i in the year prior to insolvency, t_0. Thus, eight separate regressions were run.

We start with payments as the regressor rather than net costs because recoveries occur in large lump sums and net costs may therefore be more prone to outliers.[8] As will be shown later, however, the paths using payments and net costs are qualitatively similar (and net costs are always lower since recoveries are subtracted), although as expected the estimated paths of net costs are slightly less smooth.

In table 5.1, we report the results of this regression. The specification has a nice interpretation. Each coefficient indicates the amount of payments in year t that is associated with another dollar of premiums written in the year prior to insolvency (t_0). We suppress the constant terms since they were typically insignificant and because excluding them allows the coefficients to be more easily interpreted. We estimate the coefficients to year 8 only because of the data limitations suggested earlier.

Note that all of the coefficients are highly significant. They imply that every dollar in total premiums written in the year previous to insolvency is associated with payments to the guarantee funds of about 25 cents in year 1 (the year of liquidation), 27 cents in year 2, 14 cents in year 3, and so on, to only 4 cents in year 8. The typical pattern of payments increases slightly between year 1 and year 2 and then falls, fairly smoothly, until it drops to a very small amount in year 8. It also seems clear that the vast majority of payments occur in the first two or three years following a liquidation.

Note also that the coefficients add to about 0.89, which implies that each dollar of premiums written is associated with, on average, 89 cents of payments made by the state guarantee funds in the first eight years alone.[9] We discuss *total* payments, and net costs, in subsection 5.3.3.

---

8. We reestimated all of the models in this section after trimming outliers from the data set. Our criterion for determining whether an observation was abnormally influential was based on the ratio of the determinant of the covariance matrix in the full sample to the determinant of the covariance matrix when an observation was deleted from the data set. This method and the suggested critical values are discussed in Besley, Kuh, and Welsch (1980). The deletion of abnormally influential observations did not substantively alter the results.

9. This number is consistent with the very high estimates of ratios of costs to assets that we report in the next section.

Table 5.1   **Time Path of Guarantee Fund Payments**

Year	Premiums	Adjusted R^2	N
1	.2524	.0733	51
	(.1128)		
2	.2724	.3445	51
	(.0379)		
3	.1363	.9157	30
	(.0104)		
4	.0585	.6111	34
	(.0178)		
5	.0164	.5106	34
	(.0043)		
6	.0606	.8111	23
	(.0085)		
7	.0605	.8231	23
	(.0073)		
8	.0365	.6195	23
	(.0067)		
Sum of coefficients			
for years 1–8	.8936		
Year 9 and after	.1100		
Total costs	1.0036		

Notes: Numbers in parentheses are heteroscedasticity-consistent standard errors. $\text{Payments}_{it} = \beta_{t}*$ $\text{Premiums}_{it_0} + \varepsilon_{it}$, where i = firm index ($i = 1, \ldots, n$), t = year relative to liquidation date ($t = 1, \ldots, 8$), and t_0 = year prior to insolvency. Models were estimated separately for each t. Liquidation proceedings commence in year $t = 1$.

As a check on the implied time-path pattern, we regressed payments in 1993 on payments in 1992 for each liquidation (specification 2). Since firms were liquidated in different years, this enables us to determine the relationship between costs in year t and costs in year $t - 1$ for various years since liquidation. The results are shown in table 5.2. They point to the same basic pattern. Costs are about 1.25 times higher in year 2 than in year 1 but then decline relative to the previous year in each year thereafter.

Both specifications imply a particular pattern of payments over time. The only tricky issue is what to assume about the payments in the years beyond year 8. Fortunately, the results from the first specification (payments regressed on premiums) suggest that the payments in year 8 are relatively small. Barring some unusual pattern beyond year 8, it seems likely that the out-year payments are not large. We produce "terminal value costs," which we define as the sum of total costs beyond year 8, by averaging the "rate of decline" (which is implied in the first specification and explicitly estimated in the second specification) for years 2 through 8.[10] We then assume that this rate of decline is constant

10. The rates of change between year 1 and year 2 are unlikely to tell us much about the rate of decline in the years after year 8.

Table 5.2   **Alternative Estimate of the Time Path of Guarantee Fund Payments**

Year	Payments$_{92}$	Adjusted R^2	N
1	–	–	–
2	1.2454	.7411	43
	(.3457)		
3	.5743	.9679	26
	(.0214)		
4	.4887	.8911	24
	(.0674)		
5	.8742	.9385	29
	(.0911)		
6	.6259	.8777	18
	(.1192)		
7	.7920	.9552	14
	(.0891)		
8	.7282	.9032	23
	(.0552)		

Notes: Numbers in parentheses are heteroscedasticity-consistent standard errors. Payments$_{93}$ = $\beta_t *$ Payments$_{92}$ + ε_{it}, where i = firm index ($i = 1, \ldots, n$) and t = year relative to liquidation date ($t = 1, \ldots, 8$). Models were estimated separately for each t. Liquidation proceedings commence in year $t = 1$.

for all years beyond year 8 and assume that payments increase forever at this declining rate. It turns out that for both specifications 1 and 2, the terminal value costs are small—11 and 5 percent of total payments, respectively.[11]

Table 5.3 and figure 5.2 show the implicit paths of these payments over time. For each model, and for each year, the percentages of cumulative payments are reported (i.e., the amount of payments made in that year as a fraction of implied total payments to resolve the insolvency). What is striking about the results is the similarity between the paths. In both cases, about one-quarter of total payments is made in year 1, slightly more than half by year 2, about two thirds by year 3, and three-quarters by year 4.

We now turn to estimating the time path of costs. Following our first specification for payments, we estimated

$$\text{Net costs}_{it} = \beta_t * \text{Premiums}_{it_0} + \varepsilon_{it},$$

11. Terminal values were calculated under the assumption that payments and net costs would continue to decrease at the same rate experienced in years 2 through 8. In the first specification we calculated the rate of decrease, r, and terminal value as:

$$r = (\beta_{Year8}/\beta_{Year2})^{1/6}, \qquad \text{Terminal value} = \beta_{Year8} * r/(1 - r).$$

Since our estimate of β_{Year8} is somewhat imprecise, we calculate the rate of decline using the average of β_{Year7}, β_{Year8}, and β_{Year9}. In the second specification, the rate of decrease was the average of β_{Year3} through β_{Year8}. The terminal value was calculated the same way as in specification 1.

Table 5.3   Comparison of Time Paths of Guarantee Fund Payments Implied by
Tables 5.1 and 5.2

Year	Cumulative Percentage[a]	
	From Total Premiums Regression (Specification 1)	From Regression on Previous Payments (Specification 2)
1	25.2	23.3
2	52.3	52.2
3	65.9	68.8
4	71.7	77.0
5	73.3	84.1
6	79.4	88.5
7	85.4	92.0
8	89.0	94.6

[a]Payments made by the end of year n as a percentage of implied total payments made to resolve the insolvency.

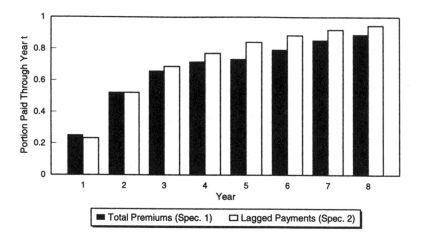

Fig. 5.2   Implied path of cumulative payments

for each of the eight cohorts ($t = 1, \ldots , 8$). The results of these eight regressions are shown in table 5.4. The results show the same basic pattern as the payments regression. The coefficient on total premiums is slightly larger in year 2 than year 1 and then declines thereafter. As suggested earlier, the declining pattern is less smooth because in some cases large lump-sum recoveries from the estate of the failed insurer may be realized late in the liquidation process. This probably accounts for the negative, but insignificant, coefficient in year 6. For the most part, the other coefficients are statistically significant and sensible; the coefficients on net costs are almost uniformly slightly smaller than the coefficients on payments, which makes sense since recoveries are always positive and net costs equal payments minus recoveries. Note also that

Table 5.4   **Time Path of Net Resolution Costs**

Year	Premiums	Adjusted R^2	N
1	.2496	.0732	51
	(.1124)		
2	.2608	.3524	51
	(.0365)		
3	.1269	.8589	30
	(.0125)		
4	.0356	.3410	34
	(.0203)		
5	.0115	.4186	34
	(.0029)		
6	−.0118	−.0178	22
	(.0365)		
7	.0506	.7563	23
	(.0059)		
8	.0252	.3233	23
	(.0124)		
Sum of coefficients			
for years 1–8	.7487		
Year 9 and after	.0750		
Total net costs	.8234		

Notes. Numbers in parentheses are heteroscedasticity-consistent standard errors. Net cost$_{it}$ = β_t* Premiums$_{it_0}$ + ε_{it}, where i = firm index (l = 1,..., n), t = year relative to liquidation date (t = 1,..., 8), and t_0 = year prior to insolvency. Models were estimated separately for each t. Liquidation proceedings commence in year t = 1.

the sum of the coefficients for the eight years is equal to 0.75, which implies that each dollar of premiums written in the year before insolvency is associated with costs to the guarantee fund of 75 cents in the first eight years. The equivalent figure for payments was 89 cents.

Using the same procedure as before, we construct the time path for net costs. This time path is shown in table 5.5 and figure 5.3, with the payment path also shown for comparison. The time paths of payments and net costs are similar, the only difference being that an even larger fraction of total costs occurs in the first few years. For example, by the end of year 4, about 82 percent of net costs are paid compared to about 72 percent for total payments. The faster pattern for net costs reflects the fact that recoveries tend to come later than payments. The clear pattern that emerges from the data is that for both payments and net costs, the vast majority of costs to solvency funds occur during the first few years following liquidation.

5.3.3   The Time Path of Costs: Long-Tail versus Short-Tail Lines

In this section, we estimate the time paths for payments and net costs and focus on how these costs vary with the types of lines that firms write. For example, we expect that firms that write significant amounts of premiums in

Table 5.5   **Comparison of Time Paths of Guarantee Fund Net Resolution Costs and Payments**

	Cumulative Percentage[a]	
Year	Net Costs	Payments
1	30.3	25.2
2	62.0	52.3
3	77.4	65.9
4	81.7	71.7
5	83.1	73.3
6	81.7	79.4
7	87.8	85.4
8	90.9	89.0

[a]Costs/payments incurred/made by the end of year n as a percentage of implied total costs/payments to resolve the insolvency.

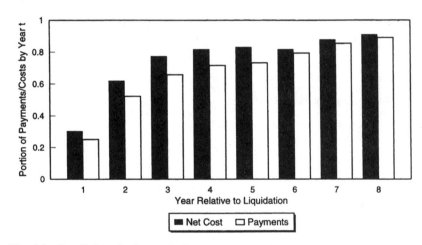

Fig. 5.3   Implied path of cumulative payments and net cost: regression of annual payments or costs on total premiums

long-tail lines such as liability coverage and workers' compensation will take longer to resolve than firms that write premiums predominantly in short-tail lines.

We run regressions of the type in specification 1 above, the only difference being that we divide premiums into two categories—long-tail lines and all "other." The lines that are placed into the long category are workers' compensation, medical malpractice, products liability, and other liability. All other lines are put into the "other" category.[12] Long-tail lines accounted for 36 percent of total premiums written by firms in our sample. Therefore, we estimate

12. We thank Sean Mooney for helpful discussion on the relative lengths of lines.

Table 5.6A   **Time Path of Guarantee Fund Payments as a Function of Failed Firm Business Mix**

Year	Long Tail	All Other	Adjusted R^2	N
1	.3675	.2219	.0557	51
	(.5969)	(.1199)		
2	.2501	.3103	.3344	51
	(.0106)	(.1215)		
3	.1569	.0987	.9457	30
	(.0083)	(.0102)		
4	.0834	.0536	.6133	35
	(.0315)	(.0223)		
5	.0182	.0161	.4959	35
	(.0069)	(.0050)		
6	.0955	.0168	.8925	23
	(.0072)	(.0103)		
7	.0736	.0423	.8189	23
	(.0117)	(.0268)		
8	.1192	.0044	.7764	23
	(.0426)	(.0112)		
Sum of coefficients for years 1–8	1.1644	.7641		

Notes: Numbers in parentheses are heteroscedasticity-consistent standard errors. $Payments_{it} = \alpha_t *$ $Long_{it_0} + \beta_t * Other_{it_0} + \varepsilon_{it}$, where i = firm index ($i = 1, \ldots, n$), t = year relative to liquidation date ($t = 1, \ldots, 8$), and t_0 = year prior to insolvency. Models were estimated separately for each t. Liquidation proceedings commence in year $t = 1$.

$$Payments_{it} = \alpha_t * Other_{it_0} + \beta_t * Long_{it_0} + \varepsilon_{it},$$

for each of the eight cohorts.

The results are shown in table 5.6A. The coefficients on long-tail premiums are generally larger and decrease at a slower rate. The slower decline in the coefficients of long-tail lines is exactly what was expected. Firms that write premiums in long-tail lines take longer to resolve than firms that write premiums predominantly in short-tail lines. In terms of differences in total payments, the sum of the coefficients is also larger for the long-tail lines. If we use the same methodology as before to calculate the terminal value payments (the implied sum of payments in year 9 and after), the total payments in long-tail lines are approximately twice as large as those in other lines, as indicated by the ratio of 1.55 to 0.80 (the last entries of the first two columns) in table 5.6B.

One possible reason why long-tail lines might be associated with higher total costs is that longer tail lines have higher costs in the future that have not been discounted. The data do not support this notion. In order to check for this possibility, we discounted the future payments with a real interest rate of 3 percent.[13] The results are shown in the third and fourth columns of table 5.6B.

---

13. We chose this rate because it is slightly higher than the average real rate of 2.5 percent on Treasury bills during the past 10 years, the time period of our data.

Table 5.6B   **Expected Guarantee Fund Payments per Dollar of Direct Premiums Written**

	Total Payments in 1993 Dollars		Present Discounted Value of Payments Assuming a 3.00% Real Interest Rate	
Years	Long-Tail Lines	All Other	Long-Tail Lines	All Other
Years 1–8	1.1644	0.7641	1.0900	0.7330
Year 9 and after	0.3896	0.0369	0.2710	0.0282
Total	1.5440	0.8010	1.3610	0.7613

Table 5.7A   **Time Path of Guarantee Fund Net Resolution Costs as a Function of Failed Firm Business Mix**

Year	Long Tail	All Other	Adjusted R^2	N
1	.3746	.2165	.0558	51
	(.5963)	(.1192)		
2	.2400	.2961	.3424	51
	(.0090)	(.1163)		
3	.1486	.0871	.8940	30
	(.0078)	(.0087)		
4	.0760	.0277	.3797	34
	(.0258)	(.0245)		
5	.0035	.0126	.4213	34
	(.0033)	(.0034)		
6	.0032	−.0305	−.0532	22
	(.0671)	(.0254)		
7	.0738	.0123	.7693	23
	(.0127)	(.0289)		
8	.1379	−.0186	.6688	23
	(.0389)	(.0174)		
Sum of coefficients for years 1–8	1.0576	.6032		

Notes: Numbers in parentheses are heteroscedasticity-consistent standard errors. Net $\text{cost}_{it} = \alpha_t *$ $\text{Other}_{it_0} + \beta_t * \text{Long}_{it_0} + \varepsilon_{it}$, where i = firm index ($i = 1, \ldots, n$), t = year relative to liquidation date ($t = 1, \ldots, 8$), and t_0 = year prior to insolvency. Models were estimated separately for each t. Liquidation proceedings commence in year $t = 1$.

Note that the discounted coefficients imply that total payments per dollar of premiums in long-tail lines (1.36) are still almost twice as high as total payments associated with other lines (0.76).

The same results with net costs substituted for payments are reported in tables 5.7A and 5.7B. The results are quite similar and consistent with expectations. Total costs associated with long-tail lines are again larger than those associated with short-tail lines; in fact, total net costs per dollar of premiums

Table 5.7B   **Expected Resolution Costs per Dollar of Direct Premiums Written**

	Total Payments in 1993 Dollars		Present Discounted Value of Payments Assuming a 3.00% Real Interest Rate	
Years	Long-Tail Lines	All Other	Long-Tail Lines	All Other
Years 1–8	1.0576	0.6032	0.9970	0.5915
Year 9 and after	0.5028	0	0.3426	0
Total	1.5604	0.6032	1.3396	0.5915

Table 5.8   **Percentage of Total Guarantee Fund Payments Made through the End of Year** *t*

	Cumulative Percentage[a]	
Year	Long-Tail Lines	All Other Lines
1	23.68	27.70
2	39.79	66.44
3	49.90	78.76
4	55.28	85.46
5	56.46	87.47
6	62.61	89.56
7	67.22	94.84
8	74.90	95.39

[a]Payments made by the end of year *n* as a percentage of implied total payments to resolve the insolvency.

in long-tail lines are more than twice as large as net costs in short-tail lines, both when costs are in 1993 dollars and when costs are discounted by the real interest rate. Again, the coefficients imply a more gradually declining path for long-tail lines than for other lines. Note that there are two negative coefficients (in years 6 and 8) in the other premium category. Though these coefficients are not statistically significant, it is possible for them to be negative since recoveries may exceed costs on average in out years.

The implied time patterns for payments associated with short- and long-tail lines are shown in table 5.8 and figure 5.4, and the analogous patterns for net costs are shown in table 5.9 and figure 5.5. Again, the striking feature about the estimated time paths is the large divergence between the time path in long-tail lines and that in all other lines. For long-tail lines, less than two-thirds of payments are made within the first six years. The similar figure for other lines is about 90 percent. For net costs, the difference in time patterns is even more striking. Only 54 percent of net costs in long-tail lines occur in the first six years. The analogous figure is 101 percent in all other lines. Again, it is possible for net costs to be negative on average (which produces a cumulative

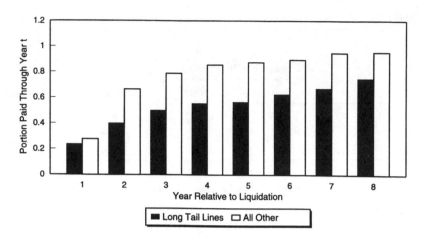

Fig. 5.4   Implied path of cumulative payments: regression of annual payments on premiums in long-tail and other lines

Table 5.9   Percentage of Total Net Resolution Costs Incurred through the End
                   of Year t

	Cumulative Percentage[a]	
Year	Long-Tail Lines	All Other Lines
1	24.01	35.89
2	39.39	84.98
3	48.91	99.42
4	53.78	104.01
5	54.00	106.10
6	54.21	101.04
7	58.94	103.08
8	67.78	100.00

[a]Costs incurred by the end of year n as a percentage of implied total costs of resolving the insolvency.

percentage that can exceed 100 percent) if recoveries exceed payments on average during a particular out year. The cumulative percentages should be viewed as rough averages since they are produced by regression coefficients, a few of which are imprecisely estimated. Nevertheless, we are comforted by the fact that the implied patterns of net costs in short- and long-tail lines are sensible and consistent with the patterns of payments. The important and robust result is that the costs associated with long-tail lines have a more slowly declining time path and represent higher total costs per dollar of premium.

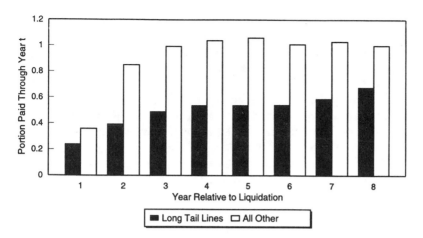

Fig. 5.5   Implied path of cumulative resolution costs: regression of annual net cost on premiums in long-tail and other lines

5.4   Estimates of Costs per Insolvency

We now use our estimates of the time paths of net costs to produce estimates of the total costs for each insolvency. We start with the cumulative net costs for each insolvency, which we have obtained from the NCIGF. The estimated coefficients from the relevant time-path regressions (from table 5.7A) along with each firm's specific percentages in each of the two premium categories (long and other) imply a unique time path for each insolvency. We use this time path, along with the number of years since liquidation, to estimate the percentage of net costs that have already been incurred for a firm with a certain set of characteristics.[14] We then combine this information with the cumulative payments to create a projection of total net costs. Note that to keep multiplicative factors small, we compute projected net costs only for firms that were liquidated at least two full years prior to the last year of our data, 1993.[15] That is, we wanted to limit the amount of "projection error" by ensuring that add-on net costs for the companies are small relative to already incurred net costs. The companies in this trimmed sample of 87 firms had mean assets of $57 million, mean premiums of $46 million, and mean surplus (i.e., capital) of $6.5 million.

A hypothetical example should help clarify our procedure for estimating net payments and costs. Assume that cumulative payments at the end of 1993 for a firm that was liquidated five years ago is $100. We use the regression coeffi-

---

14. As mentioned earlier, all costs and payments are in 1993 dollars.

15. We identified 137 liquidations involving guarantee fund action occurring between 1986 and 1991. Financial information in the year prior to insolvency was available on the NAIC Annual Statement Database for 87 of these firms. These 87 firms represented 76 percent of the net costs incurred to date for firms liquidated between 1986 and 1991.

cients in table 5.7A and the fact that the firm's premium mix was 30 percent long and 70 percent other to determine that after five years, cumulative payments are typically 92 percent of the total for a firm of this type. This implies a multiplicative factor of 1.09 (1 divided by .92), which is used to project total net costs of $109 for this firm.

As a check on our results, we also used a second procedure for producing payment and cost projections from cumulative costs. With this "additive" procedure, we sum the regression coefficients by line for the remaining years and multiply each sum by the dollar amount of premiums written prior to insolvency. This adjustment factor, used to account for future costs to the fund, is added to 1993 cumulative payments or net costs.[16] This second, additive procedure produced estimated net costs that are very similar to those from the multiplicative procedure.[17]

In table 5.10, we report some summary statistics of net costs relative to assets.[18] The first row shows, for all firms in our sample, the mean ratio of net costs to assets, with both the multiplicative and the additive scaling methods. These means indicate that the total cost of resolving firms is approximately 100 percent of the value of their assets (measured in the year before they fail), a remarkably large number. This implies that the true value of companies' liabilities are twice the value of their assets when they fail. In a later section, we show that the high ratio of insolvency costs to assets is the result of increasing liabilities (which were underestimated) rather than decreasing assets.

In the next four rows, ratios of net costs to assets are reported for sets of firms subdivided by asset size. The smallest firms tend to have higher costs than the larger firms, but no general pattern exists for the three largest quantities. In the last three rows, we divide firms according to their fraction of premiums in long-tail lines. The results show—not surprisingly, given our earlier findings—that those firms with significant amounts of premiums written in long-tail lines are more costly to resolve. In fact, the net costs of the firms in the top third of this category are approximately twice as costly as those in the bottom third. We come back to this issue in section 5.5.

The key finding, however, is that it is very costly to resolve the failures of P&C insurance companies. Net costs as a fraction of assets appear to be nearly 100 percent of assets, which we note is more than three times larger than the 30 percent estimate for commercial banks and S&Ls (Barth, Bartholemew, and Bradley 1990; Bovenzi and Murton 1988; James 1991). We discuss the validity

16. The multiplicative procedure is more appropriate if firms with abnormally large or small payments in the early stages of liquidation also experience abnormally large or small costs in the later stages. The additive adjustment procedure is more appropriate if deviations from the normal path in the later stages are uncorrelated with deviations in the early stages.

17. In section 5.5 the "failcost" regressions are estimated with both methods for estimating payments and costs. Not surprisingly, the results are very similar.

18. The results are qualitatively similar if we scale by total premiums rather than by assets. We scaled by assets because, as will be argued later, they are less prone to change sharply in the year(s) before insolvency.

Table 5.10   **Mean Value of Net Costs as a Percentage of Assets**

			Costs/Assets	
Sample	Number of Firms	Mean[a]	Multiplicative Scaling	Additive Scaling
All firms	87		1.024	1.032
Company asset size				
1 Smallest	21	2.9	2.127	2.078
2	22	13.0	.773	.797
3	22	32.4	.558	.550
4 Largest	22	176.6	.690	.748
Fraction of premiums in long-tail lines				
1 Lowest fraction	29	.000	.752	.754
2	29	.048	1.031	1.046
3 Highest fraction	29	.698	1.290	1.296

[a]Mean assets (in millions) or mean fraction of premiums in long-tail lines.

of comparisons between ratios of resolution costs to assets for insurance companies and for banks in section 5.6.

5.5   The Determinants of Insolvency Costs

In this section, we seek to determine what are the key, measurable determinants of the size of resolution costs. We use our projections of net costs from section 5.4 as a measure of the actual net costs of resolving P&C company failures. Our approach, which follows that of James's (1991) and Bovenzi and Murton's (1988) studies of the costs of bank failures, is to regress net resolution costs, scaled by total assets, on a vector of variables assumed to affect resolution costs.

The first variable that we include as a regressor is the fraction of premiums written in long-tail lines (FRACLONG). We already have established that the longer tail lines have longer resolution times and higher net costs *on average*. Here, we seek to determine whether the costs are also higher, controlling for a variety of factors.

Next, we include the ratio of book value of capital (surplus) to assets (CAPRATIO). The coefficient on the ratio of book value of capital (surplus) to assets of the insurer allows us some insight into the magnitude of unrealized losses in the insurer's assets and its book of business. We expect a higher level of (preinsolvency) reported capital to be associated with a lower cost of insolvency, ceteris paribus. If, however, the reported surplus is an unreliable measure of true capital—because, for example, insurers systematically overstate the true value of their assets or understate the true level of future losses to avoid regulatory intervention—then there may not be a strong negative relationship between the capital ratio and subsequent insolvency losses. It is noteworthy that James (1991) found this coefficient to be positive in his study of the costs of bank failures, which he interpreted to be the result of fraudulent reporting of capital.

We also consider how the reason for insolvency affects net costs. We supplemented our data set with information from the A. M. Best Company (1991) insolvency study on the cause of insurer failures. The Best study included most of the firms in our study and assigned each insolvency to one of nine categories for the cause of failure. We include dummy variables for failures deemed by Best to be caused by FRAUD (= 1) or DISASTER (= 1).

We also include several variables that may be correlated with large resolution costs. The first is high premium growth in the year preceding insolvency. As stated in the introduction, the moral hazard problem may be particularly acute for firms on the brink of bankruptcy. Such firms may undercut their competitors by offering low prices to write a large volume of premiums. For this reason, we include a dummy variable equal to one if the company's premium growth is in the top quartile of all firms. We measure premium growth two different ways: by growth in total premiums written and in earned premiums (an income statement item).

We also include two measures of asset composition that may be correlated with resolution costs. First, it is often thought that firms that own a large amount of real estate have riskier asset portfolios. Although the average proportion of real estate held by P&C insurance companies is quite small (3.7 percent of assets), we include the fraction of assets in real estate on the right-hand side as a crude measure of the riskiness of P&C asset portfolios. We include the ratio of cash plus short-term investments to liabilities as a measure of the firm's ability to meet obligations to policyholders in the preinsolvency period.

In addition, high growth in losses may be associated with unusually high costs for the obvious reason that losses erode capital. In theory, this effect should be picked up by the capital ratio. However, high loss growth may also reflect the fact that such firms are engaging in unusually risky behavior that will lead to higher resolution costs. Thus we include a dummy variable equal to one if the firm's loss growth is in the top quartile of all firms. Analogous to our measures of fast premium growth, we measure losses in two ways: total losses (from the balance sheet) and incurred losses (from the income statement).

Finally, we control for company size. The summary statistics on net costs from table 5.10 indicate that smaller firms have higher net resolution costs (as a fraction of total assets). We therefore include dummy variables, equal to one for each quartile of firms ranked by total assets, as right-hand-side variables.

The results of these regressions, with various permutations of right-hand-side variables, are shown in tables 5.11A and 5.11B as models 1–6. Heteroscedasticity-consistent standard errors (White 1980) are in parentheses. FRACLONG, the fraction of premiums written in long-tail lines, is positive

Table 5.11A   **Determinants of the Costs Resolving Insurer Failures**

Variable	Model 1	Model 2	Model 3	Model 4
N	87	71	69	67
Adjusted R^2	.3884	.4122	.4127	.5788
Intercept	1.5320	1.3548	1.4713	1.2371
	(.3734)	(.3129)	(.3287)	(.2978)
FRACLONG	1.5179	1.7231	1.6600	1.2209
	(.8365)	(.8537)	(.8115)	(.4954)
CAPRATIO	−.6133	−.5951	−.5552	−.5355
	(.2241)	(.2436)	(.2532)	(.1847)
FRAUD	.0780	−.3317	.3442	.3071
	(.2678)	(.3331)	(.3272)	(.3145)
DISASTER	5.4335	5.6018	5.4692	5.4005
	(1.8345)	(1.8196)	(1.8268)	(1.6045)
Fast growth in		.4804		
total premiums		(.3900)		
Fast earned			.5401	
premium growth			(.4235)	
Fast growth in				.5950
total losses				(.2281)
Asset size 2	−.8445	−1.7483	−.9145	−.5855
	(.5066)	(.4669)	(.5438)	(.3444)
Asset size 3	−1.2306	−1.3653	−1.4902	−1.1441
	(.5455)	(.5609)	(.6123)	(.4095)
Asset size 4	−1.5478	−1.4312	−1.5577	−1.1902
	(.7607)	(.6983)	(.7204)	(.5194)

Note: Numbers in parentheses are heteroscedasticity-consistent standard errors (White 1980). The dependent variable, FAILCOST, is the ratio of total resolution costs after scaling to preinsolvency assets of the failed insurer.

and approximately twice as large as its standard error in all six models. This is consistent with our earlier finding that firms with a high FRACLONG have higher net costs on average.

While it is easy to see why firms with a high fraction of premiums in long-tail lines have *longer* resolution times, it does not follow that such firms also have *higher* average resolution costs. While it is beyond the scope of this paper to investigate why this is the case, one intriguing possibility is a type of moral hazard induced by the solvency fund system: insolvent (and near-insolvent) companies may game the system before they are closed down by the regulators by writing premiums, perhaps at prices below expected costs, in long-tail lines. From the insurance company's perspective, the benefit of this policy is an immediate inflow of cash, which enables the company to stay in business and to continue to pay salaries, a potentially important consideration to well-paid managers and executives of the companies. The costs of this policy to the insurance company are deferred and indefinite payments to claimants. Of course,

Table 5.11B   Determinants of the Costs of Resolving Insurer Failures

Variable	Model 5	Model 6	Model 6 with Additive Scaling	Model 6 with Discounting
Observations	75	87	87	87
Adjusted R^2	.4126	.3801	.4596	.4076
Intercept	1.5035	1.6026	1.5157	1.6821
	(.3309)	(.4109)	(.3506)	(.4035)
FRACLONG	1.5920	1.5524	1.4670	1.3852
	(.7895)	(.8316)	(.6754)	(.7927)
CAPRATIO	−.6724	−.5630	−.5275	−.6367
	(.2343)	(.2369)	(.1981)	(.2337)
FRAUD	−.0467	.0986	.0449	.0786
	(.2870)	(.2655)	(.2421)	(.2723)
DISASTER	5.4858	5.3370	5.7050	5.8366
	(1.8217)	(1.8585)	(1.9059)	(1.9896)
Fast incurred loss growth	.4681 (.4279)			
Real estate to total assets		.4195 (.3784)	.3989 (.3778)	.4046 (.3947)
Liquid assets to liabilities		−.0494 (.0267)	−.0448 (.0217)	−.0491 (.0258)
Asset size 2	−.9813	−.9371	−.8126	−.9477
	(.5521)	(.5409)	(.4510)	(.5243)
Asset size 3	−1.4274	−1.3610	−1.2596	−1.3677
	(.5987)	(.5817)	(.4867)	(.5649)
Asset size 4	−1.4496	−1.6406	−1.4470	−1.5979
	(.6853)	(.7931)	(.6469)	(.7631)

Note: Numbers in parentheses are heteroscedasticity-consistent standard errors (White 1980). The dependent variable, FAILCOST, is the ratio of total resolution costs after scaling to preinsolvency assets of the failed insurer.

this gaming of the system is only possible if the regulators are either unable or unwilling to see through this game and to take quick action to close down the company when such gaming is detected.

In contrast to the finding of James with regard to commercial banks, we find a negative and statistically significant coefficient on the capital ratio (CAP-RATIO), suggesting that measured capital has at least a positive correlation with actual capital, which provides a buffer to losses and should lead, ceteris paribus, to lower levels of net costs to solvency funds. Taken together, our estimated coefficients indicate that a 1 percentage point increase in the capital ratio decreases the ratio of payments to assets by about 0.6 percentage points.

In terms of the A. M. Best rating variables, FRAUD does not seem to have any explanatory power on net costs. The coefficient on DISASTER, however, is large, positive, and statistically significant. The data suggest that disasters are associated with very large costs to the guarantee funds. They suggest that if the reason for the insolvency is a disaster, the ratio of costs to assets increases more than fivefold, ceteris paribus. Firms failing because of disasters were small and geographically concentrated. The lack of diversification may have been induced by moral hazard. When the disaster struck, the firms experienced a dramatic upward revision in their losses. This finding may suggest that the costs of resolving firms that failed because of a disaster are so large that these firms should be treated differently. As a quick check on this possibility, we removed firms that failed because of disasters from our sample. However, removal of these firms did not change our results in a substantive way.

The coefficients on fast total premium growth (model 2) and fast earned premium growth (model 3) are positive as was hypothesized. However, neither coefficient is statistically significant at the 5 percent confidence level. The coefficients on fast total loss growth (model 4) and fast incurred loss growth (model 5) are both positive as was hypothesized, and the former is significant at the 5 percent confidence level, indicating that firms that have large losses in the year before insolvency tend to be associated with large costs to the solvency funds. Neither of the asset composition variables (model 6) are statistically significant, although the coefficient on the proportion of real estate in the asset portfolio is positive and slightly larger than its standard error. Given the relatively bland nature of the typical asset portfolio of P&C insurance companies, this result is not that surprising.

The coefficients on the size dummies suggest, as was found earlier, that larger firms tend to have lower cost ratios than smaller firms. This may reflect some economies of scale in the process of liquidating the firm and administering its claim file. Alternatively, it may be that larger firms, because of their potential for sizable costs to the guarantee funds, are forced into liquidation faster or are more closely monitored by regulators *prior to* insolvency. For the same reason, large firms may be monitored more closely *during* the insolvency and liquidation proceedings.

In table 5.11B we estimate model 6 with two modifications in order to test our basic results for robustness.[19] First, we use the additive rather than the multiplicative procedure for determining net costs, as discussed in section 5.4. Second, we replace net costs expressed in real 1993 dollars with net costs expressed in present discounted value terms, using the same 3 percent (real) discount rate as before. The results are robust to both of these modifications; none of our results are substantively different from our earlier results. Taken together, a few findings stand out. The net costs of resolving P&C insolvencies (scaled by size) seem to be larger for small firms, poorly capitalized firms, firms writing significant amounts in long-tail lines, and firms that fail because of disasters.

---

19. The robustness checks of models 1 through 5 yielded the same basic results and are therefore not reported.

5.6   The Reason for Large Insolvency Costs

Our findings raise the question of why resolution costs are so high given that virtually all of the insurance companies that fail are solvent, in terms of the book value of their capital, in the year before they fail. In this section, we briefly discuss potential reasons for our key finding that the costs incurred by guarantee funds in resolving P&C insurer insolvencies are extremely high—approximately 100 percent of preinsolvency assets.

5.6.1   Assets, Liabilities, or Administrative Costs?

In an accounting sense, there are three possible explanations for such high resolution costs. First, *assets* may be the cause; assets may fall sharply or be far overstated. Second, *liabilities* may be the cause; liabilities may increase sharply or be hugely understated. And third, there may be very large *administrative, legal, and other costs* associated with resolving insolvencies. Answering this question definitively is beyond the scope of this paper. Nor do we have the necessary data to easily answer it; once a company is declared insolvent, it is removed from the NAIC database. We suspect, however, that resolution costs are so high because failed firms drastically underestimated their (expected) liabilities—that is, postinsolvency liabilities typically are about twice the size of preinsolvency reported liabilities. We provide some evidence that is supportive of this contention.

Our main reason for suspecting that costs are high because liabilities rise sharply (except for the disaster-induced failures, this is probably because liabilities were previously understated) is that the other two possibilities seem unlikely. With regard to the administrative cost possibility, we do have some data for the eight states, mostly in New England, that are managed by Boston-based Guarantee Fund Management Services. Total administrative costs—office, salaries, lawyers' fees, and so forth—for the eight state funds they administer have averaged about $8 million dollars annually since 1991. These administrative costs represent approximately 16 percent of the annual costs to the guarantee fund for these eight states. While it is difficult to know whether this number is unreasonably high, it seems unlikely that administrative costs account for a significant portion of the large resolution costs that we estimate.

The other possibility, that the large costs we estimate are associated with overstated or large decreases in assets, also seems unlikely. Approximately, 10 percent of P&C assets is in the form of cash or other liquid assets, 60 percent is in bonds of some sort, and 15 percent is in common and preferred stock. The remainder consists of receivables and tangible assets such as the firm's own buildings and data-processing equipment. While these assets can certainly fall in value, it is virtually impossible for them to fall enough to produce our resolution cost estimates. An example can illustrate why this is the case. For simplicity, assume that book assets are approximately equal to liabilities when the firm becomes insolvent (assets are actually higher, which makes our case

Table 5.12	Mean Change in Account in Annual Statements Filed by Failed Insurers between Two Years Prior to Insolvency and One Year Prior to Insolvency

Variable	Mean Percentage Change ($n = 75$)
Total assets	−1.28
Total liabilities	14.48
Loss reserves	18.65
Losses incurred during year	26.03

stronger). If liabilities do not change, and assuming away administrative costs, assets would have to fall to zero in order to produce resolution costs equal to the value of preinsolvency book assets. It seems extremely unlikely that assets fall to zero or anywhere close to that. A much more likely scenario involves increases in liabilities associated with huge (pre- and postinsolvency) losses.

One piece of evidence for the view that problem liabilities rather than problem assets cause insurance company failures is the fact that investment income is positive for the firms in our sample (averaging $3.6 million) in the year prior to insolvency, while underwriting income is negative (averaging −$10.4 million).

In addition, to get a sense of how assets and liabilities change, we looked at the change in total assets, liabilities, loss reserves (a liability that estimates future losses), and losses incurred during the year (from the income statement) between one and two years prior to insolvency. The mean of the annual percentage change for each of these variables is shown in table 5.12. The results are consistent with our expectations. In the year prior to insolvency, assets fell by only 1.3 percent while liabilities increased by 14.5 percent. Loss reserves and annual losses increased by 18.7 and 26.0 percent, respectively. It seems likely that the continuance of these trends, and not a sharp decline in assets, is what accounts for the large resolution costs of insurer insolvencies.

5.6.2 A Comparison with Bank Insolvency Costs

While insurance companies tend to fail because of rising (or previously understated) liabilities, banks tend to fail because of loan defaults. That is, to a first approximation, banks fail because of asset problems while insurance companies fail because of liability problems. This fact makes our comparison of bank and insurance company resolution costs more than fair: because our cost measures are relative to preinsolvency *assets* (which are more likely to be falling sharply for banks), our finding that the ratio of costs to assets is much higher for insurance companies is even more striking.

The large difference in resolution costs between insurers and depository institutions may be due to differences in the nature of the businesses of these institutions. Although banks make loans that are risky, these risks may be smaller on average than the risks inherent to the insurance business, where the costs of production (policyholder losses) are unknown at the time the product is sold. In such a situation, bad business judgment or opportunistic behavior on the part of management can be particularly costly. Indeed, we find resolution costs to be particularly high among firms writing large amounts of premiums in long-tail lines in which the value of future losses are particularly difficult to estimate. In addition, the resolution cost differential between banks and insurance companies may reflect differences in the way that these financial institutions are resolved. While insolvent banks are typically liquidated or quickly merged with healthy institutions, insurance company assets are liquidated and the liabilities are assumed by guarantee fund management agencies. Essentially, insurance regulatory bodies operating through the fund management systems take over the insolvent companies and run them until all claims have been paid.

5.7   Conclusion

We examine the costs of resolving property-casualty insurance company insolvencies. When a P&C insurance company becomes insolvent, solvent insurance companies are forced to pay assessments, which are a form of taxation, to state guarantee funds in order to protect the policyholders of the failed companies. Our estimates imply that the costs incurred by guarantee funds to resolve insurance company insolvencies are remarkably high—about 100 percent of the book value of assets in the year before the company was declared to be insolvent. This implies that insolvent companies have liabilities that are approximately twice as large as their assets when they are declared to be insolvent. These costs are more than three times as high as the costs incurred by the FDIC and FSLIC in resolving the failures of commercial banks and S&Ls in the 1980s.

We also find that the ratio of net costs to assets tends to be higher for small firms, poorly capitalized firms, firms writing significant amounts of premiums in long-tail lines, and firms that fail because of disasters. Our findings also indicate that the resolution of insolvencies is typically quick. More than 60 percent of all costs to the fund for a given insolvency occur within two years, and more than three-quarters of total costs occur within three years. However, we find that firms with a high proportion of premiums in long-tail lines take much longer to resolve, perhaps because companies are gaming the solvency fund system, a type of moral hazard.

Our findings raise a number of questions concerning the costs of resolving insurance company insolvencies. Although we have tried to shed some light on the subject, why the costs of resolving insurance company failures are so high remains something of a mystery. To what extent do the moral hazard effects created by the solvency fund system lead to the large costs? Are firms gaming the system by writing premiums in long-tail lines at below expected costs? Are some companies writing high-risk premiums in geographically concentrated areas? Are the high resolution costs for insurance companies relative to banks the result of the differing ways in which these insolvent institutions are resolved? Determining the reasons for the high cost of resolving P&C insurance companies is an important topic for future research.

In addition, our finding of high resolution costs raises the issue of the extent to which the solvency funds are "exposed" to various shocks (e.g., natural disasters) that may lead to very large "assessments" against healthy firms. What scenarios would cause the solvency fund assessments to reach their maximum levels, typically 1 to 2 percent of premiums per year? How exposed is the system to a very large shock or set of shocks that has the potential to create an S&L-like problem in the P&C insurance industry? All of these questions should have high priority in future research.

References

A. M. Best Company. Various years. *Best's insurance reports*. Oldwick, N.J.: A. M. Best Company.

———. 1991. *Best's insolvency study*. Oldwick, N.J.: A. M. Best Company.

Barth, J., P. Bartholemew, and M. Bradley. 1990. Determinants of thrift resolution costs. *Journal of Finance* 45:731–54.

Besley, D. A., E. Kuh, and R. E. Welsch. 1980. *Regression diagnostics*. New York: Wiley.

Bovenzi, J., and A. Murton. 1988. Resolution costs and bank failures. *FDIC Banking Review* 1:1–13.

Clarke, R. N., F. Warren-Bolton, D. K. Smith, and M. J. Simon. 1988. Sources of the crisis in liability insurance: An empirical analysis. *Yale Journal on Regulation* 6 (summer): 367–95.

Cummins, J. 1988. Risk based premiums for insurance guarantee funds. *Journal of Finance* 43:823–39.

Duncan, M. 1987. Property-liability post assessment guarantee funds. In *Issues in insurance*, 4th ed., ed. Everett D. Randall, 239–302. Malvern, Pa.: American Institute for Property and Liability Underwriters.

Epton, B., and R. Bixby. 1976. Insurance guarantee funds: A reassessment. *DePaul Law Review* 25:227–63.

Hall, D., and R. Hall. 1993. Insurance company insolvencies: Order out of chaos. *Journal of Insurance Regulation* 12:145–87.

Hiestand, J. 1986. The need for revision of state insolvency and guarantee funds laws. In *Law and practice of insurance insolvency*, 563–609. Chicago: American Bar Association.

James, C. 1991. The losses realized in bank failures. *Journal of Finance* 46:1223–42.

National Conference of Insurance Guarantee Funds (NCIGF). 1992. *Property and Casualty Guarantee Association: 1992 Assessment and financial information report*. Indianapolis: National Conference of Insurance Guarantee Funds. Mimeograph.

———. 1993a. *1993 Summary of Property and Casualty Guarantee Association acts*. Indianapolis: National Conference of Insurance Guarantee Funds. Mimeograph.

————. 1993b. *Property and Casualty Guarantee Association: 1993 Assessment and financial information report.* Indianapolis: National Conference of Insurance Guarantee Funds. Mimeograph.

Schacht, J., and P. Gallanis. 1993. The interstate compact as an effective mechanism for insurance receivership reform. *Journal of Insurance Regulation* 12:188–220.

U.S. Congress. House Subcommittee on Oversight and Investigations of the Committee on Energy and Commerce. 1990. *Failed promises: Insurance company insolvencies.* Washington, D.C.: Government Printing Office.

White, H. A. 1980. A heteroscedasticity-consistent covariance matrix estimator and a direct test for heteroscedasticity. *Econometrica* 48:817–38.

6 Organizational Form and Insurance Company Performance: Stocks versus Mutuals

Patricia Born, William M. Gentry, W. Kip Viscusi, and Richard J. Zeckhauser

6.1 Introduction

One unusual feature of the U.S. property-casualty insurance industry is the coexistence of for-profit stock companies and nonprofit mutual companies. For-profit enterprises dominate almost all other sectors of the financial services industry,[1] while cooperatives play a role in some local markets but are in general a minor organizational form. Stock insurance companies are similar to corporations in other industries: shareholders provide capital to the company, own the residual claims to the company's profits, and elect the board of directors to oversee its management. Mutual insurance companies, by contrast, are corporations that are owned by their customers: policyholders provide capital through premiums, may receive dividends (in addition to insurance) from the

Patricia Born is assistant professor of finance at the School of Business Administration at the University of Connecticut. William M. Gentry is assistant professor of economics and finance at the Graduate School of Business at Columbia University and a faculty research fellow of the National Bureau of Economic Research. W. Kip Viscusi is the John F. Cogan Professor of Law and Economics at Harvard Law School and a research associate of the National Bureau of Economic Research. Richard J. Zeckhauser is the Frank P. Ramsey Professor of Economics at the Kennedy School of Government at Harvard University, a research associate of the National Bureau of Economic Research, and a visitor at the Massachusetts Institute of Technology.

The authors are grateful to Miriam Aoins, Georges Dionne, Dwight Jaffee, Deborah Lucas, Sean Mooney, and participants at the Franco-American Seminar on Risk and Insurance and an NBER conference on property-casualty insurance for helpful comments. Views and opinions presented in this paper are solely those of the authors and do not reflect positions of any organization with which they are affiliated.

1. Savings and loans (S&Ls) are another notable example of the coexistence of stock and mutual firms. Hermalin and Wallace (1994) analyze differences in the level of efficiency of stock and mutual S&Ls. As discussed by Berger, Cummins, and Weiss (1995), comparing the efficiency of different types of insurance companies is complicated by the possibility of different organizational forms offering differentiated products. We abstract from issues of the level of efficiency of the organizational forms by concentrating on how firms respond to changes in their operating environments.

firm, and elect the board of directors to manage the business. In 1991, stock companies accounted for 67 percent of overall property-casualty premiums in the United States, compared to 25 percent for mutual companies.[2] However, the relative importance of these two forms varies across lines of insurance. For example, stock companies earned 71 percent of commercial multiple peril premiums but only 36 percent of homeowners multiple peril premiums.

Understanding the differences in how mutual and stock insurance companies respond to differences in their underwriting environments should illuminate their distribution in the property-casualty insurance market. More important, a better understanding of the competitive responses of insurance firms may help in designing insurance regulations, such as rules aimed at protecting consumers. Consumer protection regulation may have more influence on stock companies than on mutuals, given the inherent incentives facing mutual managers to take consumer welfare into account.

Insurance availability and affordability are both policy concerns, as evidenced by government's many regulations of the insurance market. Since the insurance industry has multiple organizational forms, one must understand the likely response of each significant form to predict the industry's overall response to any change in the environment, just as one must pay attention to the grazing habits of multiple animal species to predict how the grass on the Serengeti will respond to a drought. Mutual companies may be inherently more interested in making insurance available and affordable since their policyholders are also owners. They may be more reluctant to exit a market in the face of costly new regulations or a jump in claims that is expected to persist. Stock companies may be quicker to provide insurance services in new lines that have the potential for profitability and growth.

Prevailing economic theories of organizations are based on the hypothesis that a particular form will prevail in an industry if it offers the most effective solution to the industry's particular agency problems.[3] The form may be chosen consciously, or it may evolve in response to economic pressures affecting survival and growth; the most efficient form eventually prevails. For example, virtually all institutions of higher education are not-for-profit, whereas virtually all restaurants are for-profit organizations.

The coexistence of stock and mutual companies in the property-casualty insurance industry suggests that at least one of three hypotheses is true: the two organizational forms have competing advantages; the market may be rich

2. The remainder of the industry consists of reciprocals (5 percent), risk retention groups (2 percent), U.S. branches of alien insurers (less than 1 percent), and Lloyd's syndicates (less than 1 percent). Reciprocals are similar to mutuals but are not corporations and have an attorney-in-fact instead of a board of directors. We focus on stock and mutual companies since they dominate the market.

3. See Fama and Jensen (1983a, 1983b) for a general treatment of how agency costs affect business organizational form. Mayers and Smith (1981, 1988) and Hansmann (1985) discuss these problems in the specific context of stock and mutual insurance companies.

enough that different organizational forms can survive in different niches; and the market may not have reached its final equilibrium (or perhaps history may influence the equilibrium).

While stock companies have convenient access to well-developed capital markets, they suffer from a conflict of interest between shareholders and policyholders; managers of a stock company who act in the best interest of shareholders might take some opportunities to make profits at the expense of policyholders. As an extreme example, consider a stock company that is nearly insolvent. Its managers might choose to invest the firm's capital in assets that pay a high return, in part because of significant risk, rather than insure against a low-probability but catastrophic event. If nothing untoward happens, shareholders will reap the profits. However, if the assets collapse or the catastrophic event occurs, it is policyholders who suffer most from the firm's insolvency.[4] To lose their monetary claims precisely when insurance was to pay for the costs of coping with a catastrophe is doubly disastrous; it is at such times that the marginal utility of money is highest. The recent experience of Lloyd's of London, whereby some "names" (the general partners) lost vast amounts and were even thrust into bankruptcy, suggests that insolvency risks are not trivial in the insurance arena. There is considerable debate in the United States whether the insurance industry could weather the predicted catastrophic earthquake in California, the "big one."

Theoretically, the mutual form of organization eliminates managerial "opportunism" by merging the identity of the policyholders and the residual claimants.[5] The managers of a mutual do not feel a tension between serving the owners and serving the customers; the customers *are* the owners. Some insurance researchers have hypothesized that mutuals are more efficient at risk sharing since they combine policy and equity claims in a single package, which is a more efficient arrangement for risks that are not easily diversified. While the mutual form of organization may reduce this agency cost, it has distinctive costs of its own. First, mutual companies cannot raise capital from equity markets. Second, managers of mutual companies are not disciplined by the stock market and the market for corporate control to control costs and otherwise achieve efficiency. Third, the diffuse ownership of mutuals, and the inherent inability of individual policyholders to acquire significant influence, may make it difficult to monitor managerial performance. Pound and Zeckhauser (1990) show that large shareholders play a significant role within corporations in monitoring performance, promoting, for example, a long-term orientation among managers. If policyholders have little control over managers of mutuals, then managers may be more likely to act in their own best interest rather than on

---

4. Of course, this possibility also motivates government policies such as guarantee funds and investment limits. See Born (1994) and the references therein.

5. The unlimited liability of Lloyd's names was designed to provide the same reassurance, given that names had to be people of significant means.

behalf of the policyholders. For example, mutual firm managers might dissipate the insureds' surplus through expenditures yielding personal benefits.[6] Unlike nonprofit organizations in many other industries, mutual insurance companies do not enjoy tax-favored status; they are taxed as corporations and are subject to the same premium taxes as stock companies. Mutuals in other countries, such as France, do receive favorable tax treatment.

There are several kinds of mutual forms in the U.S. insurance industry. In the pure assessment mutual, policyholders pay nothing when they join but pay their assessed share of any loss after it has occurred. This form is not widespread because it is difficult to collect. A second form is a mutual that combines advance premiums with assessable policies. These mutuals return the surplus to policyholders as dividends. The mutual can levy an additional assessment, which is typically limited to an amount such as the level of the advance premium whenever the additional levy is limited by the bylaws or state law. The third and most prevalent mutual form, which is used by all of the larger U.S. mutuals, is the advance premium nonassessable mutual. These mutuals collect premiums in advance and return the surplus as dividends but do not levy additional assessments for losses. Regulations permit such mutuals to operate once they demonstrate that they have adequate financial strength to withstand foreseeable losses.

In many respects, mutuals function similarly to stock companies. They collect and invest premiums and pay any shortfall from the accumulated surplus. Unlike stock companies, however, the premium is neither fixed nor definite; any excess over cost may be returned as dividends. Policyholders theoretically control the company, serving as implicit shareholders, but they actually exercise less control. Policyholders have a weaker incentive than do shareholders to replace management by purchasing a controlling interest since they would have to undertake a proxy fight and would not capture any increases in surplus, such as those due to cost savings.

Previous empirical research on organizational form in the insurance industry has examined static questions, such as how mutual and stock companies differ. Mayers and Smith (1988) examine the geographic and line-of-business concentration of different organizational forms and test the hypothesis that mutual companies will serve more concentrated regions or types of business. Several conclusions emerge. First, stock companies serve broader geographic areas

6. Savings banks are a closely related example of a market in which mutuals and for-profit organizations compete. In recent years, there has been a major movement to "demutualize" savings banks. There have been widespread allegations of insider enrichment. In most such demutualizations a substantial capital value emerges almost overnight, suggesting that the mutual form may not have been optimal.

The hospital industry also has for-profit and nonprofit organizations competing in the same market. The nonprofits are given tax advantages and also benefit from superior trust of potential customers. The for-profits can raise equity capital. Normally, for-profits are considered more efficient, but the evidence in the hospital sector does not support this expectation (Patel, Needleman, and Zeckhauser 1994).

than mutual companies; this is consistent with the hypothesis that for-profit organizations are better able to control agency costs, particularly when operating from a distance.[7] Second, mutual companies and stock companies are about as likely to concentrate their activities in a few lines of business. Third, mutuals are relatively more important in some insurance lines, but Mayers and Smith conclude that it is difficult to see why mutuals specialize in particular lines. Lamm-Tennant and Starks (1993) explore the hypothesis that stock companies bear more risk than mutual firms. Their measure of a firm's risk is the variance of the firm's annual loss ratio from 1980 to 1987. Using this measure, they find that stock companies do bear more risk than mutuals.

This paper explores how organizational form affects a firm's responses to different situations. If stock companies are more opportunistic and less obligated to their insureds than mutuals, then they will respond more quickly to changes in regulation or the distribution of claims. For example, consider a hypothetical price cap that reduces the profitability of writing homeowners insurance in Massachusetts. The shareholders of a stock company might want the company to reduce its homeowners business in that state, just as a supermarket would stop selling products on which it expects to lose money. However, if a mutual firm reduces its business, the big losers will be policyholders, the supposed residual claimants and owners of the firm.[8] Even without changes in government policy, stock companies might give less weight to the interests of policyholders in changing premiums or quantities in response to changes in market rewards.

Exploring such dynamic questions requires an assessment over time. One way to evaluate the difference in behaviors between stocks and mutuals is to analyze firms' reactions to their past performance in a line, working on the hypothesis that there is some persistence in performance. For example, if a firm was unprofitable in writing medical malpractice insurance last year, will it raise premiums, exit the market, or do nothing? The answer may depend on the firm's loyalty to the interests of its policyholders. It may also depend on the firm's profitability in other areas, assuming that it is costly, unlikely, or impossible for the firm to secure capital from its policyholders or shareholders. That is, a substantially lesser response would be expected if the firm was unprofitable in every line last year, than if this line was the sole "loser" for the firm. Finally, the firm's sensitivity to whether a particular line is profitable may depend on the scale of the firm's operations. Big national firms can absorb losses better than small, geographically concentrated firms, so less of a response may be necessary. By comparing the current year's performance to the previous

7. Some of the geographic concentration of mutuals may result from their initial development, frequently as an offshoot of fraternal organizations or other organizations in which there were close relationships among the insureds.

8. The managers of mutuals may face pressure from different groups of policyholders, either by region or by line of business. E.g., policyholders in a profitable state would benefit if the mutual were to pull out of an unprofitable state (see Hetherington 1991, 32).

year's, we evaluate the relative influence of such factors on the behavior of stock and mutual companies.[9]

The rest of this paper is organized as follows. Section 6.2 provides background information on the relative importance and performance of stock and mutual insurers in the eight lines of business that we study. Section 6.3 discusses possible responses by stock and mutual firms to the underwriting environment: changing the premiums they charge or the quantity of insurance they write or entering or exiting particular markets. Section 6.4 presents our empirical methodology and results on changes in underwriting performance and premiums by organizational form. Section 6.5 summarizes our findings.

6.2   Performance and Size of Stocks and Mutuals

In the early nineteenth century, the property-casualty insurance industry was dominated by stock companies that were reluctant to negotiate rates for individual policyholders.[10] In response to what they felt were unfair prices, regional industry groups, such as textile mills, started mutual insurance companies—the first appeared beginning in 1843. These mutuals were able to offer lower premiums than stock companies for several reasons. First, the mutual form reassured policyholders that they were not paying inappropriately high rates due to the use of crude and unregulated actuarial tables; that is, it ameliorated monitoring problems. Second, mutuals screened prospective members in an effort to insure only the better risks. Third, they viewed their members as participants in a long-term relationship and offered helpful services; for example, they provided inspections and recommended loss prevention measures. Fourth, the common interests of a mutual's members may have reduced moral hazard: For example, farmers in a small mutual may have refrained from filing small claims because they realized that their claims would raise premiums for themselves and their neighbors. There is anecdotal evidence that an ethic against making such claims did develop and was reinforced because the farmers could monitor and sanction one another. Thus the insurance industry's problems of information monitoring may make the mutual form of organization more advantageous in certain areas.

Some of the regional mutuals began to write personal lines of insurance as the composition of demand changed over time. For example, some farm and fire mutuals formed automobile insurance mutuals. The concentration of mutuals in midwestern states suggests that ideological and regional factors also in-

9. Last year's profitability does not actually characterize a "change" in the firm's underwriting environment. Instead, the variation across firms in last year's profitability is used to describe differences in behavior in a particular line. An alternative measure from which to gauge current-year behavior would be the trend of firm profitability in the particular line and state over the past two or more years.

10. See Bainbridge (1952), Heflebower (1980, chap. 12), and Hansmann (1985) for more historical information on the industry.

fluenced their development. Yet such historical factors do not necessarily explain the survival of the form alongside for-profit firms. As mentioned above, an economic explanation for the coexistence of stock and mutual companies is that their differing approaches to agency problems allow them to prevail in different lines, or perhaps that they confront slightly different circumstances and hence must solve different problems. Under this hypothesis, one would expect the two organizational forms to behave differently, even though they might be roughly equal competitors in some markets.

To test for behavioral differences between organizational forms, we analyze eight lines of insurance: homeowners multiple peril, commercial multiple peril, medical malpractice, general liability, automobile private bodily injury, commercial automobile liability, automobile private physical damage, and commercial automobile physical damage. These lines represent the majority of the property-casualty insurance business in the United States.[11] Among these lines, stock companies wrote between 36 and 79 percent of industry premiums in 1991. This set of lines also provides a mixture of personal and commercial insurance lines as well as a combination of lines that were adversely affected by the mid-1980s liability insurance crisis and those that remained relatively stable.

Table 6.1 compares various characteristics of stock and mutual firms by line for 1991. These data are from the National Association of Insurance Commissioners (NAIC) records of property-casualty insurance companies' annual financial statements. Every firm writing insurance for each line reported its insurance information to the state insurance commissioners in response to regulatory requirements. Three conclusions emerge. First, stock firms collect greater total premiums than mutuals in all of the lines except homeowners multiple peril. Outside of homeowners, mutuals are most important in personal automobile insurance, for which they write more than one-third of all premiums. Second, in all of the lines except homeowners, considerably more stock companies write insurance than mutuals, by a ratio that is generally larger than their ratio of premiums. Third, a comparison of the mean and median firm premiums by line suggests no clear pattern in terms of whether one organizational form is generally larger or smaller than the other.[12] This is important; it suggests that organizational form is not just a proxy for size. Stock firms have the growth advantage of being able to go to the capital markets and issue equity.

11. We exclude workers' compensation from our analysis because, for the period studied, this line was subject to numerous changes in state regulations, including many changes in benefit provisions and the emergence of large residual market pools.

12. Wilcoxon rank-sum tests were performed to test whether the distributions of firm size for stocks and mutuals are the same. For premiums earned in all lines, stock companies are larger than mutuals. However, by line of insurance, this size difference is not clear. Of the eight lines analyzed, stock companies were found to be larger than mutuals in only one line: general liability. Mutuals are larger than stock companies in five lines: homeowners multiple peril, medical malpractice, automobile personal bodily injury, automobile personal physical damage, and automobile commercial physical damage. No significant difference was found for the remaining two lines.

Table 6.1   Size Comparison of Stock and Mutual Companies, 1991

Line	Stock	Mutual
Homeowners multiple peril		
Number of firms	180	200
Percentage of industry	37.5	58.6
Premiums (million $)	404.13	632.27
Mean premiums per company (thousand $)	2,245.16	3,161.37
Median premiums per company (thousand $)	255.42	661.00
Commercial multiple peril		
Number of firms	695	352
Percentage of industry	70.5	19.1
Premiums (million $)	13,661.12	3,693.33
Mean premiums per company (thousand $)	19,656.32	10,492.41
Median premiums per company (thousand $)	2,439.59	2,844.13
General liability		
Number of firms	991	352
Percentage of industry	52.4	5.5
Premiums (million $)	18,908.59	1,977.14
Mean premiums per company (thousand $)	19,080.32	5,616.86
Median premiums per company (thousand $)	1,659.16	307.74
Medical malpractice		
Number of firms	199	33
Percentage of industry	39.9	16.9
Premiums (million $)	2,620.74	1,110.26
Mean premiums per company (thousand $)	13,169.57	33,644.24
Median premiums per company (thousand $)	1,492.05	12,800.43
Automobile private bodily injury		
Number of firms	813	206
Percentage of industry	56.2	34.6
Premiums (million $)	28,823.71	17,754.63
Mean premiums per company (thousand $)	35,453.52	86,187.54
Median premiums per company (thousand $)	6,292.32	11,268.67
Automobile commercial bodily injury		
Number of firms	783	176
Percentage of industry	78.7	18.0
Premiums (million $)	10,160.48	2,324.44
Mean premiums per company (thousand $)	12,976.34	13,207.07
Median premiums per company (thousand $)	1,699.93	2,566.24
Automobile private physical damage		
Number of firms	852	209
Percentage of industry	53.3	37.7
Premiums (million $)	16,654.40	11,756.43
Mean premiums per company (thousand $)	19,547.42	56,250.84
Median premiums per company (thousand $)	3,570.74	7,737.12
Automobile commercial physical damage		
Number of firms	754	168
Percentage of industry	77.1	19.9
Premiums (million $)	3,471.47	894.93
Mean premiums per company (thousand $)	4,604.07	5,326.96
Median premiums per company (thousand $)	798.18	1,241.26

Table 6.2   **Percentage of Industry Business, 1984 and 1991**

	1984		1991	
Line	Stocks	Mutuals	Stocks	Mutuals
Homeowners multiple peril	43	54	36	58
Commercial multiple peril	75	19	70	19
General liability	87	11	52	5
Medical malpractice	58	17	40	17
Automobile private bodily injury	58	33	56	35
Automobile commercial bodily injury	79	18	79	18
Automobile private physical damage	56	35	53	38
Automobile commercial physical damage	78	19	77	20

Note: The remaining business in the industry is written by Lloyd's, reciprocals, risk retention groups, and reinsurers.

Table 6.2 presents changes in the relative importance of stock and mutual firms from 1984 to 1991. In six of the eight lines, the relative importance of stocks and mutuals remains almost constant; the exceptions are general liability and medical malpractice. These two lines were most affected by the expansion of tort liability in the mid-1980s. In these lines, the percentage of premiums earned by stock companies fell precipitously; those collected by mutuals did not rise proportionately. The decreased role of stock companies in these markets should not be regarded as a sign of organizational demise; rather responsive profit-making enterprises might well decrease their operations in markets that have become unprofitable. During this period, mutuals wrote the same fraction of total malpractice insurance and significantly decreased their fraction of general liability insurance. Risk retention groups, which emerged when insurance was hard to find, contributed to the relative decline of stocks and mutuals in these areas.[13] Table 6.2 does not show that either stocks or mutuals have been driving the other organizational form from the market in any line over the past decade. What did drive both types of firms from these markets, and bolstered the potential of risk retention pools, was a dramatic increase in rates due to losses in these areas.

Table 6.3 reports a summary measure of underwriting profitability, the loss ratio, by line for each organizational form from 1984 to 1991.[14] The table also

13. In 1986, the federal government amended the 1981 Risk Retention Act, which facilitated the formation of risk retention pools, or insurance buyers' groups, by manufacturers. The 1986 amendment extended this option to all buyers of commercial liability coverage, and it appears to have been instrumental in drawing some business away from more traditional organizational forms.

14. The loss ratios are not adjusted for administrative expenses. If stocks and mutuals differ in their administrative expenses, these comparisons may not accurately reflect differences in profitability. Several recent articles that evaluate the efficiency of insurers discuss the importance of administrative expenses. See Pauly, Kunreuther, and Kleindorfer (1986) and Cummins and Weiss (1993).

Table 6.3   **Loss Ratios of Stock and Mutual Companies by Line of Business and Year**

Line	1984	1985	1986	1987	1988	1989	1990	1991
Homeowners multiple peril								
Stock	0.76	0.73	0.62	0.51	0.61	0.70	0.65	0.68
	(0.96)	(0.57)	(0.83)	(1.50)	(1.31)	(4.95)	(1.15)	(1.01)
Mutual	0.79	0.72	0.68	0.58	0.64	0.70	0.71	0.75
	(0.23)	(0.33)	(0.30)	(0.21)	(3.15)	(0.33)	(0.24)	(0.25)
Commercial multiple peril								
Stock	0.67	0.67	0.59	0.53	0.57	0.71	0.72	0.77
	(0.76)	(0.91)	(1.71)	(1.06)	(2.53)	(2.14)	(1.42)	(1.23)
Mutual	0.64	0.65	0.58	0.53	0.56	0.67	0.65	0.69
	(0.26)	(0.28)	(0.23)	(0.18)	(0.24)	(0.55)	(0.26)	(0.27)
General liability								
Stock	0.99	1.14	0.75	0.69	0.62	0.70	0.64	0.65
	(3.82)	(9.85)	(4.65)	(16.14)	(10.99)	(12.37)	(25.29)	(4.32)
Mutual	0.81	0.83	0.67	0.70	0.59	0.58	0.64	0.56
	(1.40)	(1.64)	(0.89)	(3.91)	(1.18)	(1.48)	(1.21)	(1.46)
Medical malpractice								
Stock	0.99	1.14	0.87	0.77	0.65	0.58	0.60	0.55
	(3.95)	(11.00)	(18.63)	(15.96)	(11.34)	(13.98)	(16.93)	(8.15)
Mutual	1.21	1.21	1.10	1.10	0.90	0.48	0.54	0.55
	(13.59)	(3.10)	(2.63)	(0.61)	(1.85)	(0.56)	(0.44)	(0.58)
Automobile private bodily injury								
Stock	0.69	0.70	0.69	0.67	0.67	0.70	0.71	0.78
	(1.80)	(2.29)	(2.49)	(6.12)	(1.35)	(2.25)	(0.96)	(2.89)
Mutual	0.70	0.71	0.68	0.68	0.71	0.73	0.72	0.77
	(0.23)	(2.32)	(1.61)	(1.53)	(1.24)	(0.29)	(2.79)	(1.36)
Automobile commercial bodily injury								
Stock	0.81	0.69	0.51	0.50	0.53	0.56	0.62	0.69
	(2.59)	(3.26)	(3.72)	(7.06)	(3.79)	(2.58)	(2.90)	(6.52)
Mutual	0.79	0.67	0.55	0.55	0.65	0.66	0.64	0.66
	(0.62)	(5.41)	(0.53)	(0.34)	(0.61)	(1.33)	(0.64)	(0.76)
Automobile private physical damage								
Stock	0.66	0.64	0.60	0.56	0.58	0.61	0.61	0.55
	(0.30)	(0.32)	(0.68)	(0.29)	(0.24)	(0.74)	(0.69)	(2.77)
Mutual	0.69	0.68	0.64	0.60	0.63	0.67	0.66	0.59
	(0.12)	(0.12)	(0.13)	(0.12)	(0.19)	(0.12)	(0.11)	(0.13)
Automobile commercial physical damage								
Stock	0.69	0.58	0.45	0.41	0.45	0.50	0.49	0.45
	(0.46)	(0.58)	(0.62)	(4.05)	(8.71)	(9.51)	(0.83)	(0.62)
Mutual	0.72	0.67	0.54	0.47	0.48	0.57	0.56	0.52
	(0.41)	(0.29)	(0.20)	(0.19)	(0.19)	(0.39)	(0.21)	(0.43)

Note: Numbers in parentheses are weighted standard deviations.

reports the weighted standard deviation of the firm-level loss ratios. Figure 6.1 graphs the time series of loss ratios for each line. The loss ratio is the aggregate losses incurred by the organizational form in each line divided by premiums earned less policyholder dividends paid (for mutuals and participating policies of stock companies). This is the principal measure of insurance-underwriting profitability and can be viewed as the inverse of the ex post price of insurance. Higher loss ratios imply that the business was less profitable. These loss ratios are constructed using the premium-weighted mean of the firm-level loss ratios by line.

Figure 6.1 reinforces the lesson that neither form has a clear advantage over the other. Neither is clearly more profitable than the other, or at least not to an extent that can be discerned by visual inspection. However, in the two automobile physical damage lines, mutuals have worse loss ratios than stocks in every year. (We explore the statistical significance of differences in loss ratios across organizational form in our regression analysis below.) The loss ratios for both forms are the most volatile and the highest in general liability and medical malpractice insurance, reflecting the liability crisis of the mid-1980s. Profitability was restored, in part, by the liability reforms of 1985–87.[15]

In summary, the aggregate and firm-level statistics by organizational form do not reveal striking differences between stock and mutual firms. Thus the data provide no evidence for such simple hypotheses as "small firms organize as mutuals" or "mutuals have a special advantage in one line of business." However, these aggregate and firm-level statistics cannot confirm whether stock and mutual firms behave differently within each market. To learn this, we analyze the dynamics of firm-level data.

6.3 Stock and Mutual Company Responses to the Underwriting Environment

Different organizational forms smooth risk through different mechanisms. A stock company redistributes risk among policyholders and from individual policyholders to shareholders, who diversify their risk through the equity market. A mutual company distributes risk by pooling the risks of its policyholders. However, since the policyholders are their own residual claimants, they cannot share their risk with less affected or less risk-averse shareholders. (Some risks can be laid off on other companies through reinsurance activities, a practice used by both stock and mutual companies.) The shareholders of stock companies hire managers to maximize the value of the shareholders' claims, while customers come to the company to spread their risks. In contrast, the policyholders of mutual companies hire managers to spread risk among the policyholders by pooling.

---

15. For a discussion of the liability crisis and the reforms, see Viscusi (1991) and Born and Viscusi (1994).

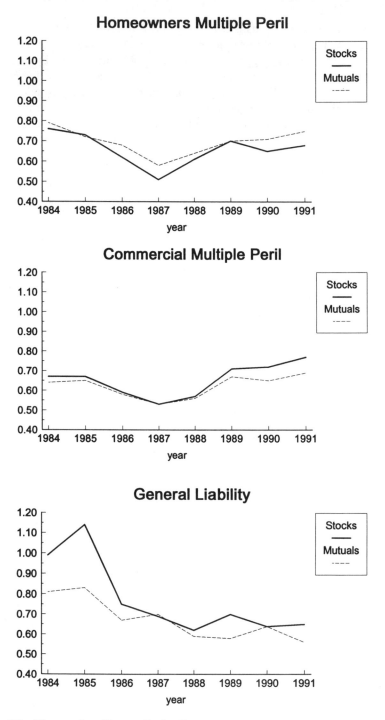

Fig. 6.1　Time series of loss ratios by line

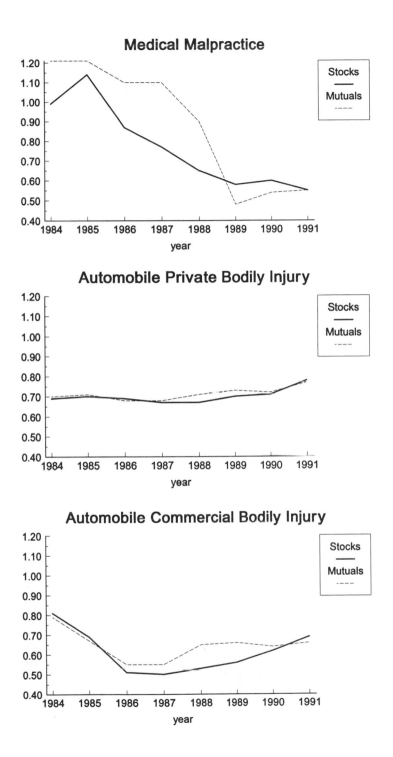

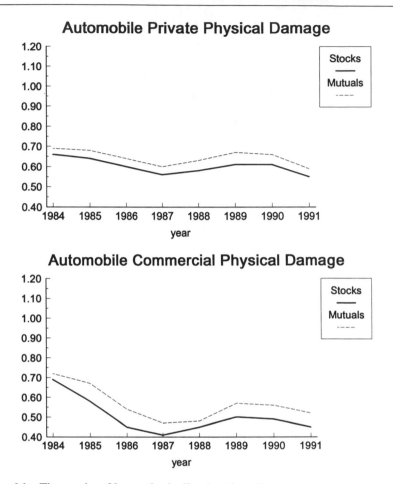

Fig. 6.1   Time series of loss ratios by line (continued)

Managers of stock companies must deal with conflicting pressures to provide shareholders with profits and policyholders with affordable insurance. By uniting owners and customers, the mutual form mitigates this agency problem. However, policyholders of mutual companies have little incentive to monitor the managers since any residual claims they have are nontransferable, last only as long as their policy is in force, and cannot be magnified by buying more shares or taking control of the company.[16] If profits on current policies are not distributed immediately, then those who hold policies when the profits are earned receive neither dividends associated with those profits while they

16. See Hetherington (1991, 31–32) for a discussion of the differences in incentives of policy-holders and shareholders.

owned the firm nor compensation in the form of a higher share price. In contrast, shareholders' claims on the firm's assets are proportionate to the number of shares they own, are transferable, and are coterminous with the life of the stock company. Hetherington (1991) hypothesizes that these differences undermine the mutuals' ability to mitigate the agency costs associated with the conflict of interest between shareholders and policyholders; thus managers of mutuals behave like firmly entrenched managers of stock companies.

To the extent that these differences in incentives to monitor managers' behavior (or other attributes of organizational form) affect performance, then, stocks and mutuals should respond differently to differences in or changes in their underwriting environments. We focus on whether stock and mutual firms respond differentially to a broad measure of profitability in their underwriting environments. Since underwriting profitability varies by line of insurance (see fig. 6.1) and, possibly, by state of business, we use a relative measure of lagged profitability for the firm in a specific line of business and state of operation. Specifically, we divide the previous year's loss ratio for the firm in an insurance line and state by the overall underwriting loss ratio of all firms operating in the specific line and state. This ratio measures a firm's relative operating environment under the assumption that firm-specific business conditions have some persistence from one year to the next. Since stock and mutual companies face similar contemporaneous shocks to underwriting profitability, differences in how their premiums, losses, and profitability respond to their previous profitability may reveal differences in firm decisions. For example, firms with relatively high loss ratios (low profitability) may want to raise their prices or lower their quantity of business.

Since state governments are responsible for insurance regulation, interstate differences in regulation could also create variation in firms' operating environments, which could be used to explore the differential responses of organizational forms. Broadly speaking, regulatory systems can be classified as either "noncompetitive" or "competitive" rate-making regimes.[17] The common element of the various regimes that would be classified as noncompetitive is that insurers cannot freely adjust rates without prior approval. In the empirical work, we focus on a state fixed-effects formulation so that the role of regulation cannot be distinguished explicitly from other state-specific differences. Formulations excluding state fixed effects but including measures of regulatory differences failed to indicate a consistent or significant effect of regulation on the performance of stocks and mutuals.[18]

17. See Cummins and Harrington (1987). More refined regulatory regime breakdowns did not generate significant effects.

18. There are several reasons why these differences in broad regulatory regimes did not differentially affect stock and mutual firms. First, we only measured legislated differences in regulation and not differences in the stringency of enforcement. Second, regulation and firm location choices could be endogenous.

6.4 Empirical Methodology and Results

The ideal measure of a firm's responses to its environment would be changes in its prices and quantities.[19] For an insurance policy with a fixed set of contractual terms, it might be possible to construct a time series of prices; however, policies vary in important details, such as the deductible or whether copayments are required, and such details are not made public. Thus we use firm-level financial data on premiums and losses by year, state, and line of business. Unfortunately, such data do not enable us to separate the price and quantity of insurance issued.

As measures of a firm's responses to its underwriting environment, we use premiums earned (the product of "price" times "quantity"), losses incurred, and firm profitability. We measure firm profitability as a firm's loss ratio in each line of insurance in each state. We use premiums earned to measure the scale of each firm's operations; losses incurred is a second measure of scale. We estimate separate ordinary least squares regressions for each dependent variable for each line of insurance.

We use NAIC data from the annual financial statements for almost all insurance firms in the United States for the years 1984–91. This data set is the most extensive information available at the firm level, as insurers are required to submit information to the NAIC on a by-line and by-state basis. For each firm in the sample, we know the losses incurred and premiums earned by line in each state. The data also specify the firm's organizational form and total assets. Since our specifications include lagged variables, our regressions use data for 1985–91.

We analyze firm-level data in each state for each line. While we could consolidate our firms into groups to get a more aggregate unit of analysis we use firm-level data since organizational form is defined at the firm level, and insurance companies often divide their business into different subsidiary firms. Some insurance groups are composed of both mutual and stock firms. The stock firms in these groups are typically privately held with a mutual firm parent owning most of the shares. These mutual-owned stock companies are an important segment of the industry; in 1991, they wrote almost one-third of total property-casualty premiums (all lines of business) in the United States (as calculated from the NAIC data). One rationale for combining mutuals and stocks within a group is that the managers of the mutual can be given or induced to buy shares of the stock subsidiary to provide a form of incentive compensation (see Hetherington 1991, 43).

As discussed by Mayers and Smith (1994), the mutual-owned stock form of organization presents a somewhat different agency problem than either widely held stock companies or mutuals. These mutual-controlled stocks could behave

19. For a review of the economic aspects of insurance market operation, see Dionne (1992).

similarly to their parent mutuals since they often have common directors. Rather than impose the assumption that these firms behave like either stocks or mutuals, our empirical specifications allow for three types of firms: stocks that are not owned by mutual parents, mutual-owned stock companies, and mutuals.

6.4.1   Premium Effects

In using premiums earned as our measure of firm behavior, we estimate the following reduced-form equation, which includes both state and year fixed effects:[20]

$$\log \text{Premiums}_{ijkt} = \alpha_0 + \alpha_1 \log \text{Premiums}_{ijkt-1} + \alpha_2 \log \text{Aggregate income}_{kt}$$

$$+ \alpha_3 \log(\text{Loss ratio}_{ijkt-1}/\text{State loss ratio}_{jkt-1})$$

$$+ \alpha_4 \log \text{National premiums earned}_{it} + \alpha_5 \text{Stock}_i$$

$$+ \alpha_6 \text{Mutual-owned stock}_i$$

$$+ \alpha_7 \text{Stock}_i \times \log(\text{Loss ratio}_{ijkt-1}/\text{State loss ratio}_{jkt-1})$$

$$+ \alpha_8 \text{Mutual-owned stock}_i$$

$$\times \log(\text{Loss ratio}_{ijkt-1}/\text{State loss ratio}_{jkt-1})$$

$$+ \alpha_9 \text{Stock}_i \times \log \text{National premiums earned}_{it}$$

$$+ \alpha_{10} \text{Mutual-owned stock}_i$$

$$\times \log \text{National premiums earned}_{it}$$

$$+ \sum_k \beta_k \text{State}_k + \sum_t \delta_t \text{Year}_t + \varepsilon_{ijkt},$$

(1)

where the subscript i denotes firms, j denotes lines of insurance, k denotes states, and t denotes years. The αs, βs, and δs are the coefficients to be estimated, and ε_{ijkt} is the error term. We estimate equation (1) separately for each line of insurance to isolate line-specific relationships. We treat each state as a separate market since firms are regulated at the state level. The logarithmic specification treats proportional effects (such as halving or doubling) equally; this reduces any large outliers.[21]

The main variables of interest are size, as measured by national premiums in all lines, and the previous year's relative profitability. The national size variable

---

20. The reported results are from unweighted ordinary least squares regressions. Alternatively, we could weight by firm asset size; however, since our unit of observation is firm activity within a state, national firm-level total assets may not be the appropriate weighting variable.

21. The logarithmic specifications also had much more explanatory power than the linear specifications.

reflects firms that are large because they write either in many states or in many lines. Since we control for the lagged dependent variable, national size is distinct from the firm's recent experience in the line in the state. A firm's lagged relative profitability is its loss ratio in the previous year divided by the overall industry loss ratio for this line in the state in the previous year. This variable captures the profitability of a line in a state relative to the typical underwriting experience in the state. If there is some persistence in the relative profitability of firms operating in a state, this variable captures which firms have relatively good or bad opportunities in the state. If the firm was relatively unprofitable in this line last year, we would expect it to try to improve the line's profitability.

To measure the effects of organizational form, we include a stock company dummy variable (equal to one for stock companies) and an analogous variable for mutual-owned stock companies. We interact these dummy variables with the key variables of interest. The coefficients on the dummy variables capture any general differences in premiums across organizational forms. The coefficients on the terms interacting with relative profitability and national premiums earned capture whether stock companies respond differently than mutuals in relation to their underwriting environments. The interaction with national premiums allows large stock companies to differ from large mutual companies. Since our organizational form variables are simple dummy variables, they are a rather crude measure of differences across types of firms and do not capture heterogeneity within types of firms. For example, stock firms include both publicly traded and privately held companies.

The state income variable is the state's aggregate income;[22] it measures differences across states in the size of their markets. Unlike the state-specific fixed-effect variables, which control for state-specific effects, this variable changes over time. The year dummy variables capture any national trends in the profitability of writing a line of insurance. We set the year dummy variable for 1985 to zero to avoid singularity.

Table 6.4 reports the results from estimating equation (1). As expected, the coefficients on the lagged value of premiums are close to but less than one; they range from 0.73 to 0.94. While the coefficients on relative profitability are often statistically significant, there is no pattern to their signs. Firms that have larger national premiums (either more states or more lines) tend to write more insurance in the state in each line. In all eight lines, the coefficients on the two types of stock companies are similar, which suggests that in terms of scale of operations within a state, mutual-owned stock companies are more similar to stock companies than to mutuals.

To test whether organizational form affects total premiums, we examine the coefficients for the stock dummy, the mutual-owned stock dummy, and the interaction terms. The coefficients on each of the two stock dummy variables

---

22. Income data are from the U.S. Department of Commerce, *Survey of Current Business* (Washington, D.C., 1985–91).

Table 6.4 Log Premiums Regression Results, 1985–91 (insurance firm-level data)

Variable	Homeowners Multiple Peril	Commercial Multiple Peril	General Liability	Medical Malpractice	Automobile Private Bodily Injury	Automobile Commercial Bodily Injury	Automobile Private Physical Damage	Automobile Commercial Physical Damage
Intercept	−0.679	−1.892*	3.412*	2.497	−0.979	1.823	−1.276	1.021
	(2.666)	(1.128)	(1.045)	(3.080)	(1.175)	(1.133)	(1.166)	(1.112)
log Premiums$_{t-1}$	0.870*	0.915*	0.753*	0.726*	0.936*	0.791*	0.912*	0.804*
	(0.005)	(0.002)	(0.002)	(0.006)	(0.002)	(0.002)	(0.002)	(0.002)
log Aggregate income	0.275	0.318*	−0.111	−0.000	0.168	0.032	0.243*	0.105
	(0.306)	(0.130)	(0.120)	(0.353)	(0.135)	(0.130)	(0.134)	(0.128)
log(Loss ratio$_{t}$/State loss ratio$_{t-1}$)	−0.024*	−0.012*	0.032*	0.026*	−0.045*	0.039*	0.002	0.058*
	(0.008)	(0.005)	(0.003)	(0.015)	(0.006)	(0.004)	(0.008)	(0.005)
log National premiums earned	0.120*	0.063*	0.119*	0.272*	0.057*	0.124*	0.070*	0.102*
	(0.010)	(0.005)	(0.004)	(0.014)	(0.005)	(0.006)	(0.005)	(0.006)
Stock	−0.416*	−0.152*	−0.258*	−0.313*	−0.258*	−0.330*	−0.208*	−0.263*
	(0.030)	(0.018)	(0.017)	(0.045)	(0.024)	(0.022)	(0.022)	(0.017)
Mutual-owned stock	−0.383*	−0.175*	−0.334*	−0.360*	−0.269*	−0.402*	−0.230*	−0.338*
	(0.030)	(0.019)	(0.018)	(0.046)	(0.026)	(0.023)	(0.025)	(0.018)
Stock * log(Loss ratio$_{t}$/State loss ratio$_{t-1}$)	−0.029*	−0.073*	−0.042*	−0.077*	−0.051*	−0.049*	−0.092*	−0.079*
	(0.010)	(0.006)	(0.004)	(0.017)	(0.006)	(0.005)	(0.009)	(0.005)
Mutual-owned stock * log(Loss ratio$_{t}$/State loss ratio$_{t-1}$)	−0.006	−0.038*	−0.046*	−0.040*	−0.027*	−0.037*	−0.041*	−0.055*
	(0.010)	(0.005)	(0.004)	(0.016)	(0.007)	(0.005)	(0.009)	(0.005)
Stock * log National premiums earned	0.013	0.015*	0.073*	0.018	0.061*	0.069*	0.047*	0.077*
	(0.013)	(0.006)	(0.005)	(0.015)	(0.006)	(0.007)	(0.006)	(0.007)
Mutual-owned stock * log National premiums earned	0.048*	0.018*	0.101*	0.012	0.047*	0.085*	0.040*	0.088*
	(0.013)	(0.006)	(0.005)	(0.014)	(0.007)	(0.007)	(0.007)	(0.007)
$\bar{R}^2$	0.847	0.879	0.844	0.861	0.873	0.811	0.851	0.809

Notes: Each equation also includes a set of six dummy variables for 1986–91 and 49 state dummy variables. Numbers in parentheses are standard errors.

*Statistically significant at the 95 percent confidence level, two-tailed test.

are negative and statistically significant at the 95 percent confidence level in all of the lines. This result suggests that even though stocks have larger firm-level national premiums, conditional on offering a line of insurance in a given state, they are smaller than mutuals. This difference is consistent with the observation that mutuals are more concentrated geographically and by line.

One would expect stock companies to be more responsive to changes in profitability since they will respond more to the interest of wealth-maximizing shareholders than of policyholders who may value stable insurance arrangements. Low relative levels of profitability (i.e., high relative loss ratios) should lead stock companies to contract their operations. The interaction between the stock dummy and lagged relative profitability is negative and statistically significant in all eight lines of insurance; this is also true of all but one mutual-owned stock company. Thus, relative to mutual companies, stock companies write less insurance in states where they are less profitable. This result is consistent with our theory that stock companies are more likely to react to their underwriting environments in determining the amount of insurance that they write. The interaction terms for mutual-owned stocks are typically about one-half as large in absolute value as the interaction terms for stock companies. This pattern suggests that the reactions of mutual-owned stock companies are somewhere between the reactions of the other types of companies.

The coefficients for the stock dummy and mutual-owned stock dummy interacted with national premiums earned are positive and statistically significant in all but three cases. The positive interaction term between stock and national premiums suggests that larger national scale has a greater influence on the premiums written by stock companies.

6.4.2   Loss Level Effects

One problem with using total premiums as a measure of behavior is that the figure can increase either because the firm writes more policies or because it charges a higher price for the same number of policies. As a second measure of firm behavior, we use the level of firm losses and control for premiums earned during the same year. By including premiums earned in the equation, the results take as given any changes in premiums due to price or quantity changes. Thus this equation measures firm behaviors aimed at reducing the level of claims, such as more stringent screening of applicants. For losses incurred, we estimate the following fixed effects equation:

$$\log \text{Losses}_{ijkt} = \alpha_0 + \alpha_1 \log \text{Losses}_{ijkt-1} + \alpha_2 \log \text{Premiums}_{ijkt}$$
$$+ \alpha_3 \log \text{Aggregate income}_{kt}$$
$$+ \alpha_4 \log(\text{Loss ratio}_{ijkt-1}/\text{State loss ratio}_{jkt-1})$$

$$+ \; \alpha_5 \log \text{National premiums earned}_{it} + \alpha_6 \text{Stock}_i$$

$$+ \; \alpha_7 \text{Mutual-owned stock}_i$$

(2) $$+ \; \alpha_8 \text{Stock}_i \times \log(\text{Loss ratio}_{ijkt-1}/\text{State loss ratio}_{jkt-1})$$

$$+ \; \alpha_9 \text{Mutual-owned stock}_i$$

$$\times \log(\text{Loss ratio}_{ijkt-1}/\text{State loss ratio}_{jkt-1})$$

$$+ \; \alpha_{10} \text{Stock}_i \times \log \text{National premiums earned}_{it}$$

$$+ \; \alpha_{11} \text{Mutual-owned stock}_i \times \log \text{National premiums earned}_{it}$$

$$+ \; \sum_k \beta_k \text{State}_k + \sum_t \delta_t \text{Year}_t + \varepsilon_{ijkt} \; .$$

Table 6.5 presents the coefficients from estimating equation (2). As expected, the coefficients on both lagged losses and current premiums are positive and statistically significant. Many of the coefficients on relative profitability and on the interaction between the stock dummy and relative profitability are statistically significant. However, there is no consistent pattern in the signs of the coefficients.

In eight of the nine instances in which the coefficient on the stock dummy or the mutual-owned stock dummy is statistically significant, it is positive. This pattern suggests that for a given amount of premiums, stock companies have more losses, a finding consistent with the historical claim that mutual companies are more careful in screening their applicants, or just secure a better mix. However, since the result is for a given amount of premiums less policyholder dividends, it is not clear that mutuals pass this savings on to policyholders either in dividends or lower premiums.[23]

6.4.3   Loss Ratio Effects

Our final measure of firm behavior is the loss ratio, a widely used measure of profitability for insurance. The loss ratio combines the effects of behaviors that change either premiums or losses. We estimate the following reduced-form fixed-effects equation:

$$\log \text{Loss ratio}_{ijkt} = \alpha_0 + \alpha_1 \log \text{Aggregate income}_{kt}$$

$$+ \; \alpha_2 \log(\text{Loss ratio}_{ijkt-1}/\text{State loss ratio}_{jkt-1})$$

$$+ \; \alpha_3 \log \text{National premiums earned}_{it}$$

---

23. While this difference suggests that mutuals have higher underwriting profits than stock companies, the two organizational forms could differ in their costs (e.g., mutuals spend more on screening) or in service levels.

Table 6.5   Log Losses Regression Results, 1985–91 (insurance firm–level data)

Variable	Homeowners Multiple Peril	Commercial Multiple Peril	General Liability	Medical Malpractice	Automobile Private Bodily Injury	Automobile Commercial Bodily Injury	Automobile Private Physical Damage	Automobile Commercial Physical Damage
Intercept	-10.553*	-7.616*	3.439	-4.618	-2.376	-2.533	-0.645	-1.358
	(6.300)	(2.017)	(2.101)	(6.023)	(1.961)	(2.510)	(1.520)	(2.227)
log Losses$_{t-1}$	0.351*	0.208*	0.252*	0.294*	0.342*	0.506*	0.066*	0.259*
	(0.022)	(0.008)	(0.007)	(0.017)	(0.007)	(0.008)	(0.006)	(0.008)
log Premiums$_t$	1.039*	1.042*	0.763*	0.621*	0.808*	0.711*	1.098*	1.045*
	(0.022)	(0.008)	(0.008)	(0.020)	(0.007)	(0.008)	(0.006)	(0.008)
log Aggregate income	0.627	0.484*	-0.496*	0.568	-0.009	-0.123	-0.231	-0.335
	(0.722)	(0.232)	(0.241)	(0.689)	(0.225)	(0.288)	(0.174)	(0.256)
log(Loss ratio$_{t-1}$/State loss ratio$_{t-1}$)	-0.121*	0.120*	0.398*	0.186*	0.086*	-0.129*	0.243*	0.057*
	(0.032)	(0.012)	(0.010)	(0.033)	(0.013)	(0.013)	(0.012)	(0.013)
log National premiums earned	-0.001	-0.031*	0.100*	0.149*	-0.035*	-0.004	-0.025*	-0.036*
	(0.024)	(0.009)	(0.009)	(0.026)	(0.009)	(0.013)	(0.007)	(0.012)
Stock	-0.117	0.255*	0.132*	0.370*	0.021	0.123*	0.063*	-0.056
	(0.072)	(0.032)	(0.034)	(0.091)	(0.040)	(0.048)	(0.029)	(0.034)
Mutual-owned stock	0.041	0.176*	0.267*	-0.107	0.018	0.219*	-0.012	-0.064*
	(0.071)	(0.034)	(0.038)	(0.093)	(0.044)	(0.052)	(0.032)	(0.037)
Stock * log(Loss ratio$_{t-1}$/State loss ratio$_{t-1}$)	0.046*	-0.011	-0.110*	0.043	0.003	0.139*	-0.026*	-0.027*
	(0.023)	(0.010)	(0.008)	(0.034)	(0.011)	(0.010)	(0.012)	(0.010)
Mutual-owned stock * log(Loss ratio$_{t-1}$/State loss ratio$_{t-1}$)	0.071*	0.028*	-0.146*	0.071*	-0.014	0.141*	-0.003	-0.020*
	(0.022)	(0.010)	(0.009)	(0.032)	(0.011)	(0.011)	(0.012)	(0.011)
Stock * log National premiums earned	0.028	-0.064*	0.022*	-0.087*	0.014	-0.006	-0.017*	-0.025*
	(0.031)	(0.011)	(0.010)	(0.028)	(0.010)	(0.015)	(0.008)	(0.013)
Mutual-owned stock * log National premiums earned	-0.045	-0.037*	-0.031*	0.054*	0.029*	-0.046*	0.020*	0.004
	(0.030)	(0.011)	(0.010)	(0.027)	(0.011)	(0.016)	(0.009)	(0.014)
$\bar{R}^2$	0.747	0.828	0.791	0.785	0.822	0.729	0.854	0.737

Notes: Each equation also includes a set of six dummy variables for 1986–91 and 49 state dummy variables. Numbers in parentheses are standard errors.

$$+ \alpha_4 \text{Stock}_i + \alpha_5 \text{Mutual-owned stock}_i$$

$$+ \alpha_6 \text{Stock}_i \times \log(\text{Loss ratio}_{ijkt-1}/\text{State loss ratio}_{jkt-1})$$

$$+ \alpha_7 \text{Mutual-owned stock}_i$$

$$\times \log(\text{Loss ratio}_{ijkt-1}/\text{State loss ratio}_{jkt-1})$$

$$+ \alpha_8 \text{Stock}_i \times \log \text{National premiums earned}_{it}$$

$$+ \alpha_9 \text{Mutual-owned stock}_i$$

$$\times \log \text{National premiums earned}_{it}$$

$$+ \sum_k \beta_k \text{State}_k + \sum_t \delta_t \text{Year}_t + \varepsilon_{ijkt}.$$

The structure of the equation is similar to that of the premium and loss equations. The size variable reflects differences in national firm size that may affect profitability. Larger firms may be able to weather worse underwriting environments if they are more efficient in other operations, such as investing.

Table 6.6 summarizes the regression results for equation (3). The lagged value of relative profitability has a positive effect on this year's profitability, suggesting that there is persistence in underwriting profitability. The mix of policies insured by a firm in the state and their relative performance tend to remain similar over time. Larger firms tend to have significantly higher loss ratios in every instance. Since these loss ratios do not adjust for underwriting expenses, the higher loss ratios of large firms may indicate that they benefit from economies of scale that give them lower administrative costs per dollar of losses. Alternatively, this may indicate that larger firms earn a higher return from investing their assets, allowing them to sustain somewhat lower underwriting profitability.

We do not find a discernable pattern whereby one organizational form outperforms the other, though the three types of firms are statistically different. This conclusion is consistent with earlier results from table 6.3. The coefficient on the stock dummy is positive and statistically significant at the 95 percent confidence level for commercial multiple peril, general liability, and medical malpractice but negative and statistically significant for homeowners multiple peril and commercial automobile physical damage insurance. For mutual-owned stocks, the dummy variable effect is positive and statistically significant in only one case but negative and statistically significant in five instances.

The coefficients for the interaction terms with relative profitability for both the stock dummy and mutual-owned stocks are mixed, with no consistent statistically significant pattern. The profitability of stock companies is statistically less persistent than that of mutual companies in four lines: commercial multiple peril, general liability, and commercial and private automobile physical damage. Similarly, less persistence is observed for stock-owned mutuals in

Table 6.6   Log Loss Ratio Regression Results, 1985–91 (insurance firm–level data)

Variable	Homeowners Multiple Peril	Commercial Multiple Peril	General Liability	Medical Malpractice	Automobile Private Bodily Injury	Automobile Commercial Bodily Injury	Automobile Private Physical Damage	Automobile Commercial Physical Damage
Intercept	−6.489 (6.622)	−8.429* (2.103)	1.844 (2.124)	−4.815 (6.163)	−1.790 (2.016)	−4.496* (2.592)	−0.889 (1.564)	−2.299 (2.303)
log Aggregate income	0.656 (0.759)	0.863* (0.241)	−0.312 (0.244)	0.494 (0.705)	0.066 (0.231)	0.295 (0.297)	−0.027 (0.179)	0.080 (0.264)
log(Loss ratio$_{t-1}$/ State loss ratio$_{t-1}$)	0.414* (0.020)	0.477* (0.009)	0.655* (0.007)	0.458* (0.030)	0.522* (0.010)	0.467* (0.010)	0.418* (0.011)	0.447* (0.009)
log National premiums earned	0.178* (0.025)	0.099* (0.009)	0.110* (0.008)	0.067* (0.025)	0.044* (0.009)	0.096* (0.013)	0.069* (0.007)	0.114* (0.012)
Stock	−0.598* (0.074)	0.126* (0.033)	0.082* (0.034)	0.437* (0.093)	0.015 (0.041)	−0.012 (0.049)	−0.009 (0.030)	−0.196* (0.035)
Mutual-owned stock	−0.521* (0.072)	−0.083* (0.035)	0.192* (0.037)	−0.023 (0.094)	−0.086* (0.045)	−0.050 (0.053)	−0.126* (0.033)	−0.288* (0.038)
Stock * log(Loss ratio$_{t-1}$/ State loss ratio$_{t-1}$)	−0.022 (0.024)	−0.037* (0.011)	−0.115* (0.008)	0.065* (0.034)	−0.011 (0.011)	0.098* (0.011)	−0.061* (0.012)	−0.072* (0.010)
Mutual-owned stock * log(Loss ratio$_{t-1}$/ State loss ratio$_{t-1}$)	0.016 (0.024)	−0.009 (0.010)	−0.153* (0.009)	0.083* (0.032)	−0.031* (0.011)	0.092* (0.011)	−0.029* (0.012)	−0.065* (0.011)
Stock * log National premiums earned	0.005 (0.032)	−0.060* (0.011)	0.030* (0.010)	−0.091* (0.029)	0.005 (0.010)	0.016 (0.015)	−0.012 (0.008)	0.017 (0.014)
Mutual-owned stock * log National premiums earned	−0.047 (0.032)	−0.014 (0.011)	−0.022* (0.010)	0.050* (0.028)	0.032* (0.011)	0.006 (0.016)	0.023* (0.009)	0.057* (0.015)
$\bar{R}^2$	0.276	0.285	0.420	0.342	0.303	0.384	0.192	0.229

Notes: Each equation also includes a set of six dummy variables for 1986–91 and 49 state dummy variables. Numbers in parentheses are standard errors.
*Statistically significant at the 95 percent confidence level, two-tailed test.

four lines: general liability, automobile private bodily injury, and both automobile physical damage lines. However, compared to mutual firms, the profitability of both stock companies and mutual-owned stock companies is statistically more persistent in two lines: medical malpractice and automobile commercial bodily injury. The profitability of stock companies and mutual-owned stock companies tends to display mixed effects with respect to the role of size variations. Again, however, the similarities between the coefficients for the two types of stock companies suggests that stock ownership is more important than who owns the stock.

6.5 Conclusion

Our results identify several differences between stocks (and mutual-owned stocks) and mutuals.[24] First, while stock companies tend to collect more premiums than mutual companies at the national level, mutuals write more business than stocks on a per line, per state basis. This result is consistent with the belief that stock companies serve broader geographical areas and write more lines of insurance than mutuals. Second, relative to mutuals, stock companies have lower total premiums in lines and states in which they were relatively unprofitable in the previous year. This suggests that stock companies are more likely than mutuals to cut back their business in unprofitable situations. Third, for a given amount of premiums, stock companies have higher losses than mutuals. This is consistent with traditional arguments that mutuals are more careful in screening or are better at attracting good risks than stock companies.

In a number of cases, we found a notable lack of differences between stock and mutual companies. For example, neither form of organization has consistently higher underwriting profitability than the other. Our most persistent and powerful result is that stock and mutual-owned stock companies are much quicker to exit unprofitable markets and expand operations in profitable markets.

---

24. Several caveats should be mentioned. First, the regressions above take the locations of stock and mutual companies as exogenous. If differences in the underwriting environment across states and lines of insurance differentially affect firms' market entry and exit decisions, then location is endogenous, and the results may be biased. Second, we have focused on agency cost differences in organizational forms. These firms also differ in their access to equity markets. To better address how this difference affects firm behavior, however, one would need to distinguish between publicly traded and privately held stock companies as well as account for the consolidated group structure of insurance firms.

References

Bainbridge, John. 1952. *Biography of an idea: The story of mutual fire and casualty insurance*. Garden City, N.Y.: Doubleday.

Berger, Allen, J. David Cummins, and Mary A. Weiss. 1995. The coexistence of alternative distribution systems for the same financial service: The case of property-liability insurance. Working paper. Philadelphia: University of Pennsylvania, Wharton School.

Born, Patricia. 1994. *Essays on insurance regulation and insolvency: Empirical evidence from the property-casualty insurance industry*. Ph.D. diss., Duke University, Durham, N.C.

Born, Patricia, and W. Kip Viscusi. 1994. Insurance market responses to the 1980s liability reforms: An analysis of firm-level data. *Journal of Risk and Insurance* 61 (2): 192–218.

Cummins, J. David, and Scott E. Harrington. 1987. The impact of rate regulation in U.S. property-liability insurance markets: A cross-sectional analysis of individual firm loss ratios. *Geneva Papers on Risk and Insurance* 12:50–62.

Cummins, J. David, and Mary A. Weiss. 1993. Measuring cost efficiency in the property-liability insurance industry. *Journal of Banking and Finance* 17:463–82.

Dionne, Georges, ed. 1992. *Contributions to insurance economics*. Boston: Kluwer.

Fama, Eugene F., and Michael C. Jensen. 1983a. Agency problems and residual claims. *Journal of Law and Economics* 26:327–49.

———. 1983b. Separation of ownership and control. *Journal of Law and Economics* 26:301–25.

Hansmann, Henry. 1985. The organization of insurance companies: Mutual versus stock. *Journal of Law, Economics, and Organization* 1:125–53.

Heflebower, Richard B. 1980. *Cooperatives and mutuals in the market system*. Madison: University of Wisconsin Press.

Hermalin, Benjamin E., and Nancy E. Wallace. 1994. The determinants of efficiency and solvency in savings and loans. *RAND Journal of Economics* 25 (3): 361–81.

Hetherington, John A. C. 1991. *Mutual and cooperative enterprises: An analysis of customer-owned firms in the United States*. Charlottesville: University of Virginia Press.

Lamm-Tennant, Joan, and Laura T. Starks. 1993. Stock versus mutual ownership structures: The risk implications. *Journal of Business* 66:29–46.

Mayers, David, and Clifford W. Smith, Jr. 1981. Contractual provisions, organizational structure, and conflict control in insurance markets. *Journal of Business* 54:407–34.

———. 1988. Ownership structure across lines of property-casualty insurance. *Journal of Law and Economics* 31:351–78.

———. 1994. Managerial discretion, regulation, and stock insurer ownership structure. *Journal of Risk and Insurance* 61 (4): 638–55.

Patel, Jayendu, Jack Needleman, and Richard Zeckhauser. 1994. Changing fortunes, hospital behaviors, and ownership forms. Faculty Research Working Paper no. R94-17. Cambridge, Mass.: Harvard University, John F. Kennedy School of Government.

Pauly, Mark V., Howard Kunreuther, and Paul Kleindorfer. 1986. Regulation and quality competition in the U.S. insurance industry. In *The economics of insurance regulation*, ed. Jorg Finsinger and Mark Pauly. New York: St. Martin's.

Pound, John, and Richard Zeckhauser. 1990. Are large shareholders effective monitors? An investigation of share ownership and corporate performance. In *Asymmetric information, corporate finance, and investment*, ed. R. Glenn Hubbard, 149–82. Chicago: University of Chicago Press.

Viscusi, W. Kip. 1991. *Reforming products liability*. Cambridge, Mass.: Harvard University Press.

Contributors

James G. Bohn
Board of Governors of the Federal
  Reserve System
20th and C Streets NW
Washington, DC 20551

Patricia Born
Department of Finance
School of Business Administration
University of Connecticut
368 Fairfield Road, U-41F
Storrs, CT 06269

David F. Bradford
Woodrow Wilson School
Princeton University
Princeton, NJ 08544

William M. Gentry
Graduate School of Business
Columbia University
602 Uris Hall
New York, NY 10027

Anne Gron
J. L. Kellogg Graduate School
  of Management
Northwestern University
2001 Sheridan Road
Evanston, IL 60208

Brian J. Hall
Harvard University
Littauer 111
Department of Economics
Cambridge, MA 02138

Dwight M. Jaffee
Haas School of Business
University of California
Berkeley, CA 94720

Kyle D. Logue
Hutchins Hall
University of Michigan
Law School
Ann Arbor, MI 48109

Deborah Lucas
J. L. Kellogg Graduate School
  of Management
Northwestern University
2001 Sheridan Road
Evanston, IL 60208

Thomas Russell
Department of Economics
Santa Clara University
Santa Clara, CA 95053

Susan J. Suponcic
Department of Public Policy
    and Management
Wharton School
University of Pennsylvania
Philadelphia, PA 19104

Sharon Tennyson
Department of Insurance and
    Risk Management
Wharton School
University of Pennsylvania
302 Colonial Penn Center
Philadelphia, PA 19104

W. Kip Viscusi
Cogan Professor of Law and
    Economics
Harvard Law School, HA 302
Cambridge, MA 02138

Richard J. Zeckhauser
John F. Kennedy School of
    Government
Harvard University
79 JFK Street
Cambridge, MA 02138

Author Index

195

Subject Index